SmartSuite®97 For Windows® For Dummies®

Cheat Sheet

SmartSuite 97 Shortcuts

SmartIcon	Keyboard equivalent	Function
	Ctrl+N	Create a n... (except in A...
	Ctrl+O	Open an exis...
	Ctrl+S	Save the current file
	Ctrl+P	Print the current file
	Ctrl+?	Print Preview
	Ctrl+X	Cut selection and store on Windows Clipboard
	Ctrl+C	Copy selection and store on Windows Clipboard
	Ctrl+V	Paste Clipboard contents into current file
	Ctrl+Z	Undo last action
B	Ctrl+B	Make selected text bold
I	Ctrl+I	Make selected text italic
U	Ctrl+U	Make selected text underlined
	Alt+Enter	Move between InfoBox and selection

Word Pro 97 Shortcuts

SmartIcon	Keyboard equivalent	Function
	Ctrl+F2	Check spelling
	Text⌐Text Properties	Open Text Properties InfoBox
	Right-click, Page Properties	Open Page Properties InfoBox
		Cycle attribute options
		Cycle alignment options
	Ctrl+L	Left-align text
	Ctrl+E	Center text
	Ctrl +R	Right-align text
	Ctrl+J	Justify text
	View⌐Show/Hide⌐Ruler	Show/Hide ruler
	Text⌐Named Styles⌐Reset to Style	Reset to style
	Text⌐Named Styles⌐Create	Create a style

...For Dummies: #1 Computer Book Series for Beginners

FOR DUMMIES

COMPUTER
BOOK SERIES
FROM IDG

SmartSuite® 97 For Windows® For Dummies®

Cheat Sheet

1-2-3 97 Shortcuts

SmartIcon	Function
	Open Workbook Properties InfoBox
	Open Sheet Properties InfoBox
	Open Range Properties InfoBox
	Copy range's format to other ranges
	Size columns to widest entry
	Sum values above or to left
	Create a worksheet
	Create a chart
abc	Create a text box
	Create an ellipse
	Create an arrow

Freelance Graphics 97 Shortcuts

SmartIcon	Function
	Run screen show
	Create a chart
abc	Create a text block
	Create or edit a speaker note
New Page	Create a new page
	Show InfoBox
	Zoom to show whole page
	Zoom in to selected area
	Select all objects
	Duplicate page
	Go to page

Approach 97 Shortcuts

SmartIcon	Function
	Go to first record
	Go to previous record
	Go to next record
	Go to last record
	Sort field in ascending order
	Sort field in descending order
	Delete current record
	Duplicate current record
16	Insert today's date
	Insert current time
	Insert value from previous record

Organizer 97 Shortcuts

SmartIcon	Function
	Return to previous page
	Open Show Through dialog box
	Create a new entry in the Calendar section
	Create a new entry in the To Do section
	Create a new entry in the Address section
	Create a new entry in the Calls section
	Create a new entry in the Planner section
	Create a new entry in the Notepad section
	Create a new entry in the Anniversary section
	Find text

...For Dummies: #1 Computer Book Series for Beginners

SMARTSUITE® 97
FOR
WINDOWS®
FOR
DUMMIES®

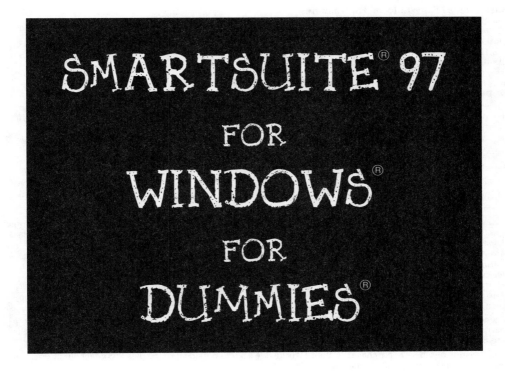

SMARTSUITE® 97 FOR WINDOWS® FOR DUMMIES®

by Jan Weingarten
with Michael Meadhra

IDG BOOKS WORLDWIDE™

IDG Books Worldwide, Inc.
An International Data Group Company

Foster City, CA ♦ Chicago, IL ♦ Indianapolis, IN ♦ Southlake, TX

SmartSuite® 97 For Windows® For Dummies®
Published by
IDG Books Worldwide, Inc.
An International Data Group Company
919 E. Hillsdale Blvd.
Suite 400
Foster City, CA 94404
`www.idgbooks.com` (IDG Books Worldwide Web site)
`www.dummies.com` (Dummies Press Web site)

Library of Congress Catalog Card No.: 96-76364

ISBN: 1-56884-610-X

Printed in the United States of America

10 9 8 7 6 5

1DD/RV/QR/ZX/IN

Distributed in the United States by IDG Books Worldwide, Inc.

Distributed by Macmillan Canada for Canada; by Transworld Publishers Limited in the United Kingdom; by IDG Norge Books for Norway; by IDG Sweden Books for Sweden; by Woodslane Pty. Ltd. for Australia; by Woodslane Enterprises Ltd. for New Zealand; by Longman Singapore Publishers Ltd. for Singapore, Malaysia, Thailand, and Indonesia; by Simron Pty. Ltd. for South Africa; by Toppan Company Ltd. for Japan; by Distribuidora Cuspide for Argentina; by Livraria Cultura for Brazil; by Ediciencia S.A. for Ecuador; by Addison-Wesley Publishing Company for Korea; by Ediciones ZETA S.C.R. Ltda. for Peru; by WS Computer Publishing Corporation, Inc., for the Philippines; by Unalis Corporation for Taiwan; by Contemporanea de Ediciones for Venezuela; by Computer Book & Magazine Store for Puerto Rico; by Express Computer Distributors for the Caribbean and West Indies. Authorized Sales Agent: Anthony Rudkin Associates for the Middle East and North Africa.

For general information on IDG Books Worldwide's books in the U.S., please call our Consumer Customer Service department at 800-762-2974. For reseller information, including discounts and premium sales, please call our Reseller Customer Service department at 800-434-3422.

For information on where to purchase IDG Books Worldwide's books outside the U.S., please contact our International Sales department at 415-655-3200 or fax 415-655-3295.

For information on foreign language translations, please contact our Foreign & Subsidiary Rights department at 415-655-3021 or fax 415-655-3281.

For sales inquiries and special prices for bulk quantities, please contact our Sales department at 415-655-3200 or write to the address above.

For information on using IDG Books Worldwide's books in the classroom or for ordering examination copies, please contact our Educational Sales department at 800-434-2086 or fax 817-251-8174.

For press review copies, author interviews, or other publicity information, please contact our Public Relations department at 415-655-3000 or fax 415-655-3299.

For authorization to photocopy items for corporate, personal, or educational use, please contact Copyright Clearance Center, 222 Rosewood Drive, Danvers, MA 01923, or fax 508-750-4470.

is a trademark under exclusive license to IDG Books Worldwide, Inc., from International Data Group, Inc.

About the Authors

Jan Weingarten is a software trainer and consultant in the Pacific Northwest. She has written or co-authored more than 20 books, including titles on SmartSuite, Windows, 1-2-3, Paradox, Excel, Microsoft Office, WordPerfect, and CorelDRAW!.

Michael Meadhra is an author and consultant who writes about Windows and a variety of Windows programs. After several years' experience in the corporate world, he began writing monthly software journals, and now writes books such as this one. To date, he has co-authored or contributed to some 16 titles on topics such as DOS, Windows, Lotus Freelance Graphics, Microsoft Works, CompuServe, the Internet, and online banking.

ABOUT IDG BOOKS WORLDWIDE

Welcome to the world of IDG Books Worldwide.

IDG Books Worldwide, Inc., is a subsidiary of International Data Group, the world's largest publisher of computer-related information and the leading global provider of information services on information technology. IDG was founded more than 25 years ago and now employs more than 8,500 people worldwide. IDG publishes more than 275 computer publications in over 75 countries (see listing below). More than 60 million people read one or more IDG publications each month.

Launched in 1990, IDG Books Worldwide is today the #1 publisher of best-selling computer books in the United States. We are proud to have received eight awards from the Computer Press Association in recognition of editorial excellence and three from *Computer Currents'* First Annual Readers' Choice Awards. Our best-selling *...For Dummies®* series has more than 30 million copies in print with translations in 30 languages. IDG Books Worldwide, through a joint venture with IDG's Hi-Tech Beijing, became the first U.S. publisher to publish a computer book in the People's Republic of China. In record time, IDG Books Worldwide has become the first choice for millions of readers around the world who want to learn how to better manage their businesses.

Our mission is simple: Every one of our books is designed to bring extra value and skill-building instructions to the reader. Our books are written by experts who understand and care about our readers. The knowledge base of our editorial staff comes from years of experience in publishing, education, and journalism — experience we use to produce books for the '90s. In short, we care about books, so we attract the best people. We devote special attention to details such as audience, interior design, use of icons, and illustrations. And because we use an efficient process of authoring, editing, and desktop publishing our books electronically, we can spend more time ensuring superior content and spend less time on the technicalities of making books.

You can count on our commitment to deliver high-quality books at competitive prices on topics you want to read about. At IDG Books Worldwide, we continue in the IDG tradition of delivering quality for more than 25 years. You'll find no better book on a subject than one from IDG Books Worldwide.

John Kilcullen
John Kilcullen
CEO
IDG Books Worldwide, Inc.

Steven Berkowitz
Steven Berkowitz
President and Publisher
IDG Books Worldwide, Inc.

**Eighth Annual
Computer Press
Awards ≥1992**

**Ninth Annual
Computer Press
Awards ≥1993**

**Tenth Annual
Computer Press
Awards ≥1994**

**Eleventh Annual
Computer Press
Awards ≥1995**

Authors' Acknowledgments

This book couldn't have happened without the help of the following people:

John Weingarten, who not only made significant contributions to the book itself, but also managed to keep his sister, Jan, sane in the process.

Wallace Wang, a funny guy and a heck of a writer who was there when we needed him. His contributions to the book were invaluable. We can't thank you enough, Wally.

Deborah Christy's hard work and contributions also were of great help.

Rev Mengle and Bill Barton, project editors, without whose Herculean efforts, diligence, and patience (which we put to the test) this book would never have seen the light of day.

We also want to thank the rest of the IDG Books team, who performed small and large miracles to complete this project.

And, of course, thanks to Matt Wagner, Jan Weingarten's terrific agent at Waterside Productions, for getting her this cool gig.

Publisher's Acknowledgments

We're proud of this book; please register your comments through our IDG Books Worldwide Online Registration Form located at: http://my2cents.dummies.com.

Some of the people who helped bring this book to market include the following:

Acquisitions, Development, and Editorial

Project Editors: Rev Mengle, Bill Barton

Acquisitions Editor: Gareth Hancock

Copy Editors: Tamara S. Castleman, Diana R. Conover, Diane L. Giangrossi, Jennifer Ehrlich, Suzanne Packer

Technical Editor: Jim McCarter

Editorial Manager: Seta K. Frantz

Editorial Assistant: Constance Carlisle

Production

Project Coordinator: Debbie Stailey

Layout and Graphics: Cameron Booker, Dominique DeFelice, Angela F. Hunckler, Tom Missler, Brent Savage, Ian A. Smith

Proofreaders: Nancy L. Reinhardt, Christine Sabooni, Joel K. Draper, Rachel Garvey, Dwight Ramsey, Robert Springer, Carrie Voorhis, Ethel M. Winslow, Karen York, Michelle Croninger

Indexer: Steve Rath

Special Help: Chris Collins, Editorial Assistant; Stephanie Koutek, Proof Editor; Kelly Oliver, Project Editor

General and Administrative

IDG Books Worldwide, Inc.: John Kilcullen, CEO; Steven Berkowitz, President and Publisher

IDG Books Technology Publishing: Brenda McLaughlin, Senior Vice President and Group Publisher

Dummies Technology Press and Dummies Editorial: Diane Graves Steele, Vice President and Associate Publisher; Mary Bednarek, Acquisitions and Product Development Director; Kristin A. Cocks, Editorial Director

Dummies Trade Press: Kathleen A. Welton, Vice President and Publisher; Kevin Thornton, Acquisitions Manager; Maureen F. Kelly, Editorial Coordinator

IDG Books Production for Dummies Press: Beth Jenkins, Production Director; Cindy L. Phipps, Manager of Project Coordination, Production Proofreading, and Indexing; Kathie S. Schutte, Supervisor of Page Layout; Shelley Lea, Supervisor of Graphics and Design; Debbie J. Gates, Production Systems Specialist; Robert Springer, Supervisor of Proofreading; Debbie Stailey, Special Projects Coordinator; Tony Augsburger, Supervisor of Reprints and Bluelines; Leslie Popplewell, Media Archive Coordinator

Dummies Packaging and Book Design: Patti Crane, Packaging Specialist; Lance Kayser, Packaging Assistant; Kavish + Kavish, Cover Design

◆

The publisher would like to give special thanks to Patrick J. McGovern, without whom this book would not have been possible.

◆

Contents at a Glance

Cartoons at a Glance

By Rich Tennant

page 9

page 45

page 289

page 175

page 261

page 345

page 123

Fax: 978-546-7747 • E-mail: the5wave@tiac.net

Table of Contents

Introduction

*W*elcome to *SmartSuite 97 For Windows For Dummies*. Just the fact that you're holding this book in your hands proves — at least to us — that you're no dummy. You're just someone who wants to get the essential information about how to use all those terrific features you know must be lurking somewhere in the Lotus SmartSuite 97 package.

So, what the heck is SmartSuite 97, anyway? Glad you asked. We'll start with what Lotus SmartSuite 97 is not. SmartSuite 97 has nothing to do with fancy first-class hotel rooms — although you get plenty of room to "spread out" with this package. SmartSuite is actually an integrated set of first-class computer programs (a "suite" in computerese) that can make your day-to-day work at the computer a whole lot easier. In fact, by using the SmartSuite 97 programs individually or in combination, you can perform just about any computing task you can possibly imagine — if, of course, you take the time to learn a bit about how SmartSuite operates. Well, you're in luck. Showing you what SmartSuite can do — and how you can best use its interconnected programs — is exactly what we're here for.

About This Book

This book is a reference. You don't need to read it front-to-back or cover-to-cover. Instead, think of a topic that piques your interest. Look it up in the index, turn to that page, and just start reading. Generally, each topic has its own section, and no section assumes that you've read anything else in the book. (If you need some background knowledge, or you want more information, you can use the references sprinkled throughout to guide you to the pertinent topic.)

This book can help you perform any of the following feats:

- ✔ Use Lotus Word Pro to create beautiful word-processing documents, such as letters, memos, reports — even (dare we say it?) the great American novel! — without breaking a sweat.

- ✔ Put together Lotus 1-2-3 spreadsheets to juggle numbers and perform death-defying calculations. You can even persuade your boss that you actually *know what you're talking about.*

- ✔ Keep track of vast amounts of data by using SmartSuite's Approach database program. Yes, thanks to Lotus, database management is finally approachable.

✔ Conquer your paralyzing fear of public speaking by using Lotus Freelance Graphics to create professional presentations. The next time you need to make a presentation, instead of yawns you'll get "Ooohs!" and "Aaaahhhhs."

✔ Organize your life by using (what else?) Lotus Organizer. What's Organizer? (Funny you should ask. . . .) It's much like a computerized version of one of those pocket day planners — on steroids. If you can't get organized by using this program, you just can't get organized.

✔ Create even more complex documents than any one of these programs can handle by itself. (But don't worry. The documents themselves may be complex, but the steps to create them aren't.)

How This Book Is Organized

This book is arranged so that you can easily find the information you're looking for. The first step on your quest to knowledge is to head toward the appropriate part of the book. To help you in that goal, here is a handy description of the book's eight main parts:

Part I: A Suite Deal

This is the part of the book that looks at SmartSuite 97 as a whole — how to use SmartCenter, for example, to launch the SmartSuite 97 programs, open documents, and access other features; how to work with SmartIcons and save your work; how to use SmartSuite 97 with the Internet; how to get help if you're stuck; and how to figure out exactly which SmartSuite 97 program to use — and when. If you haven't played around with SmartSuite 97 at all yet, we strongly suggest you read through this part of the book before jumping ahead to another section that catches your fancy.

Part II: Take a Letter, Word Processor

The average computer user spends more time using a word-processing program than any other computer-related activity. This part shows you all the skills you need to put Word Pro's wordsmithing capabilities to work. By using Word Pro as outlined in this part, you can create, edit, format, and print documents — pieces of paper with words on 'em — in less time than you used to take to change a typewriter ribbon. You'll never need to dust off that old typewriter again. (You *do* remember typewriters, don't you . . . ?)

Part III: Spreadsheets As Easy As, Well — 1-2-3!

If working with numbers is your middle name (hmmm, that's a really weird middle name), 1-2-3's your game. If you think pocket calculators are cool, wait till you get a load of what 1-2-3 can do for you. Spreadsheet programs are generally credited with starting the personal computer revolution. After reading this part of the book, you'll know why. You'll be shown how to create and format worksheets for any purpose you can imagine, use formulas to automatically calculate results, and turn those results into charts and graphs to make the results understandable even to those folks whose eyes routinely glaze over at the sight of too many numbers.

Part IV: Caution — Database Approaching

If you need to manage piles of data; create forms, reports, and queries; and deal with other strange-sounding stuff about which you're currently clueless (if you have a life, that is), Approach should be your SmartSuite 97 tool of choice. This part of the book covers all the database basics you'll need to create anything from a simple name and address list to an integrated accounting system. Okay, so you need to know about accounting to create an integrated accounting system, but we still show you the basic steps you need to get rolling.

Part V: Freelance's Presentation Power

Whether you're pitching next year's budget to your corporation's board of directors or making a proposal to the local homeowners' association, presentations can be scary. If giving presentations makes you sweat, turn to this part of the book before you even *start* thinking about your next presentation. Freelance Graphics makes preparing and organizing all your presentation materials as easy as . . . well, *easy!* (Trust us.) This part shows you how to put together all the bits and pieces you need for a top-notch presentation, including title pages, charts, bulleted lists, text — you name it. You'll even find information on how to put together an on-screen electronic presentation. Gee, maybe you won't even need to show up at all.

Part VI: Organize Your Life

This is the part of the book to turn to if you want to computerize all the entries you *should* have made in your pocket day planner. These chapters tell you how to keep track of appointments, names and addresses, anniversary dates, and notes. You'll still need to enter the data yourself, but by using Organizer, at least you can *find* that data when you really need it.

Part VII: The Part of Tens

You want the top ten shortcuts for the SmartSuite 97 programs, ten best tips, ten of this and ten of that? Here they are. If you can't find the answer to your SmartSuite 97 questions or dilemmas elsewhere in the book, check out this part. You may get lucky.

A Word about Teamwork and Passing Notes

SmartSuite 97 includes some powerful features to facilitate team computing. The component programs all incorporate specific features to help you share your work with others and collaborate on projects. In particular, the SmartSuite 97 programs are designed to integrate with Notes, Lotus' popular groupware program. However, these are relatively advanced features that involve using networks of computers more than using the SmartSuite 97 programs themselves. As such, these features are beyond the scope of this book. Once you've gotten comfortable with SmartSuite 97, we encourage you to check with your network administrator to find out more about how you can reach out across the network to extend the capabilities of SmartSuite 97.

Foolish Assumptions

We don't make too many assumptions about our readers. We do, however, assume several things:

- ✔ You have a computer.
- ✔ You use Windows 95.
- ✔ You have SmartSuite loaded onto your computer. (If not, go immediately to our handy installation appendix at the end of this book.)

We don't assume that computers are your life — or even that you like computers, for that matter. We figure that you just want to find the answers to your questions so that you can use SmartSuite to get your work done with the least amount of fuss and bother. If any of the following items apply to you, we wrote this book for you:

✔ You're scared to death of computers and want gentle guidance through the SmartSuite minefield.

✔ You know a bit about computers in general, but haven't a clue about SmartSuite and don't want to remain clueless.

✔ You hate computers and want nothing to do with them, but your boss is forcing you to learn this stupid program.

Read More Dummies Books

Because this book covers all the SmartSuite programs in a limited number of pages, we can't cover every aspect of every program. We also don't cover a great deal about what you may need to know about computer basics and Windows.

Don't despair — ...*For Dummies* books can be found for every occasion. If you want to know more about the basics of computer operations, for example, check out *PCs For Dummies,* 3rd Edition, or *Windows 95 For Dummies.* For specific terms you don't recognize, try the *Illustrated Computer Dictionary For Dummies.* If you want more detail about some of the individual programs in SmartSuite, look for *1-2-3 97 For Windows For Dummies* and *Approach 97 For Windows For Dummies.*

Conventions Used in the Book

If you believe the old saw, consistency is the hobgoblin of small minds. Okay, we admit to having small minds when it comes to making things easy for you so that you have no trouble figuring out what the heck we mean when we tell you something about SmartSuite 97. So we adopted some conventions for this book.

You may notice that whenever we tell you to choose menu commands to perform some task, the names of these commands usually contain underlined letters. These underlined letters are called the *hot keys* for those commands. You can either use the mouse to click menu commands directly off the menu bar or opened menus, or you can use these hot keys instead. If we tell you to choose Edit⇔Undo, for example, you can either click the name of the Edit menu, as it appears on the menu bar, and then click the Undo command after the Edit menu opens — or you can press the Alt key and hold it down as you press the E key and then press the U key, all on your keyboard. (Pressing keys together like this is called using *key combinations.* Oh, and whenever you see that little arrow between a couple of menu commands, as in Edit⇨Undo in this example, it always means that you first open the menu named before the arrow and then choose from that open menu the command named after the arrow. Got it? No? Well, hang in there; we'll cover this more later, too. And if you don't know what we mean when we tell you to *click* a command, well. . . .)

If we tell you to *click* the mouse (or click a command or even to *single-click* something), that means to press and rapidly release the left mouse button. *Double-click* means to press and release the left mouse button *twice* in rapid succession. *Right-click* means to press and release the right mouse button.

If we want you to type something specific, such as on a page in a document, in a text box of a dialog box, or in a cell of a spreadsheet, that something appears in **boldface** type, just like the following:

Type **this text** in the Filename text box.

(Oh, and if we *really* want to be tricky, we put the words you type in regular text if the rest of the surrounding text is bold, as is the case in numbered list paragraphs that tell you specific actions to take.)

If we want to show you something that appears on-screen — particularly text that appears in list boxes — we put that text in a special typeface (like `this`). Just remember whenever you see that kind of type that you're seeing something here on the page that you should also be seeing on-screen.

Text that appears in *italic* type indicates a new term (which we try to explain in the surrounding text) or something we think is important enough to emphasize. Italics are also used for book titles, words in foreign languages (no, not computerese), and so on.

If you see several paragraphs of text with a gray background surrounded by a box stuck smack-dab in the middle of a page of regular text, you've encountered a *sidebar*. Sidebars provide useful, or at least interesting, information that you can often safely skip. The following is an example of a sidebar:

Sidebars are cool!

You don't have to read any of the sidebars to get all the essential information you need to use SmartSuite. On the other hand, you'll usually find the sidebar information interesting and enjoyable. Well, at least we enjoyed writing them.

Icons Used in This Book

The following *icons* (little circled pictures clueing you in to special portions of the text) are strategically placed in the margins to point out stuff you may — or may not — want to read right away.

This alerts you to nerdy technical discussions you may want to skip (or read — for the nerd in each of us).

Any shortcuts or new insights on a topic are marked with this icon.

This icon provides a friendly reminder to do something.

This icon provides a friendly reminder *not* to do something.

This icon indicates a feature that two or more SmartSuite programs share or a way to use the various SmartSuite programs together.

This icon indicates a link to the Internet or a feature that enables you to use the Internet.

Figures and features

SmartSuite 97 has many options and customizable features. We have tried to write instructions and descriptions and capture screens for figures using the default settings for each SmartSuite 97 program. However, the programs may look slightly different on your screen, depending on the settings you are using and your computer system.

Where to Go from Here

Before diving into the text, scour the table of contents to find the topic you want to learn more about — and *then* jump right in. If you don't find what you seek in the table of contents, check the index. Remember that this book is a reference, not necessarily a cover-to-cover read. (If you're having a *really* good time reading it, however, we certainly won't mind if you devour every word.)

Ready to get going with SmartSuite 97? Well, what are you waiting for? Go to it!

Part I
A Suite Deal

The 5th Wave   By Rich Tennant

"ALL THIS STUFF? IT'S PART OF A SUITE OF INTEGRATED SOFTWARE PACKAGES DESIGNED TO HELP UNCLUTTER YOUR LIFE."

In this part . . .

SmartSuite 97 is more than just a group of independent computer programs. SmartSuite is actually a tightly integrated suite of programs (Smart*Suite*, get it?) with a ton of features that are the same in each of its programs. This part looks at SmartSuite as a whole entity — how to launch and switch among the programs and how to use its common features. So don't be a SmartSuite dummy — read this part and become a SmartSuite . . . er, *smarty*.

Chapter 1
Boot Camp for SmartSuite

. . . .

In This Chapter

▶ Introducing the SmartSuite family members

▶ Learning about the SmartSuite family's common commands

▶ Getting caught up in SmartSuite's Internet capabilities

. . . .

A *suite* is more than just a collection of popular programs in the same box. Although all the component programs in SmartSuite 97 are powerful, stand-alone applications designed to fulfill specific computing needs, each program is also designed to work with all the other programs in the suite. SmartSuite enables you to easily share information among its component programs. You can develop a table in 1-2-3, for example, add that table to a letter you write in Word Pro, and then merge names and addresses into the letter from an Approach database.

All the SmartSuite programs share a strong family resemblance. They look alike (or at least as much alike as a word processor and a spreadsheet or other program can look). But the family resemblance goes beyond appearances — the various SmartSuite programs work alike, too. Common actions are exactly the same in all the SmartSuite programs. That makes learning to use all the SmartSuite programs easier for you. After you figure out how to open a file in one SmartSuite program, you know how to open a file in all the other SmartSuite programs.

This chapter and Chapter 2 show you how to do all sorts of things in 1-2-3, Word Pro, Approach, Freelance, and Organizer, even though the individual programs aren't covered till later. Amazing — *but true!*

How Suite It Is: The SmartSuite Family

Now that you know what a suite is, you need to meet the members of the SmartSuite family. Each family member has its own specialty and a distinctive character that makes that program the tool of choice for particular tasks. But remember that each SmartSuite program is also designed to complement all the other SmartSuite programs.

Word Pro is the SmartSuite word processor. You use this program to dash off a quick memo, write a letter to Aunt Gertrude, prepare a report, or write a manuscript. Word Pro is likely to be your most-used SmartSuite program.

Lotus 1-2-3 is SmartSuite's resident number-crunching expert. You can use 1-2-3's columns and rows of numbers and formulas to prepare a budget or a price list, compare the cost of buying or leasing your next car, or calculate how much retirement income you are going to need. But 1-2-3 does more than numbers — the program also creates charts, graphs, and more to help you make sense of your calculations.

If you need to make a presentation, SmartSuite's *Freelance Graphics* can help you make your best impression. Freelance can help you organize your thoughts and turn your ideas into colorful visuals to support your presentation. Freelance may not make the knot in your stomach go away, but the knot may loosen a bit after you know you're well-prepared, thanks to this program.

Approach is the name of SmartSuite's database program. The idea of working with a computer database may seem intimidating, but this database is very, well, approachable. A database is, after all, just a place to keep lists. Approach can handle everything from simple mailing lists to inventory systems.

Organizer helps you clean up the clutter of a busy life by providing a place for you to keep track of all your appointments, telephone calls, to do lists, and addresses. Best of all, you already know how to use the program. Organizer looks just like the pocket calendar systems that are so popular — except that Organizer taps the power of your computer to do things that no paper calendar can do.

SmartCenter provides a convenient master control for all the SmartSuite programs and documents. With SmartCenter running, no SmartSuite program is more than a couple of mouse clicks away. SmartCenter also provides you with quick access to Internet sites, addresses, e-mail, and online Help for SmartSuite programs.

ScreenCam is a nifty little utility that lets you record screen activity and, if you have a sound card and microphone installed, a narration in your own voice. It's great for creating training demos that simultaneously show and tell someone how to do something on the computer. Of course, like your VCR, you're more likely to use ScreenCam to play back recordings someone else makes than to create your own "movies." You don't need special training for simple playback of ScreenCam movie files created by someone else, so we won't cover it in this book.

It's All in the Family

As already described, all the SmartSuite programs share some of the same features — after you know how to use a common feature in one program, you know how to use that same feature in all the SmartSuite programs. This interchangeability is all part of that family resemblance we've been talking about.

The following sections briefly describe just a few of the many features shared by all (or most of) the SmartSuite programs. We introduce many more of these common features in later chapters. We mark each of these common features with the Linking icon (described in the Introduction to this book) — so get into the habit of looking for the ubiquitous little critter.

Get smart — icons, that is

All the SmartSuite programs (except ScreenCam) include a variety of icon palettes, called *SmartIcons,* that put access to many common features a mere click away. So what exactly is a SmartIcon? A SmartIcon is simply a button that displays a little picture (called, naturally enough, an *icon*). Clicking a SmartIcon causes the program to perform some common task, such as saving your document. You can also perform the same action by choosing the equivalent command from a menu — the SmartIcon is just faster and more convenient to use.

Sets of SmartIcons designed for performing related tasks are grouped together into *palettes*. In most SmartSuite programs, you usually find palettes of SmartIcons positioned just below the menu bar. You can, however, drag SmartIcon palettes to any on-screen position that is convenient for you. SmartIcon palettes can cling to the sides of the SmartSuite program window or even float on top of your document, as shown in Figure 1-1.

That different SmartIcons exist for each different SmartSuite program only makes sense. After all, each program performs different functions. Those nice folks at Lotus, however — always trying to make your lives easier — tried their best to make as many of the SmartIcons as possible appear and work exactly the same from program to program. Figure 1-2 shows typical SmartIcon palettes.

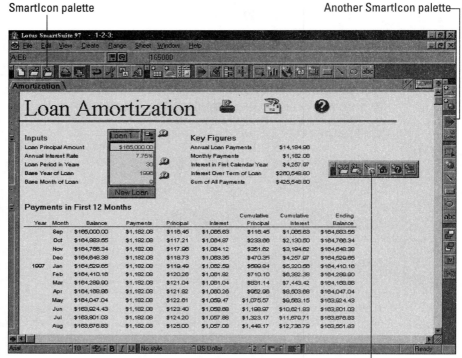

Smartlcon palette

Another SmartIcon palette

Floating SmartIcon palette

Figure 1-1:
SmartIcon
palettes
aren't
locked to
any one
place in the
program
window.

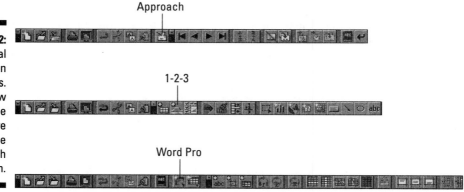

Approach

1-2-3

Word Pro

Figure 1-2:
Typical
SmartIcon
palettes.
Notice how
many of the
icons are
the same
for each
program.

As you work with SmartIcons, keep the following points in mind:

✔ You don't need to remember what each SmartIcon does (although you're likely to start remembering them as you use them regularly). Whenever you position the mouse pointer on a SmartIcon for a couple of seconds, a bubble appears describing the icon.

✔ To use any of the SmartIcons, just point to one and click the left mouse button. If you know how to use the SmartIcons in one program, you know how to use them in all the programs.

Note: As you read through the chapters of this book, you see the most useful SmartIcons for each program pointed out and described.

✔ Although you can use most features in SmartSuite without a mouse, you must use your mouse to access SmartIcons. (Fortunately, alternatives are available for most SmartIcon functions. You could, for example, choose File⇨Save from the menu bar or press Ctrl+S instead of clicking the Save SmartIcon.)

Checking your status (bar)

Each of the SmartSuite programs (except Organizer and ScreenCam) features a *status bar* at the bottom of the screen. As you discover in each of the book's SmartSuite program sections, the status bar provides valuable information; you can also click various portions of the status bar to display a list of options, which enables you to make changes to your document and window more easily than you can by choosing commands from a menu.

You can choose which paragraph style to use, for example, by clicking the portion of the status bar displaying the paragraph symbol and style name, as shown in the Word Pro status bar in Figure 1-3.

Figure 1-3:
The Word
Pro status
bar displays
a list of
paragraph
styles.

Keep the following points in mind about status bars:

✔ Although the status bars in each program are a bit different from one another, each status bar generally offers you the most efficient way to change styles and formats, fonts (typefaces), and type sizes.

✔ Get used to looking at the status bar for useful information about your current document or environment. You can usually ascertain such information as the current style, font, type size, and page number.

✔ The status bars are discussed in each of the program sections of the book, but all work pretty much the same.

✔ You can completely avoid status bars if you have some sort of status bar allergy. You miss out on some good information, but anything you can do with the status bar you can also do with menus and dialog boxes. Give status bars a try, however, as they save you a lot of time.

Keeping tabs on dialog boxes

Many of the dialog boxes in the SmartSuite programs are *tabbed* dialog boxes, such as the one shown in Figure 1-4. These dialog boxes have a row of labels across the top that look similar to the tabs in a three-ring binder or a box of index cards. The tabs enabled Lotus to squeeze more information or options into these dialog boxes than would normally fit and enable you to work with several related groups of settings without opening multiple dialog boxes.

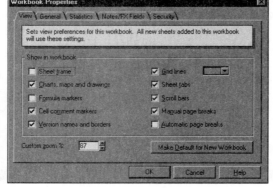

Figure 1-4:
Click a tab
to access
another
page of
options.

Each tab represents a separate page of options. You just click a tab to bring that page of options to the front where you can work with them. Then you can select another tab and adjust the settings on that page and so on. You can jump back and forth among the tabs as much as you want. After you're through working in the dialog box, just click the OK button to apply the settings and close the dialog box. You can also close the dialog box by clicking the Close button (the button with the X, located in the upper-right corner of the dialog box).

InfoBox — the super dialog box

The major SmartSuite programs (1-2-3, Word Pro, Approach, and Freelance) all use a special kind of dialog box for formatting text and such. Called an *InfoBox,* this handy little feature pulls all sorts of formatting options together.

An InfoBox, such as the one shown in Figure 1-5, is essentially a tabbed dialog box that displays the properties of a selected object. The InfoBox, however, is a little more unusual. Unlike with normal dialog boxes, any settings that you change in the InfoBox take effect immediately. You don't need to click OK to close the dialog box and apply the settings. You can also leave the InfoBox open and select another object (a block of text, a picture, or whatever), and the InfoBox displays the settings for the newly selected object, which replace those of the previously selected object. The InfoBox also features a drop-down list at the top to enable you choose between different levels of formatting — for example, between Text formatting and Page Layout formatting.

Figure 1-5:
The InfoBox
handles
formatting
chores.

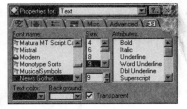

Use Fast Format to make quick work of copying styles

Suppose you format a row of numbers just so in 1-2-3. You select a different font and color for the numbers and add a shaded background to make the numbers stand out from the surrounding information. Now you need to add the same formatting to another area of your spreadsheet. Instead of tediously noting the formatting settings and then manually duplicating the same settings elsewhere, you can use the *Fast Format* feature to copy formatting with a sweep of your mouse. This feature is available in Word Pro, 1-2-3, Approach, and Freelance.

Simply select a spreadsheet cell or range that's formatted the way you want. Then choose the Fast Format command. (In 1-2-3, for example, the command is Range⇨Fast Format. In other programs, the command appears on other menus, but it always operates the same.) The pointer changes to a paint brush, as shown in Figure 1-6. All you need do is drag the pointer across another range of numbers to apply the formatting from your sample to the new area. Pretty slick, huh?

After you finish "painting" with the Fast Format brush, choose the command again to turn Fast Format off and return to normal operations.

Impress your mom — spell it right

If you've used most any modern word processing program recently, the fact that SmartSuite enables you to check the spelling in your documents probably comes as no great surprise. You would, in fact, be more surprised if SmartSuite *didn't* have this capability. Okay, so what's the big deal?

Figure 1-6:
The Fast
Format
feature
enables you
to easily
copy
formatting
from one
area to
another.

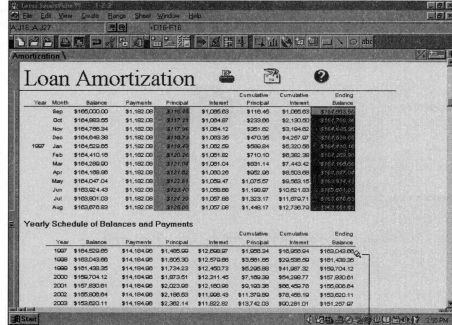

Paintbrush pointer

The big deal is that all the SmartSuite programs (except poor little Organizer, which has no spell checker) share the same spell-checking dictionary. After you tell one SmartSuite program that how you spell your name really is correct, you don't need to tell any of the other programs the same thing. They already know. Trust us when we tell you that this feature is really cool. You start the spell-checking process in all the programs exactly the same way — by choosing Edit⇨Check Spelling. The Spell Check dialog boxes that appear vary somewhat depending on which program you're using. The Spell Check dialog box in Approach, for example, offers different options than the one for 1-2-3 does, as you can see in Figure 1-7.

Figure 1-7:
The Spell
Check
dialog boxes
vary slightly
but perform
the same
basic
operation.

Spell Check dialog box for Approach

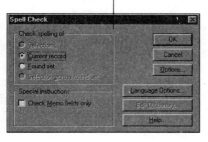

After you choose the portion of the document to check, the Spell Checker searches for possibly misspelled words. If the Spell Checker finds an unfamiliar word, the dialog box displays the word, along with suggested replacements.

As you use the Spell Checker feature in the various SmartSuite programs, keep the following points in mind:

✔ If the word the Spell Checker flags is spelled just the way you want, you can click the Skip button to ignore this one occurrence or you can click Skip All to ignore all occurrences of this spelling in the document.

✔ If the word is one you think that you intend to use again in the future — and you're sure the word's spelled correctly — you can click the Add To Dictionary button so that the Spell Checker doesn't bother you if it encounters that word again.

✔ If the Spell Checker offers some suggested alternatives, you can click the correct alternative and then click the Replace button to replace this occurrence with the alternative, or you can click Replace All to replace any occurrence of this word in the document with the alternative.

As important as spell-checking is to your documents, using a spell checker is no substitute for proofreading. The Spell Checker doesn't stop at a correctly spelled word that just isn't the right word for the context. The feature is not that smart. Suppose that you type *to* or *two,* but you really meant to type *too.* The Spell Checker can't catch that error. Distinguishing between such words is still a job for real people. (Thank goodness *something* is left for us to do.)

Save your stuff

No matter which SmartSuite program you use, you need to save the stuff you're working on in a file on your disk. And no matter which program you use, you save files in exactly the same way. Simply choose File⇨Save As to open the Save As dialog box, as shown in Figure 1-8. You can select the disk drive and folder to which you want to save the file and give your file a name. Depending on which program you're using, you can also select different options, such as saving a portion of the document or using different file formats for compatibility with other programs. After you name the file and select any appropriate options, click the dialog box's Save button to record the information on your disk.

Figure 1-8: You can name your file in the Save As dialog box — in this case, the one used in Word Pro.

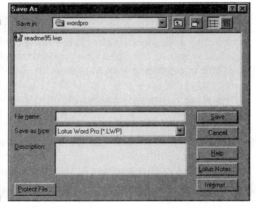

After you save a file the first time, subsequent saves are even easier. If you're working on a file, you can choose File⇨Save (or press Ctrl+S) to update the file with your latest changes without bothering with the Save As dialog box or entering the name of the file each time.

If you want to reuse or edit a file you saved, choose File⇨Open to open a dialog box very similar to the Save As dialog box. Just as you did when you saved the file, you can select the drive and folder and then select the file from the large list box. Then click the Open button to open the file. This operation works the same in all the SmartSuite programs.

A quick trip to the printer

Another operation that's essentially the same in all the SmartSuite programs is printing. Regardless of which program you're using, you start the printing process by choosing File➪Print. This command opens a dialog box. The Print dialog box enables you to choose which printer to use (assuming you installed more than one printer) and to specify what portion of the current document to print. The details of this dialog box vary slightly depending on which program you're using. After you adjust the settings as needed, click OK to start printing.

Click the Properties button in the Print dialog box to open a standard Windows dialog box in which you can adjust your printer settings.

Before you print, check the document's page layout to make sure that margins and such are set correctly. In Word Pro, press Alt+Enter to open the InfoBox and then select Page Layout from the drop-down list in the InfoBox title bar to access the margin settings. In the other programs, choose File➪Page Setup (or a similar command) to open a dialog box containing settings appropriate to that program's output.

Go team!

All the SmartSuite programs include features that make the often-complicated task of collaborating on projects with other members of a team or work group easier. The *Team Computing* features, as they are called, include some or all of the following, depending on which program you're using:

- *TeamMail* — enables you to send an e-mail message to a colleague and include all or part of the document you're working on.

- *TeamReview* — enables you to send a document, spreadsheet, or presentation to other team members for review and comments. You control who gets what editing privileges and can review their comments and suggestions.

- *TeamConsolidate* — helps you evaluate review comments by combining multiple documents into one.

- *TeamShow* — enables you to show a presentation to several team members simultaneously over a network.

- *TeamSecurity* — makes handling file-sharing controls for Approach and Word Pro files easier on a network.

These Team Computing features are cool stuff — provided that you and the other members of your team have access to the SmartSuite programs, network connections, and e-mail systems required in order to make them work.

We're not going to delve into SmartSuite's Team Computing features in this book, however, because many readers probably aren't able to take advantage of them. Those who can surely also have access to system administrators and a corporate computing services staff to help in using these features. If you're one of those lucky ones, make sure that you check out the Team Computing capabilities in SmartSuite.

Caught Up in the Net

The Internet is in the process of revolutionizing the way many of us work.

All the SmartSuite programs are Internet-aware to one extent or another. This awareness starts with the simple (but unusual) capability of each program to open files from and save files to remote computers that are connected to the Internet. All the SmartSuite programs except Organizer and ScreenCam can also use the Net's File Transfer Protocol (FTP) to save files to an FTP site — and can do so directly from within the program. You don't need to save the file on your local hard disk and then use a separate utility to transfer the file across the Net to the FTP server.

You can use the File⇨Save As command to open the Save As dialog box, and then just click the Internet button to open the Save to Internet dialog box, where you can enter all the information your SmartSuite program needs to locate the other computer on the Internet. Then just click the Save button to save your file.

Word Pro, 1-2-3, and Freelance Graphics can all save their respective documents as HTML files (the standard file format for World Wide Web pages) that can be posted on a server on the Internet or a corporate intranet and viewed by anyone with a standard Web browser such as Netscape Navigator or Internet Explorer.

SmartSuite's Internet connections aren't confined to the output of the SmartSuite programs either. SmartCenter has its own links to the Net that give you instant access to Web sites for news, reference, technical support, and more. You can find out more about SmartCenter in Chapter 2.

Chapter 2

Taking Control: Working with SmartCenter

· ·

· ·

*Y*ou can think of *SmartCenter* as the glue that holds all the SmartSuite 97 programs together. It's not — but you're welcome to think of it that way. SmartCenter is really a group of buttons that make starting — and switching among — your SmartSuite programs unbelievably easy. SmartCenter is your central command center for SmartSuite — and more.

What Is SmartCenter?

SmartCenter is a little like the Windows 95 taskbar — a button bar that always lurks at the edge of your computer screen to help you launch and switch among programs. But SmartCenter is more than just a convenient way to start SmartSuite programs. SmartCenter also provides easy access to document files, Internet sites, an address book, and much more. In other words, SmartCenter helps you organize your computer desktop so that everything is kept neatly in its place.

SmartCenter normally resides in a strip situated across the top of the computer screen. And SmartCenter jealously guards its turf. Even if you maximize a program window, SmartCenter stays visible — and available — right at the top of your screen. Other program windows never cover up SmartCenter (unless, of course, you configure SmartCenter to act otherwise).

If you installed SmartSuite on your computer by using the standard installation procedure — and you didn't change the setup — SmartCenter automatically swings into action right after you start Windows 95. After Windows starts, you see the Welcome to Lotus SmartSuite logo. Then the row of buttons that make up SmartCenter appears on-screen, as shown in Figure 2-1. If all the buttons don't fit on your computer screen, a couple of arrows appear at the right end of the SmartCenter bar. Just click the right arrow button to slide more SmartCenter buttons into view. Click the left arrow button to bring the other buttons back into view.

Figure 2-1:
This row of buttons is the Lotus SmartCenter.

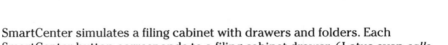

SmartCenter simulates a filing cabinet with drawers and folders. Each SmartCenter button corresponds to a filing cabinet drawer. (Lotus even *calls* the buttons *drawers*.) Click a drawer button, and the "drawer" itself slides open revealing — you guessed it! — *folders* (see Figure 2-2).

SmartCenter menu button

Open drawer

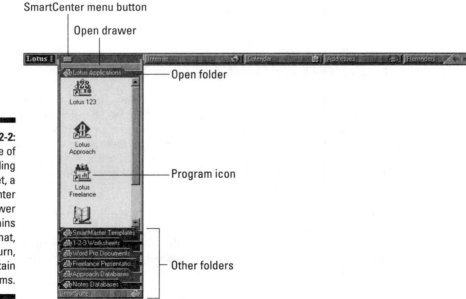

Open folder

Figure 2-2:
Like those of a real filing cabinet, a SmartCenter drawer contains folders that, in turn, contain useful items.

Program icon

Other folders

Folders can contain a variety of items depending on the kind of drawer in which the folder is located. The Lotus Applications folder, shown open in Figure 2-2, for example, contains shortcut icons for all the SmartSuite programs. Other folders in the drawer contain shortcut icons for the documents you create using your SmartSuite programs. The folders in other drawers may offer address-book entries, access to reference materials, links to Internet sites, and so on.

Opening Drawers and Folders

You can start your SmartSuite program just as you start other Windows programs — click the Start button in the taskbar, point to Programs, point to Lotus SmartSuite in the cascading menu that appears, and finally, select (or click) the SmartSuite program you want to start from yet another cascading menu. Yeck! Surely SmartSuite offers an easier way to get started. (Fortunately, it does.)

If SmartCenter is visible on-screen, any SmartSuite program is just a few clicks away (and you don't need to concern yourself about menus that seem to slip from your grasp and close unexpectedly). To start a program, just click the SmartSuite drawer button in the SmartCenter to open its drawer, click the Lotus Applications folder tab, and then double-click the icon for the program you want to start. Before you realize what's happening — or shortly thereafter — that program appears on-screen. To close the SmartCenter drawer, simply click the drawer front again.

- ✔ SmartCenter is always visible, no matter which Windows program you're running. Even if you're using a Windows program that isn't one of the SmartSuite programs, SmartCenter stays with you like a guardian angel.

- ✔ Don't worry about remembering which SmartSuite programs are running. You don't end up with two copies of the program hogging your computer's memory if you click the icon of a program that is already running. If, for example, you're creating a Word Pro document, clicking its SmartCenter icon does absolutely nothing. If you're working in another program, but Word Pro is running in the background, clicking its SmartCenter icon brings Word Pro to the foreground without closing the current program.

- ✔ If you want to get rid of SmartCenter, click the SmartCenter menu button (the black button at the left end of SmartCenter with Lotus written on it), and choose Exit SmartCenter. SmartCenter goes away and the other program windows get a bit bigger to use the space previously occupied by SmartCenter.

- ✔ If SmartCenter isn't running, and you want to use it, click the Start button in the taskbar, point to Programs, point to Lotus SmartSuite, and then select (click) Lotus SmartCenter 97.

SmartSuite programs and documents

The first of the default SmartCenter drawers is the one you're likely to use the most. The SmartSuite drawer, as it's aptly named, provides quick access to your SmartSuite programs and documents. In addition to the Lotus Applications folder you've already seen in action, this drawer contains folders for templates and for documents (files) that you create in each of the major SmartSuite programs. The SmartSuite drawer even contains a folder set up for Notes Databases for those of you using Lotus Notes to share information among members of your workgroup. The following list details some things you can do with SmartCenter drawers:

✔ You can add shortcut icons to a folder in a SmartCenter drawer by simply dragging a shortcut from your Windows desktop or from an Explorer window and dropping the icon on an empty space in an open folder.

✔ You can drag a file icon from a Windows Explorer window and drop that icon onto a program icon in the Lotus Applications folder. SmartCenter starts the program and tries to load the file you dropped.

✔ You can easily get rid of any folder you don't need. Just right-click the folder and choose Delete Folder from the pop-up menu that appears. Confirm the action by clicking Yes in the dialog box that appears, and — poof! — the folder is gone.

Note: If you are not experienced in the ways of using shortcut icons and drag-and-drop techniques, you can read up on these subjects in *Windows 95 For Dummies,* by Andy Rathbone (published by IDG Books Worldwide, Inc.).

Internet

SmartCenter's Internet drawer enables you to reach out beyond the limits of your own computer and tap into the resources of the Internet, putting some handy information at your fingertips. SmartCenter uses your existing Internet connection and World Wide Web browser software to deliver the information you select in the Internet drawer. For the most part, SmartCenter's Internet drawer just provides a collection of useful Web sites in a convenient and easy-to-use format. On the other hand, some of the folders, such as Headlines, Stock Quotes, Weather, and Web Reference, can display Internet information right in the folder.

Obviously, you need an Internet connection for this to work. SmartCenter is designed to work best on a computer that has a full-time Internet connection (usually provided by a local area network that is linked to the Internet), but SmartCenter also works pretty well over a dial-up connection to an Internet service provider. Configuring an Internet connection and Web browser are beyond the scope of this book. Fortunately, once your Internet connection and Web browser are set up to work properly in Windows 95, SmartCenter requires little or no additional setup to use the same connection.

If your connection to the Internet is via a local area network, your network system administrator should be able to get you set up. (If your network uses a security device called a proxy server, you'll need to enter its address in the Internet Settings dialog box — which you can reach by opening the Folder Properties dialog box, as explained below — and then click the Internet Settings button.) If you use a dial-up Internet connection, try to get a knowledgeable colleague to configure the various settings for you. Otherwise, you probably need to consult with the technical support staff at your Internet service provider, and perhaps read up on the subject in *The Internet For Dummies,* 4th Edition by John Levine, Carol Baroudi, and Margaret Levine-Young (published by IDG Books Worldwide, Inc.).

If possible, you want your system configured to automatically launch your Web browser and initiate a dial-up network connection when you attempt to open or run a URL (a *Uniform Resource Locator,* or Internet address). Getting this to happen automatically requires some add-on utility software as well as all the right settings in Windows 95 — which is why it's probably worth bribing your favorite computer geek with a free lunch to set your computer up for you.

The features of the Internet drawer require a full-featured Internet connection capable of supporting a connection to the World Wide Web. Most direct network connections will work just fine, as will dial-up connections that go by names such as SLIP and PPP. However, a text-only, e-mail Internet connection just won't get the job done. Talk to your network administrator or Internet provider to find out if your Internet connection has what SmartSuite needs.

SmartCenter's Internet drawer comes with an assortment of folders that provide you with easy access to Internet resources for news, weather, reference material, and more. The default folders include the following:

- ✔ **Headlines.** The Headlines folder connects to Yahoo! — a powerful and popular Internet index and search site — to download the wire service headlines displayed in the folder. Click on an underlined headline to retrieve the story from Yahoo! and display it in your Web browser.

- ✔ **Stock Quotes.** After you tell SmartCenter what stock ticker symbols you want to track, you can view reasonably current (15-minute delayed) price quotes for those stocks in the Stock Quotes folder.

- ✔ **Weather.** Just tell SmartCenter what city you're interested in and it will display a brief summary of current and forecast conditions in the Weather folder.

- ✔ **Web Reference.** This folder is a collection of links to useful reference sites on the World Wide Web. Click on an underlined item to launch your Web browser and connect to that site.

✔ **Bookmarks.** Do you have favorite Web sites you want to revisit? If you saved the locations as bookmarks in your Web browser, SmartCenter displays the list of bookmarks in this folder. To visit a bookmarked Web site, simply click on an underlined item in the Bookmarks folder. SmartCenter will launch your Web browser and load the Web page.

✔ **Favorites.** This folder works like the Bookmarks folder. It provides easy access to Web sites, documents, files, and other shortcuts saved in your Windows 95 Favorites folder.

The folders in the Internet drawer need to be customized in order to meet your needs and make the best use of your Internet connection. For instance, you need to select what news category you want to see in the Headlines folder, what city you want weather reports for, and what stocks you want to track in the Stock Quotes folder. You can also specify whether you want to update the information in the folders manually or whether you want SmartCenter to handle the updates automatically at preset intervals. To customize a folder's settings, follow these steps:

1. **Right-click on the folder tab you want to customize and choose Folder Properties from the pop-up menu that appears.**

   This opens the Folder Properties dialog box for that folder. The dialog box contains a Basics tab plus another tab, depending on what kind of folder it is. For instance, the Folder Properties dialog box for a Headlines folder contains a Basics tab and a News tab.

2. **Click the Basics tab and adjust the folder's color, label, and icon settings, if desired.**

   You probably won't need to adjust these settings, but it's easy to do. To change the folder label, simply type the new label text into the Folder label text box. To change the color of the folder's tab, click the arrow button at the right end of the Color box and select a color by clicking on the desired color in the color palette that appears. To change the icon, simply choose a new icon from the Icon drop-down list.

3. **Click the News (or Weather, or Stocks) tab and select the options specific to that folder type.**

   The options available on this tab vary depending on the folder type. For example, on the News tab, you can choose what news category you want to see in the folder. Your choices include the following: Top Stories, World News, Technology, Business, and Sports.

   Want to see news from more than one category? No problem. Just create another folder for the additional news category. See the "Adding drawers and folders" section later in this chapter for instructions.

   Other folder types have other options appropriate to those folders. You can specify what stocks you want to track in a Stock Quote folder or the city for which you want weather reports in a Weather folder.

4. **If you want SmartCenter to update the information in the folder automatically, click the <u>R</u>efresh every check box and enter an appropriate number in the <u>m</u>inutes text box.**

   Note: Automatic updates are great if you enjoy the luxury of a full-time Internet connection. However, if you have a dial-up Internet connection, you probably want to leave the automatic refresh option disabled and refresh the folder information manually after establishing an Internet connection.

5. **If your Internet connection goes through a proxy server, click the Internet Settings button to open a dialog box where you can enter the proxy settings; then click OK to close the Internet Settings dialog box.**

   This is an advanced setting. You need to consult your network system administrator to determine whether your network uses a proxy server and get the address of the server.

6. **Click OK to close the Folder Properties dialog box and record your settings.**

   Now your folder is ready to use.

If you have a dial-up Internet connection you need to establish your Internet connection manually and then update the folders in SmartCenter's Internet drawer. To manually update the information in a folder, right-click the folder tab and choose Refresh from the pop-up menu that appears.

Addresses and mail

The Addresses drawer is another of SmartCenter's default drawers. After you open the Addresses drawer, you see a display reminiscent of those flip-top phone directories with the alphabet tabs along the side. Click a letter tab to display a list of address entries that start with that letter. Next, click an entry name to display more details on an address card for that listing, as shown in Figure 2-3. The buttons on the address card that appears enable you to start a letter in Word Pro, dial the phone number, dial the fax number, or send an e-mail message.

To add a new name and address to the folder, just click the Add Name entry in the address list. SmartCenter opens a dialog box in which you can fill in the information for the new entry. Then click OK to record the name and address in the folder.

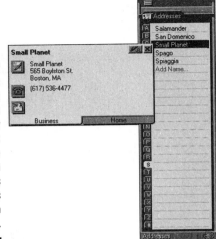

Figure 2-3:
Each
address
card entry
has room
for home
information
as well as
the business
information
shown here.

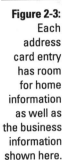

SmartCenter can maintain a separate list of addresses but is at its best if you use the feature to access the address section of your Organizer file. To link the Addresses folder to your Organizer file, right-click the Addresses folder tab and choose Folder Properties from the pop-up menu that appears. In the Folder Properties dialog box, click the Name & Address tab, select Lotus Organizer file in the File Type drop-down list box, fill in the filename for your Organizer file in the Name of Lotus Organizer file text box, and then choose your Address Book section from the Section drop-down list box. Click OK to complete the link.

Although SmartCenter doesn't offer one among its default folders, you can create a special folder type for handling e-mail. If you get your e-mail service through Lotus Notes, cc:Mail, or a compatible VIM mail program, the capability to access to your e-mail from SmartCenter can be really handy. (Check with your network system administrator to find out if your e-mail system is compatible with SmartCenter.)

Calendar

The Calendar drawer in SmartCenter is another one that you can link to your Organizer file. Just open the Calendar drawer to view a display of your appointments for the day, as shown in Figure 2-4. Need to see appointments at earlier or later times? Simply click the Morning or Evening arrows, which are located above and below the Time column, respectively, to scroll the calendar display up or down. To view entries for a different date, click the date number icon. SmartCenter opens a Calendar dialog box in which you can click another date to display appointments for that day. The following list tells you more stuff you can do with the Calendar drawer:

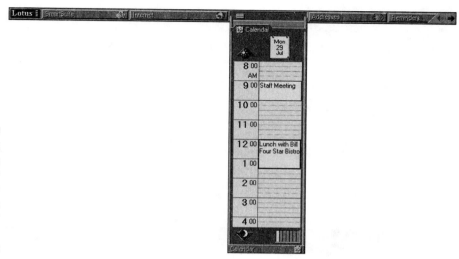

Figure 2-4:
The Calendar drawer keeps track of your appointments.

✔ To link the Calendar folder to your Organizer file, right-click the Calendar folder tab and choose Folder Properties from the pop-up menu that appears. This action opens the Folder Properties dialog box. Click the Calendar tab, open the File Type drop-down list box and choose Lotus Organizer file, fill in the filename for your Organizer file in the Name of Lotus Organizer file text box, and then choose the appropriate section in the Section drop-down list box. Click OK to complete the link.

✔ You can set the Calendar drawer to open automatically to remind you of appointments. The Open Drawer check box is located at the bottom of the Calendar tab in the Folder Properties dialog box. You can even set how much in advance of each appointment you want to be notified.

✔ To add an appointment to the Calendar folder, simply drag the mouse pointer down across the appropriate time span in the Calendar display. For example, to schedule a two-hour meeting starting at 2:00 p.m., simply click at the top of the 2:00 time block and drag down to 4:00. SmartCenter displays a small Create Appointment dialog box in which you can enter a description of the appointment and then click OK to record that appointment in the Calendar. To enter more information about an appointment, however, you need to set up the appointment in Organizer. (See Chapter 22 for more details.)

✔ You can display appointments for more than one day by clicking the corresponding columns in the Days to Display box, located in the lower-right corner of the Calendar folder. For example, to see three consecutive days of appointments, click the third column. SmartCenter automatically widens the Calendar drawer to accommodate the additional days.

✔ To make a drawer wider (or narrower), open the drawer and position the mouse pointer anywhere along the right edge of the drawer. After the pointer changes to a double-headed arrow, you can drag right or left to make the drawer wider or narrower.

Reminders

The SmartCenter Reminders drawer (as shown in Figure 2-5) is a convenient place to keep a simple to-do list. By default, the Reminders drawer contains folders for Home and Business reminders. But you can add folders for projects and other special uses if you want. (See the section "Customizing SmartCenter," later in this chapter.)

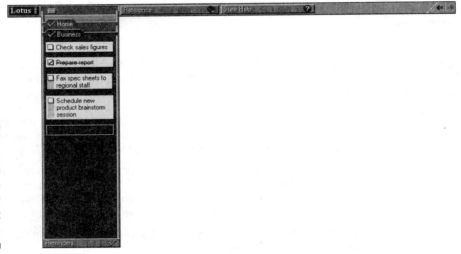

Figure 2-5:
The Reminders drawer keeps your to-do list handy.

Note: Unlike the Calendar and Addresses drawers, the Reminders drawer does not have any provision for linking to your Organizer file. You must keep track of which items you list in the Reminders drawer and which items you track in Organizer.

The following list describes some of the things you can do in the Reminders drawer:

✔ To add a reminder, select a reminder folder to open that folder, click the empty rectangle, and type in the reminder text.

✔ You can mark a reminder as completed by clicking the check box beside the reminder item.

✔ To delete any reminder item from the list, right-click the item and choose <u>D</u>elete Reminder from the pop-up menu that appears.

   ✔ You can delete all the completed reminder items at once by right-clicking the folder tab and choosing Delete <u>C</u>ompleted Reminders from the pop-up menu that appears.

Reference

Did you ever wish you had a dictionary or thesaurus at your fingertips as you worked on some project? Well, now you do. The SmartCenter Reference drawer contains Dictionary and Thesaurus folders.

To use the dictionary, open the Reference drawer, click the Dictionary folder tab, type a word into the text box, and press Enter. SmartSuite's dictionary responds by displaying the definition, part of speech, and pronunciation guide for the word.

The Thesaurus folder works just like the Dictionary folder except that the display includes only a very brief definition of the word you type, followed by some synonyms for the word.

The Business Productivity drawer contains an assortment of templates and SmartMasters that Lotus thoughtfully includes with SmartSuite. In this drawer you can find templates for many routine business documents you need to create, all arranged in folders according to functional groups — not which program you use to create them — so you can just double-click an icon for what you want to do. For example, if you choose Amortize a loan in the Business Management folder, SmartSuite launches 1-2-3 and loads a workbook with a template for doing loan calculations. If you choose Positioning Proposal in the same folder, SmartSuite opens Freelance and starts a presentation based on the proposal SmartMaster.

Suite Help

The Suite Help drawer puts lots of resources that help you use SmartSuite just a mouse click away. The drawer contains folders for Help files, online documentation, Tours (instructional on-screen movies), and links to Internet Web sites. You see more of the Suite Help drawer in Chapter 3.

Customizing SmartCenter

If SmartCenter isn't set up just the way you want, you can make some modifications so that the feature performs more to your liking. You can, for example, make SmartCenter appear at the bottom of the screen instead of the top. (No, we don't know why you'd want to do that, but you can.) You can change the look of the drawer fronts, add and remove drawers and folders, and add items to folders. The point is that you can have it your way, as the folks at one of those fast-food burger joints used to say.

To start customizing, click the SmartCenter menu button — the first one on the left end of the SmartCenter (the black one that reads Lotus). Choose SmartCenter Properties from the menu that appears to open the SmartCenter Properties dialog box, as shown in Figure 2-6. This dialog box is one of those tabbed ones we talk about in Chapter 1. You find the first set of options on the Basics tab.

Figure 2-6:
Most of SmartCenter's customization options are contained in the SmartCenter Properties dialog box.

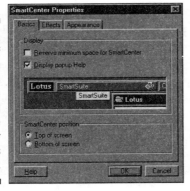

Redecorating SmartCenter

So you want to know what you can — and should — customize? Fair enough. Here's a bit about the Basics tab:

✔ You can reduce the amount of screen space SmartCenter requires by clicking the check box next to the Reserve Minimum Space for SmartCenter option. A check mark in this box tells SmartCenter to share its little strip of your computer screen with other programs.

✔ If you don't want to see the pop-up Help labels that appear as you rest the mouse pointer on a SmartCenter button for a few seconds, you can hide these labels by removing the check mark from the Display Popup Help option. Just click the check box to deselect this item.

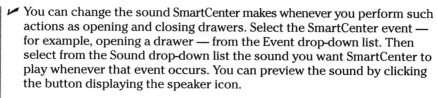 ✔ You can move SmartCenter to another portion of the screen by choosing the Top of Screen or Bottom of Screen option button.

Click the Effects tab in the SmartCenter Properties dialog box to see the next set of options, as shown in Figure 2-7. Now take a look at the customization options you find on this tab:

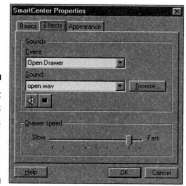

Figure 2-7:
The Effects
tab controls
sound
effects in
SmartCenter.

✔ You can change the sound SmartCenter makes whenever you perform such actions as opening and closing drawers. Select the SmartCenter event — for example, opening a drawer — from the Event drop-down list. Then select from the Sound drop-down list the sound you want SmartCenter to play whenever that event occurs. You can preview the sound by clicking the button displaying the speaker icon.

✔ To silence the sound of a SmartCenter event, select None in the Sound drop-down list. (Sounds are cool, but some sounds can become annoying after a while.)

✔ By adjusting the Drawer Speed slider at the bottom of the Effects tab, you can change how fast the SmartCenter drawers open and close after you click a drawer. Drag the marker to the left to make the drawers open slower. (We don't know why you'd want to do that, but you can.) Drag the marker to the right to make the drawers open faster.

The Appearance tab of the SmartCenter Properties dialog box is where you can get fancy with your SmartCenter redecorating. SmartCenter provides many textures you can apply to your drawer buttons. To select a different texture, simply scroll down the list to see your options and click the one you like.

After you make your choices in the SmartCenter Properties dialog box, click OK to apply the changes to SmartCenter.

Adding drawers and folders

So much for the cosmic effects; now to examine how to do something useful — such as adding your own drawers and folders. After all, SmartCenter is supposed to help you organize your work. For SmartCenter to succeed at that goal, you must be able to adapt the feature to your own style and to the projects on which you work.

To add a drawer to SmartCenter, click the SmartCenter menu button (the black Lotus button) and choose New Drawer from the menu that appears. The New Drawer dialog box appears. Type a name for your drawer in the Drawer Label text box. Then select an icon for the drawer from the Drawer Handle drop-down list box. After you click OK, the new drawer is added to SmartCenter.

Of course, an empty drawer doesn't do you much good. You want to put something in the drawer. You start by adding folders to a drawer. To add a new folder, follow these steps:

1. **Right-click the drawer to which you want to add a folder and choose New Folder from the pop-up menu that appears.**

    This action opens the New Folder dialog box, as shown in Figure 2-8.

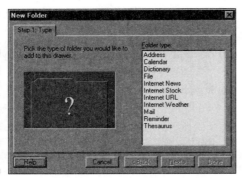

Figure 2-8:
The New
Folder
dialog box
starts out
with a
single tab.

The first step in creating the folder itself is deciding what type of folder you want. (Folder type is an important distinction, because the different folder types hold different kinds of information.)

2. **Choose the appropriate folder type by clicking its name in the Folder Type list.**

    The New Folder dialog box suddenly acquires some extra tabs. The exact nature of these tabs varies depending on the folder type you select.

3. **Click the Next button to proceed to the next step in creating a new folder.**

   For most folder types, that is the Basics tab, which is similar to the one shown in Figure 2-9.

Figure 2-9:
The Basics tab is where you label your new folder.

4. **Type a name for your new folder in the Folder Label text box.**

   You can also choose a color and icon for the folder from the Color and Icon drop-down list boxes.

5. **Click Next to move on to the next step.**

   The Step 3 and Step 4 tabs vary somewhat depending on what kind of folder you are creating. For a File folder type, for example, you need to specify whether you want to see large or small icons and whether the SmartCenter folder is linked to a Windows desktop folder; for an Internet Weather folder, you need to specify the location for which you want to receive weather reports and how often you want those reports updated.

6. **Fill in the information requested on each tab and click Next to move on to the next step (if you have one).**

7. **After you fill in all the information in the dialog box, click Done to create the folder.**

That's it! You created a new folder.

What can I put in a SmartCenter drawer?

The short answer to the question of what you can put in a SmartCenter drawer is — folders. The more pertinent question, however, is what can you put in a SmartCenter folder? The answer to that depends on what kind of folder you create.

Most of the folder types are designed to hold a specific kind of information. Address folders hold addresses, calendar folders hold appointments, and a dictionary folder provides access to the dictionary database built into SmartSuite.

The File folder type is a notable exception. This folder holds Windows shortcut icons. You can use file folders to hold shortcuts to programs (including non-SmartSuite programs) and shortcuts to files of all descriptions — even shortcuts to other Windows folders. (See Andy Rathbone's *Windows 95 For Dummies* — published by IDG Books Worldwide, Inc. — for more information on working with shortcut icons.)

SuiteStart: A Tray Full of SmartSuite Programs

SmartCenter and the Start menu aren't the only ways to start SmartSuite programs. The standard SmartSuite setup also installs *SuiteStart*, a set of icons for SmartSuite programs that appears in the system tray — the expandable section at the right end of the taskbar that is home to the clock display and speaker volume control icon. (See Figure 2-10.)

Figure 2-10:
The SuiteStart icons in the taskbar's system tray.

Taskbar   System tray   SuiteStart icons

To start a SmartSuite program by using SuiteStart, simply click the icon for the program you want to start. The program starts (almost) instantly. This method is by far the fastest way to start a SmartSuite program. Also, you can do the following with SuiteStart:

   ✔ If you decide you don't want SuiteStart in your taskbar, you can remove the feature by right-clicking any of the SuiteStart icons and choosing Exit from the pop-up menu that appears. SuiteStart removes itself from the taskbar.

   ✔ If SuiteStart isn't running and you want to use the feature, click the Start button, point to Programs, point to Lotus SmartSuite, point to Lotus Accessories, and select (click) Lotus SuiteStart 97.

Chapter 3

Moving On

● ●

● ●

*F*iguring out how to get unstuck — that's what this chapter's all about. Whether you're having trouble using a particular feature in a SmartSuite program or you don't even know which program to use to do what you want to do, we show you the way.

Help! What Do I Do Now?

What's the scariest thing about using computers for most people? It's not the fear that you may get sucked into the darned thing like the guy in the movie *Tron*. If you're like most folks, you're more likely to worry that you may panic if you can't figure out how to perform a task that's necessary to your work. That's probably why you bought this book — for which we thank you profusely. This book doesn't cover every SmartSuite feature, however, or even all the possible ways to use the features it does cover. So where can you turn?

Good news! All the SmartSuite programs are chock-full of helpful instructions and sage advice that can be called on whenever you need them. You can also tap the treasure trove of information in SmartCenter's Suite Help drawer.

Taking a tour

Each SmartSuite program includes a guided tour feature so that you can obtain a good overview of how the program works. So where exactly do you go to make reservations for these tours? Try the following locations:

  ✔ In SmartCenter, open the Suite Help drawer (by clicking the Suite Help drawer button), open the Tours folder by clicking its tab, and then double-click the icon for the tour you want to take.

✔ In each program, you can choose Help⇨Tour to start the tour for that program.

✔ Most of the SmartSuite programs (all except Organizer) offer the tour as an option in the Welcome dialog box that appears after you start the program. Just click the Take a Tour button to start the tour.

Note: Each of the tours leads you by the hand and tells you where to click and what to do to move through the tour. Also, the tours must run at a standard (640 x 480 pixels) screen resolution. So don't be too shocked if your screen blinks and everything changes sizes before the tour starts to run. After the tour is over, your screen returns to normal automatically.

The tours are a good way to get an overview of a program and some of its key features. Tours, however, aren't much help in learning how to perform some specific action in a program. You must look elsewhere for that help. Fortunately, plenty is available.

Hey! How about some help over here?

Most of the time, what you really need from SmartSuite's Help system is — help. Imagine that. You can get help in several ways, and the methods vary slightly among the SmartSuite programs, but you do have one consistent way to get the help you need in any SmartSuite program — by pressing F1 (the Help key). The F1 function key accesses *context-sensitive* Help — Help that's relevant to what you're doing at the moment. Most of the time, the SmartSuite program you're using knows what you're trying to do and displays the appropriate Help screen. Amazing! Suppose, for example, that you're in Word Pro and you notice the Frame command on the Create menu. You can't remember — or never knew — how to create a frame, and you want to know how . . . now. Just choose Create⇨ Frame, and then, when Word Pro opens the Create Frame dialog box, press F1. A Help window appears to instruct you on how to create a frame.

Your Help windows may be larger or smaller than the one shown in the figure. Just as you can resize other windows, you can resize Help windows by positioning the mouse pointer over one of the window's edges so that the pointer turns into a double-headed arrow; then hold down the left mouse button and drag the window's edge until the window becomes the size you want.

As you work with Help windows, remember the following points:

✔ Context-sensitive Help works for just about any menu command or dialog box option.

✔ More help for a topic is often available than can fit in one window. You may need to use the scroll bars to move down the window to bring the additional Help information into view.

✔ At the bottom of Help screens (you usually must scroll down to get there), you often find a small gray button beside some text such as See related topics. Click the button to view a list of related topics. Then you can select a topic from the list and click the Display button to view that topic. Don't be afraid to explore. In addition to the See Related Topics button, you sometimes see other buttons (such as See Details). Clicking these items takes you to related Help screens.

Finding Help on a topic

If context-sensitive Help doesn't give you the help you need, you can usually find what you need by searching for that information. You can choose Help⇨Help Topics or click the Help Topics button in most Help windows to open a dialog box similar to the one shown in Figure 3-1.

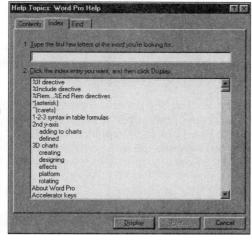

Figure 3-1:
Search for help on the topic you need in the Help Topics dialog box.

The Help Topics dialog box is another one of those tabbed dialog boxes. The three tabs give you three different ways to locate information in the Help file. The three tabs in the dialog box function as described in the following list:

 ✔ Perhaps the most useful of the three is the Index tab. This tab lists a program's Help topics in a format similar to that of the index in a book.

 To use the Index to search for information, type a word in the text box to display the portion of the list of Help topics that includes the word you want help with. Select a specific topic from the list by clicking the topic name and then click the Display button to display that Help topic in a Help window.

- ✔ The Contents tab of the Help Topics dialog box arranges the Help topics in a collapsible outline style similar to that of the table of contents of a book. If a topic displays a small, closed book icon next to its name, one or more subtopics are listed under the main topic. Double-click the book icon to view a list of those subtopics. (Guess what? Yep, the icon changes to an open book if the subtopics are visible. You can double-click the open book icon to hide the subtopics again.) If you see a Help topic listed with a question mark icon instead of a book, you can select that topic and click the Display button to view its information.

- ✔ The Find tab of the Help Topics dialog box provides a more detailed search of the Help topics for a program. You can use this feature to search for topics that may contain key words or phrases anywhere in the text — not just in the topic title. Using the Find tab, however, is more time-consuming than using the other tabs, and you usually don't need to bother with such a detailed search. You can usually find what you need by using one of the other techniques.

The Help Topics dialog box disappears after you display a specific Help topic in its own window. You can access the dialog box again if you want to look for another topic; just click the Help Topics button located below the menu bar of the window displaying the current Help topic.

In case you're wondering what version of a particular program you own, you can choose Help⇨About (whatever program you're in) to open a dialog box containing that information. In Word Pro, for example, choose Help⇨About Word Pro to display a dialog box showing the release (or version) number of the program. By the way, this tip works for most Windows programs — not just for SmartSuite.

Taking in a movie

Some Help topics include prerecorded demonstrations to show you how to perform some action. You can recognize these demos, if they're available, as they're accompanied by a button displaying a movie camera icon. Just click the button to play the demonstration lesson.

We just cover the basics of getting Help in this chapter. The best advice we can give you is to explore the various Help facilities in the individual SmartSuite programs. In addition to the basic information available in all the SmartSuite programs, specific programs offer more ways to help you learn to use their features. In Word Pro, for example, you can choose Help⇨Ask the Expert and complete the sentence How do I . . . in the Ask the Expert bar that appears across the top of the workspace to get help on a feature or procedure. In Freelance Graphics, you can click the Guide Me button to get context-sensitive advice.

Reading manuals on-screen

Tired of having to go dig up the manuals if you need to look up something? Well, you may be able to find the information you need with just a few mouse clicks instead. A wealth of documentation for the SmartSuite programs is available for you to read on-screen. You find these on-screen manuals in SmartCenter's Suite Help drawer. Just open the DocOnline folder and double-click the icon for the manual you want to read. A special document viewer program opens and displays the book on your computer screen.

To save hard disk space, most of the SmartSuite installation options do not install the online document files on your hard disk. The document reader retrieves the files it needs from the CD-ROM disc as you view the online documents. Of course, that means you must have the SmartSuite CD-ROM disc available in the drive before you can read the online documents.

Casting the Net

Another source of information about SmartSuite and the SmartSuite programs is the Internet. Lotus maintains Internet sites to provide information about the products, updates, and add-ons, as well as access to technical support.

One way to access help on the Internet is to open the Suite Help drawer in SmartCenter and then open the Helpful Web Sites folder. The folder is a mini-Web browser that automatically opens to the Lotus SmartSuite home page (provided you have a live Internet link). From there, you can follow links to other helpful Web pages.

Note: If you use a dial-up Internet connection, the Web page does not appear automatically after you open the Helpful Web Sites folder. To remedy the problem, establish your Net connection and then right-click the Helpful Web Sites folder tab; choose Refresh from the pop-up menu that appears. The Web page appears after a brief delay and you can then use the page normally.

Most of the SmartSuite programs provide access to Internet-based help directly from within the program. Choose Help⇨Lotus Internet Support and then choose Lotus Home Page for information via the Web, Lotus Customer Support for technical support, or Lotus FTP Site for access to update files.

What Program Do I Use — and When?

Deciding which of the SmartSuite programs to use for a particular project is your first and often most difficult challenge. These applications offer some overlap in capabilities, so you can complete many projects by using any of the programs. Choosing the best one, however, makes the job go more smoothly and gives you greater flexibility to do the work the way you want.

Picking the correct program may seem just a matter of common sense — if working with words, use Word Pro; if manipulating numbers, use 1-2-3; if creating a presentation, use Freelance Graphics; if attempting complex database management, use Approach. You get the idea. You can't go too far wrong by just following this line of reasoning. Because of the shared capabilities of the SmartSuite programs, however, the choice is not always quite that easy.

Often, projects need to include elements that are the forte of more than one of the SmartSuite programs. To create a report that contains mostly text but also includes a chart, for example, you have several options. You could create the text portion of the document in Word Pro and the chart in 1-2-3 or Freelance and then join them together. Or you could create the entire document in Word Pro, because Word Pro also enables you to create charts. Or you could create the whole thing in Freelance Graphics, which can handle text elements reasonably well, too.

The following are a few examples of the SmartSuite programs your authors would choose for various kinds of activities:

- ✔ Word Pro makes putting together almost any written document a breeze. For business or personal letters, book-length manuscripts, memos, and annual reports, Word Pro is the SmartSuite program of choice.

- ✔ For household or company budgets, forecasts, and cash-flow analyses, 1-2-3 is our choice.

- ✔ For keeping track of inventories, maintaining a large customer database, processing sales orders, and other data-intensive work, we use Approach.

- ✔ Whenever we think of putting together the materials for making a presentation, whether in front of the board of directors or the local homeowners' association, we turn to Freelance Graphics.

Don't feel limited to using just one program to complete a project. The beauty of SmartSuite is that you can use elements from several programs and combine them in one glorious document.

You never really have an absolutely right (or absolutely wrong) program choice. In most cases, the decision on what program to use is simply a matter of personal preference. So don't let anyone — except maybe your boss — tell you anything different.

Part II

Take a Letter, Word Processor

The 5th Wave   By Rich Tennant

YEAH, BUT YOU SHOULD SEE HOW NICELY IT CENTERED EVERYTHING.

In this part . . .

You may as well make friends with Word Pro — SmartSuite 97's powerful word processing program. After all, if you're anything like most computer users, you spend most of your time working with words. Whether you need to write a simple letter or a hefty novel, this part covers all the basics you need to know to get started quickly and painlessly. We can't teach you to write well, but we do show you how to put Word Pro's tools to good use.

Chapter 4

Boot Camp for Word Pro

· ·

In This Chapter

▶ What's a Word Pro — and what happened to my friend Ami?

▶ Starting 'er up

▶ First things first — starting a new document

▶ Say hello to Word Pro's screen

▶ Typing stuff in (that's what you do in a word processor, isn't it?)

▶ Word Pro's modus operandi

▶ Moving around in your document

▶ Selecting this and that

▶ Moving this and copying that

▶ Oops, I didn't mean to do that

▶ Saving documents you don't want to lose

▶ Getting from screen to printer

· ·

*A*nyone out there still using a typewriter? Man, was that white ribbon correcting stuff a pain (even though it had that liquid white-out stuff all beat to heck)! If you discovered one tiny little mistake after you took the paper out, trying to line the paper back up was virtually impossible. Those *weren't* the good old days! But we digress. If you're reading this book, presumably you own Lotus Word Pro word-processing software (and maybe even a computer), so you're hearing no more typewriter talk from us. Ever.

What's a Word Pro?

Un ami est quelqu'un que vous aimez et qui vous aime aussi. Oops, that was a flashback from high school French class. See, Word Pro used to go under the name Ami Pro and *Ami* is a French word that means *friend*. And Word Pro is a word processor that wants to be *your* friend. (Is that cute enough for you?) But seriously, Word Pro is a really cool word processor that goes far out of its way to make your life easier. And that's what friends are for, *n'est-ce pas*?

A word processor, you're thinking. That means that I can type letters and reports and maybe even change the margins around and add such nifty stuff as footers, footnotes, and fonts. Yeah, sure. But hey, this is the information age. Technology is king and queen. You think Lotus is gonna give you a word processor that can't do anything but process words? No way!

Along with all the preceding, you can cook up some nifty tables and charts, add clip art pictures, draw your own pictures, and (as they say in the ad biz) do a whole lot more. So get with the program.

Starting Word Pro

Can't do much with Word Pro until you do something to get the program going. No problem — getting Word Pro to pop up on your screen is no biggie. Just make sure that Windows 95 is running.

The easiest way to start Word Pro is from SuiteStart. If SuiteStart's running, all you need to do is click the Word Pro icon in the taskbar's system tray (that collection of miniature icons in the lower-right corner of your computer screen — next to the clock). Here's a clue to help you find the icon: As you hold the mouse pointer over the correct icon, a little tag appears that reads Lotus Word Pro.

Note: You can also start Word Pro from SmartCenter. Just open the SmartSuite drawer, open the Lotus Applications folder, and then double-click the Lotus Word Pro icon. For more information about SmartCenter, check out Chapter 2.

The other way to start Word Pro is from the Windows 95 Start menu. Click the Start button in the taskbar, point to Programs, point to Lotus SmartSuite, and finally choose Lotus Word Pro 97 from another cascading menu.

If any of the preceding stuff didn't work for you (maybe you don't have any such animal as a Lotus Applications folder, for example), you could possibly find some nice technoid-type person to set up your system in a different way. Just ask that person nicely what you need to do to get into Word Pro. Not to worry — whatever your setup, starting Word Pro is most likely just a matter of clicking or double-clicking something or other.

Welcome to Word Pro

After you first start Word Pro, a logo briefly appears and then the program shows up on-screen with the Welcome to Word Pro dialog box open, as shown in Figure 4-1. The tabs and buttons in the dialog box give you the following options:

- ✔ The Take A Tour button launches a screen show that takes you on a get-acquainted tour of Word Pro.
- ✔ The Open An Existing Document tab presents a list of documents you've worked on recently in case you want to reopen one of them.
- ✔ The Create A New Document From A SmartMaster tab enables you to create a document based on a template. (We cover SmartMasters in the section "Understanding SmartMasters," in Chapter 5.)
- ✔ The Create A Plain Document button does just what the name implies: creates a plain document, ready for you to start typing.

At this point, you probably don't have any existing Word Pro documents, and we haven't gotten to SmartMasters yet. So, unless you're in the mood to take a tour, take the other document creation option in this dialog box by clicking the Create a Plain Document button. This action starts Word Pro out with a simple, blank document — kind of like slipping a blank sheet of paper into a typewriter. (Yeah, that same typewriter we promised not to mention again. Ah, well . . . .)

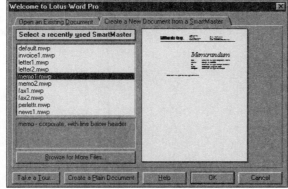

Figure 4-1:
The
Welcome to
Word Pro
dialog box.

Later, if you decide you want to create another new document, you can choose File➪New Document to open the New Document dialog box, which, not coincidentally, is very similar to the Welcome to Word Pro dialog box. For more information on creating a new document, see Chapter 5.

If you really want to take a tour after you close the Welcome to Word Pro dialog box, you can always choose <u>H</u>elp⇨<u>T</u>our.

Making Friends with Word Pro's Screen

"Hullo, screen." "Hullo, *mon ami*." There. Now you're friends. But in any good relationship, you want to find out as much as possible about the other party. So in that spirit . . . .

Right about now, your screen should look something like the one shown in Figure 4-2 (except without all the lines and words that tell you what all the different components are for).

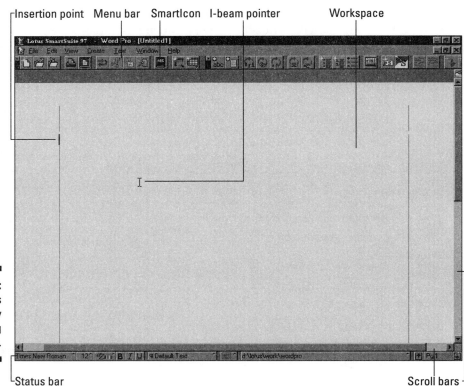

Figure 4-2:
Word Pro's
friendly
opening
screen.

The elements of the Word Pro opening screen are described in the following paragraphs:

- The white space in the middle of the screen represents a piece of paper where you type stuff. The vertical lines on the left and right sides of the "paper" indicate the margins. And the whole thing, including the gray area around the page, has its very own name — it's your *workspace*.

- The *insertion point* is that flashing line near the top of the left margin — it marks where the text you type appears. As you type stuff, the text gets inserted to the left of the insertion point, and the insertion point graciously moves over to make room.

- The thing that looks like a capital letter I is the *I-beam pointer*. The I-beam pointer is really just your regular old mouse pointer in disguise. Whenever you're somewhere in Windows where you can enter text, you get an I-beam instead of an arrow pointer.

- The Word Pro *menu bar* works just like any Windows 95 menu bar. Click an item (or press the Alt key in combination with the underlined letter) to open the menu and then click one of the menu item names to make a choice from the menu itself.

- The cute little buttons with pictures on them, located just below the menu bar, are the *SmartIcons*. Just click one of these buttons to make something happen in Word Pro, such as saving or printing your document. SmartIcons provide a quick alternative to choosing commands from the menus.

  Unless you *love* surprises, you may want to know what is going to happen *before* you click a SmartIcon. If you hold your mouse pointer over a SmartIcon button for a fraction of a second or so, the button actually *speaks* to you. (Well, really the button "speaks" in the form of a bubble that appears right there on-screen and tells you what the button is for.)

- The *status bar* is a very cool place to hang out. Not only does this area give you all sorts of useful info, such as what page you're on and what font you're using, but the status bar also actually *does* stuff. Try selecting some text and clicking some of its buttons — such as the typeface, type size, or bold attribute button — and see what happens. (But be ready for a few — *sigh* — surprises . . . .)

Entering Text

Entering text in Word Pro is easy. Just start typing and stop whenever you're tired, hungry, or done, whichever comes first. Ah, but what happens when you come to the end of a line? Keep typing (unless you're tired or hungry). We're not talking typewriters here — you don't need to press Enter to move the text to the next line. Word Pro does all the moving for you. You see, word processors offer this cool feature called *word wrap*. If no more words can fit on a line, Word Pro automatically moves (or *wraps*) the text to the next line.

We get into all sorts of stuff you can do elsewhere in this chapter and in the other chapters of this part, but for now, here are a few rules of the road to send you merrily on your way:

✔ As you're typing along, sooner or later you're bound to make a mistake (or so we've been told). If you notice the error right away, simply press the Backspace key to get rid of the character you just typed. If you want to get rid of more than one character, just keep pressing the Backspace key. Backspace keeps deleting a character at a time as long as you keep holding down the key.

✔ But what about the Delete key? If the Backspace key deletes stuff, why do you need another key to do the same thing? We have our own conspiracy theory on this oddity — basically, we think that, at the beginning of computer time, the ubiquitous *they* decided to stick in *two* deletion keys just to make the rest of us feel dumb. Here's the scoop:

• The Backspace key deletes the character to the left of your insertion point.

• The Delete key deletes the character to the right of your insertion point.

✔ What if you don't notice a mistake until you've typed several more lines? Piece of cake. Move the I-beam pointer (*remember* — the I-beam pointer is your mouse pointer in disguise) to the place you want and click the mouse to move your insertion point to the I-beam's new position. Now you can use the Backspace and Delete techniques just described.

✔ To start a new paragraph, press Enter. And that's the *only* time you're to press Enter — never, never, never press Enter just because you're at the end of a line; if you do, you end up with major headaches whenever you change your margins or make other formatting changes. See, Word Pro's pretty smart, and the program knows to wrap text to the next line as it reaches the right margin. If you change the margins, Word Pro stays right on top of the situation and rewraps all the lines to fit into the new margins. If you press Enter at the end of a line, Word Pro can't perform its word wrap magic.

✔ You don't need to do anything special after you get to the end of a page either. Word Pro automatically starts a new page for you. If you want to force Word Pro to start a new page at a spot other than where the program would automatically do so, choose Text⇨Insert Page Break from the menu bar.

✔ You can always tell what page you're on by looking at the status bar. (The page number is located at the far right of the bar, between the two arrow buttons.)

What's Your Mode?

Do you know what Word Pro *mode* you're working in? Did you know that Word Pro had modes? No? Well, Word Pro has the following three modes:

- ✔ In *Insert* mode, Word Pro inserts text to the left of your insertion point as you type, and the text pushes the insertion point over to the right. Insert mode is the default mode, meaning unless you have changed your mode without telling us, you're in Insert mode right now. Insert mode is where you want to be most of the time.

- ✔ In *Typeover* mode, whatever you type replaces the text that's already there. For example, if you move the insertion point in front of the word *example* at the beginning of this sentence and turn on Typeover mode, the first letter you type replaces (or *types over*) the *e*, the second letter replaces the *x*, and so on.

- ✔ In *Markup Edits* mode, anything you add or delete gets marked with a different color or text style so that you can tell what has been changed. This mode is handy if you're editing someone else's work or just trying to keep track of changes between drafts for your own stuff.

To switch between Insert and Typeover modes, press the Insert key. Before you do that, however, take a peek at the status bar. Notice the Document Info button? (The button probably shows the drive and folder name where you save your file.) Click that button and check out the items in the pop-up menu that appears. The second line should read `Insert`. That line tells you that you're in Insert mode. Click anywhere to close the info list and then press the Insert key. Check Document Info again and you see that you're in Typeover mode.

To switch into Markup Edits mode, choose Edit⇨Markup Edits from the menu bar. This command is a *toggle command*. Choose the command once to activate the Markup Edits mode. After the feature is active, a check mark appears beside the command name in the File menu. Choose the command again to turn Markup Edits mode off. (See — the command *toggles* from one mode to the other, hence the name of this type of command.)

Getting from Here to There on the Word Pro Screen (Wherever "There" Is)

After you enter a bunch of text on-screen, the fun has just begun. You get to rearrange your text, format the text (as described in Chapter 5) — or even give your golden prose to your boss to hack to death (not the desired choice). Your first order of business, however, is simply moving around the screen — because how can you rearrange or hack up your text if you can't get to it? (Rhetorical question.)

We already told you that you can move your insertion point just by clicking at a new location on-screen. You can also use the up-, down-, left-, and right-arrow keys on your keyboard to move the insertion point (wow — what a concept!). The up- and down-arrow keys move you up or down one line at a time; the left- and right-arrow keys move you left or right one character at a time. Unless you're gunning for terminal tediousness, however, hang in there while we add to your navigational repertoire.

Keyboard kapers and shortkuts

Word Pro offers a bunch of keyboard shortcuts that keep you from having to press an arrow key 9,354 times. And we're going to tell you about them right here.

Time for a quick review here, however, just in case you're staring in glazed amazement at the following list. If we list something along the lines of *Ctrl+Home* (or tell you to *press* Ctrl+Home), we're actually telling you to press and hold down the Ctrl key while you press the Home key. Do not pass Go, do not collect $200, and *do not* release the Ctrl key until after you press and release the Home key. The plus sign (+) between the two keystrokes always means that you hold down the first key while you press the second key. Simple, eh? Carry on.

The following keystroke shortcuts enable you to easily move your insertion point around in Word Pro:

- ✓ **Ctrl+Home:** Moves the insertion point to the beginning of the document (or to the beginning of a division if you've broken your document into multiple sections).

- ✓ **Ctrl+End:** Moves the insertion point to the end of the document (or to the end of the current division).

- ✓ **Ctrl+Page Up** or **Ctrl+Page Down:** Moves the insertion point up or down a page at a time.

- ✓ **Page Up** or **Page Down:** Moves the insertion point up or down a screenful at a time.

- ✓ **Ctrl+↑** or **Ctrl+↓:** Moves the insertion point to the beginning of the current or next paragraph, respectively. If you're already at the beginning of a paragraph, Ctrl+↑ moves you to the beginning of the previous paragraph.

- ✓ **Ctrl+period:** Moves the insertion point to the beginning of the next sentence.

- ✓ **Ctrl+comma:** Moves the insertion point to the beginning of the previous sentence.

> ✔ **Ctrl+→ or Ctrl+←:** Moves the insertion point to the right or left a word at a time.
>
> ✔ **Home:** Moves the insertion point to the beginning of the current line.
>
> ✔ **End:** Moves the insertion point to the end of the current line.

Stupid mouse tricks

(Before you skip past this section, we'd better tell you that these really aren't *stupid* mouse tricks. That was just our lame attempt at a cute heading. These are *super-important* — dare we say even *brilliant*? — mouse tricks that are sure to cause your friends to gasp at the mere mention of them! Hmmm. Did we just go too far in the other direction?)

We already told you about the super-easiest mouse trick of all — just click anywhere in a document and your insertion point moves to wherever you click. Easy, yes. Efficient . . . not always. What if you want to move your insertion point somewhere that you can't see on-screen? Kind of hard to click something you can't see, and those brilliant keyboard shortcuts we told you about in the preceding section don't cover all the bases.

Ah, but that's what scroll bars are for. *Scroll bars* are those vertical and horizontal bars located along the right and bottom edges of your screen (see Figure 4-3). If you single-click the vertical scroll bar's up- or down-arrow button (located at the top or bottom of the bar, respectively), the document view moves up or down one line. And if you hold down the mouse button as you click the up or down arrow, the view keeps moving up or down until you release the button. The horizontal scroll bar functions the same way but moves side to side instead of up and down. Nothing too fancy so far.

But take a look at the box or button inside each scroll bar. (By some strange coincidence, this item's called the *scroll box*.) That box is the key to scroll bar mastery. You can tell where you are in a document by looking at the scroll box. If the vertical scroll box is about halfway down the scroll bar, that means that what you're looking at on-screen is about halfway through the document. So what can you do with this information? Well . . .

> ✔ You can drag the scroll box up or down to move to a different relative location. If you want to move toward the beginning of the document, drag up; if you want to move toward the end, drag down.
>
> ✔ You can also click the shaded area anywhere above or below the scroll box to move up or down a screenful at a time.

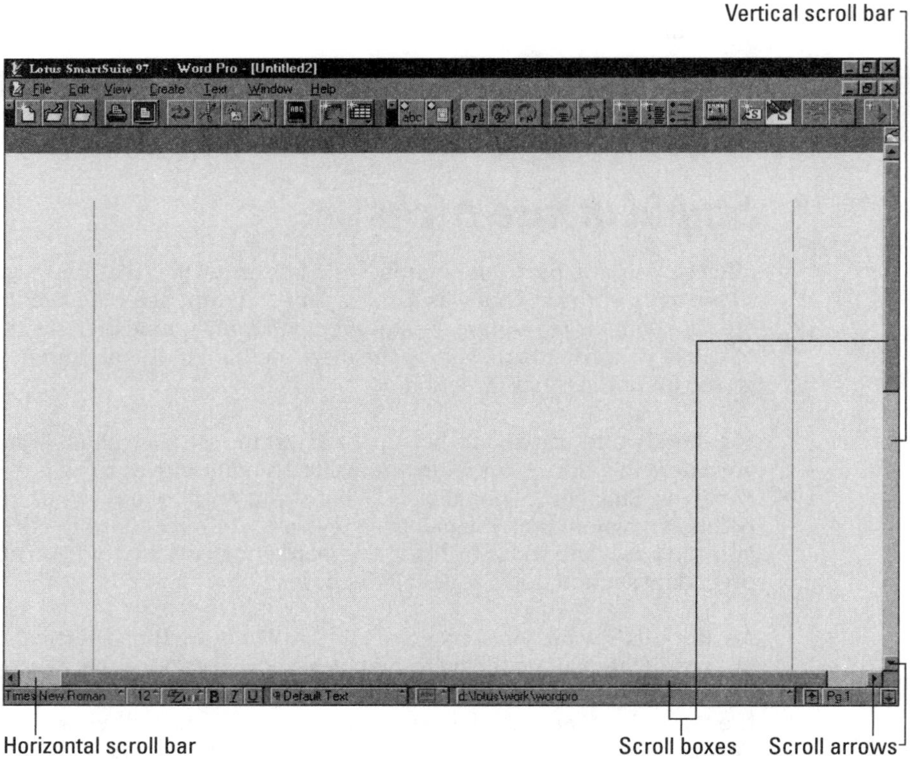

Vertical scroll bar ⌐

Figure 4-3:
Use the
scroll bars
to move up
or down or
from side to
side in your
documents.

Horizontal scroll bar   Scroll boxes   Scroll arrows⌐

Repeat after me: Scrolling *isn't* clicking

So you think you're pretty cool — you've got this scrolling thing down. You started on the first page and, with a combination of the scroll arrows and the scroll box, you moved to just the right location on page eight. Yup, there it is — page eight, right in front of you. You start typing and — wait just one doggone minute! The stuff you typed ended up back on page one! What in tarnation happened?

What happened is that you forgot that moving to a different location by using the scroll bar doesn't do anything to change the position of your insertion point. Scrolling changes your *view*, but the insertion point stays where it was before you scrolled — until you click somewhere else in the document. As soon as you click, the insertion point moves to the place you click. The scroll bars are great for navigating vast distances, but just remember that final click.

Being Selective

Word Pro (and all the SmartSuite 97 programs) enables you to do all kinds of things to text and other parts of a document. The rest of the Word Pro section talks about all the things you can do. But before you find out how to do this kind of stuff, you must find out how to tell Word Pro exactly to *what* you want to do stuff. If you want to make some text bold, for example, you need to tell Word Pro *which* text you want to make bold *before* you apply the bold attribute.

This process is called *selecting*. Before you do just about anything to text, you select the text you want to affect. After the text is selected, you can delete that text, move it, copy it, or make the text look different. The following section talks about moving and copying text; to know how to *delete* selected text, however, you don't need an entire section of explanations — just press the Delete key.

You can use the mouse or the keyboard for selecting text — use whichever one makes more sense to you at the time. The simplest way to select text by using your mouse is just to place the insertion point where you want the selection to start and then hold down the mouse button while you drag the mouse over the text you want selected. As you drag, you highlight that text.

The *Shift+click* trick is a great way to select a bunch of text with precision. If you drag to select text, you must make sure that you release the mouse button at just the right place or you end up with more or less text selected than you want. And if you need to select text that starts on one page and ends on another, dragging can be a real . . . drag. The Shift+click trick is just what it sounds like. You place your insertion point at the beginning of the text you want to select. Then you scroll to the end of the text you want selected and hold down the Shift key as you click to place the insertion point there.

The following list describes a few other mouse-selection shortcuts:

- ✔ To select a word, double-click anywhere in that word.
- ✔ To select a sentence, press and hold the Ctrl key and then click anywhere in the sentence.
- ✔ To select an entire paragraph, press and hold Ctrl and then double-click in the paragraph.
- ✔ To select text a word at a time, double-click the first word you want; then, without releasing the mouse button, drag to the last word.
- ✔ To select text sentence by sentence, press and hold Ctrl and then click anywhere in the first sentence. Without releasing the mouse button, drag to the last sentence.
- ✔ To select text paragraph by paragraph, press and hold Ctrl and then double-click anywhere in the first paragraph. Without releasing the mouse button, drag to the last paragraph.

To select text by using the keyboard, just press and hold the Shift key and then press any of the arrow keys. Suppose, for example, that you want to select the word *word*. Put your insertion point in front of the *w* and press and hold the Shift key as you press the right arrow key four times.

Amaze your friends with this little-known selection tip. Did you know that you can use any of the keystroke combinations that move your insertion point (the ones we talk about in the section "Keyboard kapers and shortkuts," a little earlier in this chapter) to select text? Well, you can. The trick is to press and hold the Shift key as you press the regular keystroke combination. Say, for example, that you want to select all the text from where your insertion point is to the end of the document. Press and hold Shift while you press Ctrl+End, which is the keystroke that moves your insertion point to the end of the document.

Don't get caught by the disappearing text gremlin. Whenever text is selected, the first thing you type *replaces* the selected text. So if you have two pages selected and then type a word, your two pages are gone and that one lonely little word is all that's left. A couple of things you can do may help you avoid this disaster. First, just be aware how this selection stuff works. Unless you want to get rid of the selected text, click anywhere to deselect that text *before* you start typing. Second, if you forget and wipe out the selected text anyway, you can always use Word Pro's Undo feature to nullify that last action (as described in the section "I Didn't Mean to Do It — So Now What?" later in this chapter).

Moving and Copying Text

One of the cool things about using a word processor instead of a typewriter is that text doesn't need to stay where you put the words initially. You can move or copy any amount of text from one place to another. You can keep juggling words and phrases around 'til the cows come home. Heck, you can even keep juggling after those cows have turned in for the night.

You already know how to do the most important part of moving and copying — you can select text. *Remember:* First you select and then you tell Word Pro what to do with the selection. With text selected, moving or copying that text anywhere else (even to another document or application) is a piece of gooey chocolate cake. The only problem is that, here again, Word Pro gives you too many choices. You can use the mouse or the keyboard; you can cut and paste, or you can drag and drop. Decisions, decisions.

But don't fret. Coming right up — the most straightforward way to move or copy stuff from one place to another: Just *drag and drop*. With your text selected, you just place your mouse pointer on the text and drag the selection wherever you want. As you drag, a fist clutching a note attaches itself to your mouse pointer and a small red bar shows where the text you're dragging is going to land. After the mouse pointer is located at the place in your document where you want the text moved, release the mouse button. That's the entire process. If you want to copy instead of moving the text, press and hold the Ctrl key while you drag the selection. (A plus sign appears below the fist to show that you're copying instead of moving the selected text.)

So what's the difference between moving and copying? If you move text, you actually delete the selected text from its original location and insert the selection in a new location. If you copy text, you leave the selected text where it is and insert a copy of the text in the new location. Got it?

Here's another way to move and copy text. Use this method if you want to make several copies of a block of text, move or copy text to another document or another application, or move or copy text to a distant location inside your document. Just follow these steps:

1. **Select the text you want to move or copy.**

2. **Click the Cut SmartIcon (that's the one displaying the scissors) to move the text, or click the Copy SmartIcon (the one with two little A's in boxes) to copy the text.**

    This action places a copy of the selected text in a special section of Windows memory called the Clipboard.

    Pressing Ctrl+X or choosing Edit➪Cut from the menu bar is the same as clicking the Cut SmartIcon. Pressing Ctrl+C or choosing Edit➪Copy from the menu bar is the same as clicking the Copy SmartIcon.

3. **Put your insertion point at the place in your document where you want to move the text.**

4. **Click the Paste SmartIcon (the one displaying the little paste pot).**

    Pressing Ctrl+V or choosing Edit➪Paste from the menu bar is the same as clicking the Paste SmartIcon.

    The selected text stays in the Clipboard until you put something else there, so you can paste that same text in as many times as you want.

Moving or copying stuff to another application is just as easy as moving or copying stuff to another place in a Word Pro document. After you cut or copy text, that block of text ends up in the Windows Clipboard, where the poor thing just sits and waits for you. (This particular piece of text doesn't wait forever, though; the Clipboard can hold only one thing at a time, so as soon as you cut or copy something else, the new stuff replaces whatever's already there.) For example, if you want to copy some text from Word Pro and paste that text into a

1-2-3 worksheet, all you need to do is select the text in your Word Pro document and copy the text to the Clipboard by clicking the Copy SmartIcon; then open 1-2-3, put your insertion point in the worksheet cell where you want to paste the text, and click the Paste SmartIcon. All SmartSuite 97 applications (as well as most other Windows applications) use the same techniques for moving and copying, so you don't need to worry about learning a different method of working with text this way from one application to another. You can paste stuff into any SmartSuite 97 program by pressing Ctrl+V, choosing Edit⇨Paste from the menu bar, or clicking the Paste SmartIcon.

I Didn't Mean to Do It — So Now What?

By now (provided, of course, you've looked at the other sections in this chapter), you know just enough to be really dangerous. You can type and select and move and copy. Terrific. But knowing how to do all that stuff also means that you can do things you didn't mean to do, such as moving something that should've stayed where it was or deleting a bunch of text that, as soon as you hit Delete, you realize is the most brilliant, incisive work you ever created. Are you panicking yet? If so, carry on for a few more seconds, just to get your heart pumping, and then read on.

If you do something you wish you hadn't, just undo that action. Word Pro's *Undo* feature enables you to reverse your last action. In fact, you can reverse your last several actions, but that's a story for another time and place — or maybe for the section "Making Undo do its thing," a bit later in this chapter.

 So how do you do this magical thing? Just choose Edit⇨Undo from the menu bar or click the Undo SmartIcon (the one with the arrows that can't decide which way to go). You can also press Ctrl+Z. Undo automatically does its thing.

Note: The Undo command on the Edit menu changes to reflect what action it can undo. The command may appear as `Undo Typing` or `Undo Drag & Drop` or some other variation. But the exact wording doesn't matter. You still use the command the same way to undo the last action you performed.

 Undo can even help save you from itself. If you undo something you didn't mean to undo, just choose Edit⇨Undo/Redo Special, choose the action you want to fix from the lists in the Undo/Redo dialog box, and click the Undo or Redo button (depending on which list the item is in).

What can Undo undo?

Undo can undo just about anything. If you type stuff you didn't mean to type, Undo can delete the unwanted text. If you delete stuff you want back, Undo can take care of that problem, too. If you make a formatting change and decide the new format stinks, just click that Undo SmartIcon.

What can't Undo undo?

Undo is a very cool thing, but the feature has its limits. Here are some things that Undo can't fix:

- If you saved your document since you did the thing you want to undo, you're out of luck.
- Undo can't undo anything if Undo's turned off. By default, Word Pro's set up to undo the last editing change. If you try Undo and nothing happens, some sneaky person or gremlin may have done something to your User setup. Read the following section so that you know how to foil that dastardly plan to confuse you.

Making Undo do its thing

You can set up Undo to reverse your last several editing changes. Sounds great, right? If Word Pro can do that, why on earth would anyone want to tell the program to undo only one or two levels or even — dare we say it — none?

We have two words for you: speed and memory. To keep track of the last several edits you've made, Word Pro must store information about *everything* you did, in case you decide to change any of it. The fewer levels of Undo you activate, the less stuff Word Pro has to think about, so the program can go about its business at a faster pace. The general rule is to activate as many levels of Undo as your computer can handle without slowing down. The more power-ful your computer, the more levels of Undo your machine can handle gracefully.

To control the Undo levels, choose File⇨User Setup⇨Word Pro Preferences to open the Word Pro Preferences dialog box, as shown in Figure 4-4. The Undo Levels text box on the General tab shows how many actions Undo can reverse. Click the up or down increment arrow beside the Undo Levels text box to select the number of levels you want. (Select 0 if you don't want to use Undo at all.) After you're done, click OK. Your Undo levels are set.

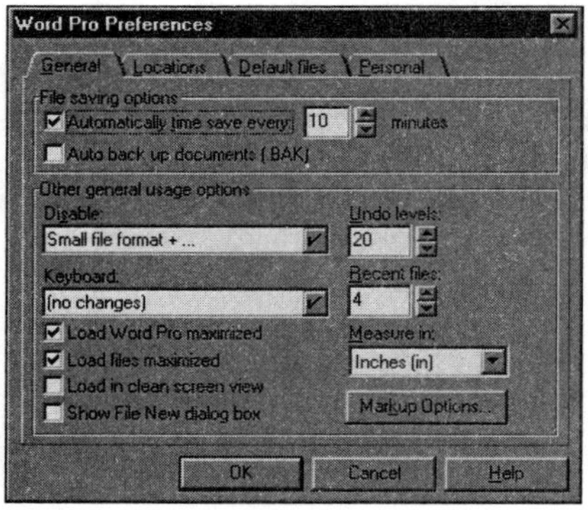

Figure 4-4:
You can
change
Undo levels
(and other
stuff) in the
Word Pro
Preferences
dialog box.

Saving Stuff

If you've been typing anything other than practice garbage up to this point, stop immediately and read this section. And if you ever plan to type anything except practice garbage, stop immediately and read this section. In other words, if you ever type stuff that you don't want to lose, saving is a very good thing to know about. Until you give your document a name, all those glowing words exist only in your computer's temporary memory. So if you stumble over the power cord, pulling it out of its socket and breaking your leg in the process, you not only end up hobbling around in a cast, but you also must retype the whole stupid document. Wouldn't your mood improve as you're hobbling around if you knew that your document was waiting for you on your hard drive, all safe and sound?

So save your text. Now. And often. Here's how:

1. Choose File⇨Save As.

The Save As dialog box appears.

You can do a bunch of stuff in here, but all you need to know about for now is the File name text box. Notice that the Save As Type box already has Lotus Word Pro (*.LWP) selected. This state means that Word Pro automatically adds a period and the letters LWP to the end of the name you assign to your file. *LWP* is the *extension* (kind of like a last name) that Word Pro gives its documents. (Because LWP is already selected as the dialog box opens, all you need to do is start typing a document name; the name you type goes into the File name text box.)

2. Type a name in the File name text box.

You can call a document just about anything you want. Word Pro supports Windows 95's long filenames, which means that you can use any combination of letters, numbers, and spaces.

Actually, your filename can be up to 255 characters long (including the period and extension Word Pro adds automatically). That's the theoretical limit, but you'd never really *use* that many characters in a filename. And, if you did, you'd have trouble viewing such monstrous filenames in most dialog boxes.

If you need to swap documents and files with others, using long filenames for your documents may not be a good idea. Many other programs and networks are still restricted to filenames that are only eight or fewer characters. You may need to be creative to come up with a filename using only eight characters, but doing so can avoid a lot of hassles if your document file must go to someone whose program can't recognize long filenames.

3. Click Save or press Enter.

Your document's safe — for now. But as soon as you add more stuff to what you already saved, that stuff isn't safe until you save the document again. Save whenever you think about doing so — and save whenever you think about something else, too. Save, save, save! Have we made our point?

After you save a document the first time and give that document a name, you can save the file again without opening the Save As dialog box each time. Resaving a document with the same name is quick and easy. You can click the Save SmartIcon (the one with the arrow pointing down into an open file folder), choose File⇨Save from the menu bar, or press Ctrl+S. We like to use the keystroke shortcut Ctrl+S to save while working on a document. We've trained our fingers to start tingling if they haven't pressed Ctrl+S in more than a few minutes.

You can even sit back and have Word Pro do some of the driving for you by using its Auto Backup or Auto Timed Save options. These options are set in the Word Pro Preferences dialog box. (To open the dialog box, choose File⇨User Setup⇨Word Pro Preferences from the menu bar, just as you did to set Undo levels.) Check out the following options in the Word Pro Preferences dialog box:

✔ If you check the Auto backup documents (.BAK) option in the Word Pro Preferences dialog box, you see that Word Pro makes another copy of your document every time you use any of the saving techniques. The program gives both of the copies the same name but adds the BAK extension to the backup copy. You can also tell Word Pro to put the backup copy into a different directory by clicking the Locations tab and entering in the Backups text box a path name (the drive and folder where you want Word Pro to put the files). (If you think a directory is just something you use to look up phone numbers and a path is found only in the woods, *Windows 95 For Dummies,* by Andy Rathbone, published by IDG Books Worldwide, Inc., can set you straight.) We like Auto Backup a whole lot better than we do the Automatically Time Save feature — and we're just about to tell you why.

✔ You can click the check box for Automatically Time Save Every *X* Minutes and tell Word Pro how often you want to perform this procedure. If you type **5** in the text box, Word Pro automatically saves your document every five minutes to protect you against the whims of fate. Even if the power goes out or your cat jumps onto your keyboard and stands on the Delete key, you never lose more than five minutes of work because Word Pro saves your document for you. The problem with this option is that Word Pro saves your document on schedule, no matter what's happening. Here's the rub: Word Pro may save your document when you don't want the document saved. We'd rather control the process ourselves — and the earlier "save, save, save" advice still applies.

We're Off to See the Printer

You created this really cool document, and now you want to share your masterpiece with the world. So send the file to the printer already. What're you waiting for? Oh, we understand. You're waiting for us to tell you how. Okay. Follow these steps:

1. **Click the Print SmartIcon (the one displaying the little printer).**

   You can also choose File⇨Print from the menu bar or press Ctrl+P.

   The Print dialog box appears.

2. **To print more than one copy of your document, type a number in the Number of copies text box.**

   If typing a number is too hard, you can click the up or down increment arrow on either side of the box, and Word Pro automatically increases or decreases the number for you.

3. **To print the entire document, just click Print or press Enter.**

   To print just the current page, click the Current Page radio button before you choose Print. To print some other grouping of pages, type or choose the page numbers in the from and to text boxes and then choose Print.

And that's all you do. Your document's on its way to the printer. Hooray! (Just make sure that your printer's turned on before you get too excited.)

Chapter 5
Format with Style

● ●

In This Chapter

▶ Formats for everything

▶ Making text **bold**, *italic*, and <u>more</u>

▶ Learning to rule your tabs and indents

▶ Left, right, or center (we're talking alignment — not politics)

▶ Between the lines — changing line spacing

▶ Setting margins

▶ Crossing the border

▶ Dressing up your page from head to foot

▶ Treating paragraphs with style

▶ Mastering SmartMasters

● ●

*I*f you just want to type a whole bunch of text and don't care too much what that text looks like, you may as well just use a typewriter. (Oh, oh — the dreaded T-word again!) Sure, a typewriter enables you to change your left and right margins and adjust your tab settings, but that's about all. For fancy formatting, however, nothing beats a word processor such as Word Pro.

Formatting Basics

Formatting is just a catch-all term for all the things that affect the appearance of your document. If you change the margins or add a border to a page, you're changing the document's format. Word Pro formatting falls into three categories: *text formatting, paragraph-level formatting,* and *document-level formatting.* The following paragraphs describe these three levels of formatting:

✔ If you apply features to one character or selected characters, you're applying formatting at the *text level.* Type styles and attributes such as bold and italic are examples of text formatting.

> ✔ If you add features that affect an entire paragraph or selected paragraphs, you're applying *paragraph-level formatting*. Line spacing, tab settings, and alignment are examples of paragraph-level formatting.
>
> ✔ If you add features that affect the whole document, that's *document-level formatting*. Paper size, headers and footers, and page numbering are all examples of document-level formatting. (*Headers* and *footers*, in case the terms are unfamiliar, are those lines of text, numbers, and so on that appear at the top — the *head* — or the bottom — the *foot* — of a page. Don't you just *love* body part analogies?)

Doing Stuff to Text

One of the simplest ways to add emphasis to a document is to add boldface, italics, or underlining to some of your text. Another way is to change the text's size or type style. If you need a quick refresher on selecting text for such changes, just review the pertinent sections in Chapter 4 before you move on, because all this text formatting stuff revolves around working with selected text.

Making text bold, italic, or underlined

We're lumping all these attributes together because you use exactly the same technique regardless of which attribute you want. Just select the text to which you want to add the attribute; then click the appropriate button on the status bar, make a choice from the Text menu, or use the keyboard shortcut, as described in the following list:

> ✔ To make text bold, click the Bold button on the status bar (the one with the big B — you can't miss it) or choose Text➪Attributes➪Bold from the menu bar. *Keyboard shortcut:* Ctrl+B.
>
> ✔ To italicize text, click the Italic button on the status bar (the one with the tipsy I) or choose Text➪Attributes➪Italic from the menu bar. *Keyboard shortcut:* Ctrl+I.
>
> ✔ To underline text, click the Underline button on the status bar (the capital U with a line under it) or choose Text➪Attributes➪Underline from the menu bar. *Keyboard shortcut:* Ctrl+U.

After you apply an attribute, notice that the text remains selected. You can continue to add more attributes without reselecting the text. If you want some text to be both bold and italic, for example, just select the text and click first the Bold button and then the Italic button. (Or vice versa, as you prefer. Doesn't really matter which is first as long as the text remains selected.)

Changing the type style or size

SmartSuite 97 comes with a whole bunch of type styles (a.k.a. *fonts*) that can be used in just about any size you want. Changing fonts is just as easy as adding attributes. Just follow these steps:

1. **Select the text you want to affect.**

2. **Choose Text⇨Font & Color from the menu bar to open the Text Properties InfoBox to its default Font, Attribute, and Color tab, as shown in Figure 5-1.**

Font, Attribute, and Color tab

Alignment tab

Bullet tab   Style tab

Lines and Border tab

Figure 5-1:
The Font,
Attribute,
and Color
tab of the
Text
Properties
InfoBox.

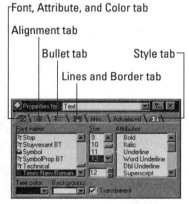

You can also open the Text Properties InfoBox by right-clicking the selected text and choosing Text Properties from the pop-up menu that appears.

3. **Choose a type style from the Font name list.**

In Figure 5-1, Times New Roman is selected. Notice that any change you make in the InfoBox takes effect immediately. You can see the result right there in your document.

4. **Select a type size from the Size list.**

If the size you want isn't listed, you can type a specific size in the Size text box, just below the Size list, or use the increment arrows next to the text box to choose a size.

5. **To add attributes to the text, select one or more attributes from the Attributes list.**

Note: More attributes are included on this list than are available by clicking status bar buttons. For example, you can choose double underlines and superscript.

6. **To add color to the text, click the arrow button next to the Text Color box.**

   This action opens a palette of color choices. Click a color swatch to make that color appear in the Text Color box and change the text to that color. (Just remember that the color doesn't print unless you use a color printer.)

7. **Click the Close (X) button to close the InfoBox after you finish making your choices.**

Text sizes are specified by measuring the height of the characters in points. *Point* is a typesetting term for a measurement that equals $1/72$ of an inch. So a 72-point font is one inch high. (Fonts are measured from the top of the capital letters to the bottom of the descenders — or tails — of letters such as *g*. A 72-point capital *M,* therefore, isn't really quite one inch high.)

Going overboard with type styles and text attributes is all too easy. Unless you're actually writing a ransom note, try to avoid using too many type styles and attributes on a page. A good rule of thumb is to use no more than two type styles per page — one for headings and one for regular text. As far as the attributes go, remember that <u>underlining strictly for emphasis</u> is generally considered <u>tacky</u>. Also remember that you use **bold** and *italic* type for *emphasis*. If **you** use them ***too much***, the attributes *lose* **their** *effectiveness*.

Getting rid of text formatting

Okay, so you're really upset and you dash off a nasty letter to your state senator. In the first paragraph, you use three type sizes, boldface 15 words, and underline the bold words for additional emphasis. Then you cool down a bit and decide that the senator may be more open to your message if you tone the text down a bit (visually, at least). No problem. To remove all the text formatting at once, simply follow these handy steps:

1. **Select the text from which you want the formatting removed.**

2. **Choose Text⇨Normal from the menu bar.**

   You can also press Ctrl+N instead of using the menu commands.

And like magic, all the bold and underlining disappears! Ta daaaaa!

Adding Tabs and Indents

The simplest way to add a tab to your document is just to press Tab at the beginning of a paragraph to indent the first line. But this tab and indent thing has much more to it than that. As shown in Figure 5-2, Word Pro enables you to create four kinds of tabs. And for indenting the first line of each paragraph, Word Pro offers an Indention feature that can automate the process for you.

Figure 5-2:
Different
types of tab
settings and
how they
appear in
Word Pro.

Left	Center	Numeric	Right
Tomfoolery	Tomfoolery	Tomfoolery	Tomfoolery
90210	90210	90210	90210
98.6	98.6	98.6	98.6
789.4321	789.4321	789.4321	789.4321
.02	.02	.02	.02
Neverland	Neverland	Neverland	Neverland
The End	The End	The End	The End

Notice the ruler at the top of the workspace, just below the SmartIcons. As the following section makes clear, the ruler enables you to easily set and adjust tabs in Word Pro.

Setting tabs

Word Pro comes with tabs preset every one-half inch. Unless you change the tab settings, the insertion point moves one-half inch to the right every time you press Tab. Here's how you change the tab settings for any given paragraph:

1. **If the ruler isn't visible on-screen, choose View➪Show/Hide➪Show Ruler from the menu bar or click the Show/Hide Ruler SmartIcon.**

   This SmartIcon looks, unsurprisingly, like a little ruler.

2. **Right-click anywhere in the ruler and choose the kind of tabs you want to create from the pop-up menu that appears.**

   You can choose Left, Centered, Right, or Numeric (decimal) tabs. Whenever the pointer is over the ruler, a small arrow attaches itself to the pointer to indicate the kind of tab you're creating.

3. **To add a new tab stop, click the ruler at the location where you want the new tab to appear.**

After you click the ruler, a new tab marker — a small arrow — appears. You can place several tabs just by clicking different locations on the ruler. You don't need to right-click the ruler to open the pop-up menu each time unless you need to change the kind of tab you want to create. Word Pro assumes that you want to continue creating the same kind of tab until you tell it something different.

Moving a tab is exceptionally easy. Just point to an existing tab on the ruler. A small double-headed arrow attaches itself to the pointer to indicate that you are in Move Tab mode. Then you can simply drag the tab marker to a new position on the ruler.

4. **To clear all the current tab settings, right-click the ruler and choose Clear** <u>**All**</u> **Tabs from the pop-up menu.**

To delete a single tab stop, you just drag its marker off the ruler.

To quickly create a centered tab in the center of the page, right-click the ruler and choose Quick Center Tab from the pop-up menu. For a right tab on the right margin, right-click the ruler and choose Quick Right Tab from the pop-up menu. Cool shortcut, don't you think?

Note: After you change tab settings, the new settings apply only to the paragraph your insertion point is in (or to any paragraphs you select before changing the settings). If you want to change tab settings for the entire document, do so from the Page Layout dialog box. Changing page layouts is covered in the section "Changing the Page Layout" (what else?), later in this chapter.

Tabs are great for lining up columns of stuff, but tables are even better. Tables are much easier to set up, provide a lot more options, and are covered in Chapter 6 (see the section "Tabular, Dude!" in that chapter).

Changing indents

If you want to indent the first line of every paragraph, has SmartSuite 97 got a feature for you! First, select the paragraphs you want to affect; then right-click the selected text and choose Text Properties from the pop-up menu that appears to open the Text Properties InfoBox. Click the Alignment tab (the second tab from the left) to view the options shown in Figure 5-3. Notice the four buttons under the Indent label. To indent the first line of each selected paragraph, click the second button from the left. Below the Indent buttons you find the Indent from Margin text box. You use this setting to determine the amount in inches the first line of the paragraph indents from the left margin. Type in a value or use the up and down increment arrows to adjust the setting. Close the Text Properties InfoBox by clicking the Close (X) button.

Figure 5-3:
Set Indents
in the
Alignment
tab of the
Text
Properties
InfoBox.

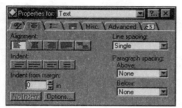

Word Pro offers you the following indent options:

✔ The All option (the first Indent button) indents every line in the selected paragraphs from the left margin.

✔ The First option (the second Indent button) indents the first line of each selected paragraph.

✔ The Rest option (the third Indent button) indents every line except the first line of each selected paragraph.

✔ The Both option (the fourth Indent button, at the far right) indents selected text from both the left and right margins. This style is often used to set off quotations.

All indents except Both measure from the left margin. So if your left margin is set at one inch and you specify a first-line indent of one-half inch, the first line of each paragraph will be indented one-half inch from the left margin, or one and one-half inches from the left edge of the page.

If you need more control over your indents, click the Options button at the bottom of the Text Properties InfoBox to open the Indent Options dialog box, where you can set each indent distance individually.

Lining Up Text

Take a look at this book. The text is all lined up at the left margin, but the right margin is uneven. Left alignment is considered somewhat informal, and that's why we use that variety — we want you to feel right at home. Check out Figure 5-4 for examples of this type of alignment and the other Word Pro alignment styles.

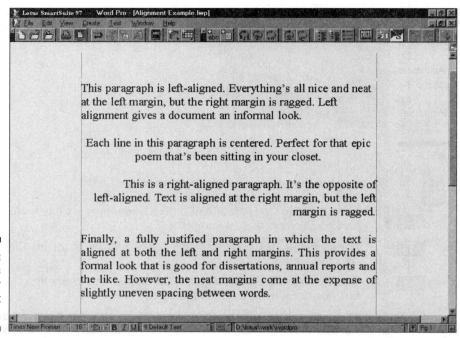

Figure 5-4:
Word Pro's
four
alignment
styles.

All the alignment options affect either the paragraph in which your insertion point is currently located or all selected paragraphs. You can set the alignment by clicking one of the alignment buttons on the Alignment tab of the Text Properties InfoBox, or you can use the shortcut keys or menu commands in the following list:

 ✔ To left-align text, press Ctrl+L or choose Text⇨Alignment⇨Left.

 ✔ To center text, press Ctrl+E or choose Text⇨Alignment⇨Center.

 ✔ To right-align text, press Ctrl+R or choose Text⇨Alignment ⇨Right.

 ✔ To justify text (line the text up on both the left and right margins), press Ctrl+J or choose Text⇨Alignment⇨Full Justify.

 Individual SmartIcons for each alignment option are not part of the default SmartIcon palettes for Word Pro. One SmartIcon, however, enables you to cycle through the alignment options. Click the Cycle Alignment Options SmartIcon to apply the next option. Click the SmartIcon again to apply another alignment option. Continue until you reach the alignment option you want.

You can also change alignment settings by right-clicking the selected text and choosing Text Properties from the pop-up menu to open the Text Properties InfoBox. After the InfoBox opens, click the Alignment tab and then click one of the Alignment buttons.

Spacing Out

Need a triple-spaced draft that gives your boss room to mark up your text to the point of unrecognizability? No problem. Word Pro enables you to adjust line spacing just about any way you want. To change line spacing, just follow these steps:

1. **Select the paragraphs you want to change.**

   If you want to change the spacing for only one paragraph, you don't need to select that single paragraph — just place your insertion point anywhere in the paragraph.

2. **Right-click the selection and choose Text Properties from the pop-up menu to open the Text Properties InfoBox; then click the Alignment tab.**

   (Refer back to Figure 5-3 to see this tab of the Text Properties InfoBox.)

3. **In the Line Spacing drop-down list box, select the line spacing you want or select Multiple, Leading, or Custom to specify nonstandard line spacing.**

   Selecting Multiple, Leading, or Custom opens a small dialog box for each specific selection. The Multiple dialog box enables you to enter nonstandard fractions of lines (2.75, for example) for line spacing. The Leading and Custom dialog boxes enable you to specify a unit of measure (inch, centimeter, point, or pica) and a specific measurement. Enter the desired line spacing in whichever dialog box you open and click OK to return to the Alignment tab of the Text Properties InfoBox.

4. **Click the Close (X) button to close the InfoBox.**

As with alignment changes, line spacing changes apply *only* to the paragraph you're in at the time you make the change or to any paragraphs you selected before changing the spacing.

You can change line spacing for an entire document by selecting the document first: Just press Ctrl+Home to get to the top of the document and then press Shift+Ctrl+End to select to the end of the document. Then follow the instructions for changing line spacing as described in the preceding steps.

Changing the Page Layout

The *page layout* consists of a whole bunch of stuff such as the tab settings, margins, and paper size. You already saw earlier in this chapter how to change tab settings by using the ruler, but that's just one way of changing these settings. If you use the ruler, you're changing tabs only for the paragraph you're in or any paragraphs you select before you make your changes. To get to a place where you can make changes that affect the entire document, right-click anywhere in the workspace and choose Page Properties from the pop-up menu that appears. This action opens the Page Layout Properties InfoBox. Figure 5-5 shows the first tab (Size and Margin) of this InfoBox.

Figure 5-5:
This tab of the Page Layout Properties InfoBox box is where you tell Word Pro what size paper to use.

Size and Margin tab

Color, Pattern, and Line Style tab

The first thing you should remember about this InfoBox is that the box itself is composed of several tabs. Notice that the Size and Margin tab is open in Figure 5-5. Well, if you click another tab, a whole new set of options appears.

To make changes in the InfoBox, all you need to do is select the options you want. You see the effect immediately (provided you're in layout view). Experiment until you get the effect you want and then click the Close button to close the InfoBox after you finish. The following sections provide a quick rundown of what you can do in this InfoBox.

Selecting pages

The selection in the Settings for drop-down list determines which pages of your document that you affect with the settings you choose in the Page Layout Properties InfoBox. The pages you choose here are the ones that your changes in this InfoBox affect, no matter which tab you're in at the time. Your choices include the following:

✔ Choose All pages to apply your settings to every page in the document.

✔ Choose Right pages or Left pages to apply your settings only to odd-numbered (right) or even-numbered (left) pages.

If you choose Right pages or Left pages and change some settings, you can click Mirror pages to have Word Pro reverse your new layout settings for the opposite type of pages (right or left). If your left margin is set at one inch and your right margin at two inches on *left* pages, for example, mirroring places the left margin at two inches and the right margin at one inch on *right* pages. This option is great for any material that you plan to bind together, because you usually need a larger margin in the middle to leave room for the binding.

Setting page size and margins

The Size and Margin settings are shown in Figure 5-5 and function as described in the following paragraphs:

- ✔ Use the Page size drop-down list box to tell Word Pro what size paper you want to use. Word Pro comes with a generous selection of preset page sizes. If your paper doesn't fit any of the predefined settings, you can select Custom from the list and enter your own measurements in the dialog box Word Pro opens.

- ✔ Click one of the Orientation buttons to tell Word Pro how you want the text oriented on the page. Word Pro avoids the sometimes confusing Portrait and Landscape terminology by labeling the buttons with icons representing tall (portrait) or wide (landscape) pages.

- ✔ Change margin settings by typing numbers in the appropriate text boxes or by clicking the up or down increment arrows next to each box.

Adding lines

Impress your friends by adding a border around every page or maybe just a slick-looking line down the left margin. Click the Color, Pattern, and Line Style tab in the Page Layout Properties InfoBox to access these options, as shown in Figure 5-6.

The best way to figure out what you want to do here is just to play around. Click the different options and see what happens to the page currently on-screen.

To better appreciate the effects of page borders, make sure that you're in Layout view (by choosing View⇨Layout) and choose View⇨Zoom to Full Page to make the entire page visible on-screen.

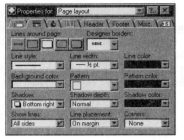

Here's a rundown on the main options you find in this tab of the InfoBox:

- ✔ The Lines around page buttons offer a quick way to add a standard border to your page.

- ✔ For a fancy border, try one of the selections from the Designer Borders drop-down list box.

- ✔ Choose the first Lines around page button — None — to quickly get rid of a border.

- ✔ The twelve drop-down list boxes below the row of Lines around page buttons enable you to fine-tune your border by changing such details as the thickness and color of the lines, drop shadow effects, and whether the line should surround the page or appear on only one side.

Note: Many computer printers incorporate what's called an *unprintable zone*. This zone is usually about a quarter-inch wide, all the way around the sheet of paper. If your printer can't print all the way out to the edge of the page, your lines don't show up on the printout if you select Page edge in the Line placement drop-down list box.

Inserting a page layout

If you modify the page layout, you change the entire document. If you want to change the page layout in the middle of a document (such as to set different margins for one section), choose Text⇨Insert Page Layout from the menu bar to open the Insert Page Layout dialog box. This dialog box lists the existing page layouts in your document. You can choose one of the existing layouts from the list and click Insert to insert a new page with a copy of the existing page layout settings or click Insert & Edit to insert a copy of the default page layout and open the Page Layout Properties InfoBox you're already familiar with. Then just make the changes you want there and close the InfoBox. Word Pro inserts a manual page break and a small page icon appears in your text to indicate where page layout settings change.

To remove from your document a page layout you inserted, you need to select and then delete the page layout icon. Because the page layout icon is also a page break, selecting just the icon can be a bit tricky. The easiest way to select a page break (whether or not it's also a page layout icon) is to position the text cursor just to the left of the page layout icon and then press Shift+right-arrow. The next page jumps into view, but if you scroll back to the previous page, you find the icon alone selected. Press the Delete key to delete the icon.

You can insert as many page layouts in your document as you want. Here's what Word Pro does with these layouts: Word Pro uses the settings for the original layout until the end of the document or until the program encounters an inserted page layout. Word Pro then uses the settings for that new layout until encountering yet another inserted layout (or until the program reaches the end of the document, whichever comes first). If you want to revert back to the default layout at any point in your document following an inserted page layout, you need to insert another page layout with a copy of the default layout.

Creating Headers and Footers

Look no farther than the top of this page to see what a header is. In this book, the chapter number and title are printed at the top of each odd-numbered page, and the part number and title are printed at the top of each even-numbered page. These are *headers* — repeating information that appears at the top of succeeding pages. *Footers* are exactly the same, except that they appear at the bottom of the page.

Before you create a header or footer, make sure that you're in Layout mode. No doubt, you've seen the header and footer areas as you worked in Layout mode (although you may not have realized what they were). The portions of the screen where the left and right margin lines extend above and below the normal text area are the header and footer areas, respectively.

You can change your view by selecting View➪Layout, View➪Draft, or View➪ Page Sorter from the menu bar.

To create a header, just place your insertion point anywhere in the header area (the space above the main document area) and start typing. You can create a footer the same way, the only difference being that, to create a footer, you put your insertion point in the area below the main text before you start typing. After you finish entering header or footer information, just click anywhere in the main document area and get back to work.

You can use all the normal formatting tools to control the appearance of your header and footer text. You can adjust text attributes such as font and color and you can set tabs and paragraph alignment for headers and footers — just as you do for any other text paragraph.

If you need to adjust the position of headers and footers on the page, you find those settings in the Page Layout Properties InfoBox. Just right-click the text page and choose Page Properties from the pop-up menu to open the InfoBox and then click the Headers tab to adjust your headers (see Figure 5-7). You can adjust the margins for the header space just as you adjusted the margins for the page as a whole. The Footers tab provides similar settings to control footer positions.

Figure 5-7: Use these settings to control the position of the header in your document.

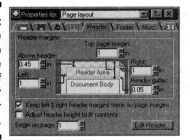

If you want different headers and footers for odd and even pages (such as the ones in this book), open the Page Layout Properties InfoBox (by right-clicking the text page and choosing Page Properties from the pop-up menu, remember?) and select Right pages from the Settings for drop-down list box. Then place your insertion point in the top or bottom margin of any odd-numbered page (depending on whether you want a header or footer), and type what you want. Return to the InfoBox and choose Left pages, click back in the main document area, move to an even-numbered page, and then create another header or footer the same way.

If you don't want the header or footer to appear on the first page of your document, go to the Page Layout Properties InfoBox, click the Header or Footer tab (depending on which one you want to affect), and change the page number in the Begin On Page text box. Usually, headers and footers begin on page 2, but you can specify another page if you want.

You can add page numbers to a header or footer by choosing Text⇨Insert Page Number from the menu bar to open the Insert Page Number dialog box. Use the options in the Insert Page Number dialog box to specify a style for the numbers.

Inserting the Date or Time

Word Pro can automatically insert the date or time in your document. Because a header or footer is a likely location for the date or time, we cover this feature here, following the section on headers and footers. Follow these steps to place the date or time in a document:

1. **Position your insertion point where you want to insert the date or time.**

   To put the date or time in a header or footer, place the insertion point in the header or footer area, as described in the preceding section.

2. **Choose Text⇨Insert Other⇨Date/Time from the menu bar.**

   The Insert Date/Time dialog box appears.

3. **Click the option button for the Date or Time and select the date or time you want to insert from the drop-down list boxes.**

4. **Highlight one of the options in the Date format list box and then click OK.**

The date or time you chose is now inserted into the appropriate location in your document in a . . . well, *timely* manner. (Sorry.)

Understanding Paragraph Styles

Paragraph styles are nothing mysterious. A *paragraph style* is simply a set of formatting information that is given a name. (This formatting information can include text formatting, such as font and size, and paragraph formatting, such as tabs and indents.) After you create a certain paragraph style, you can then apply that named style to a paragraph. When you apply a named style to a paragraph, you are applying to that paragraph all the formatting information recorded in that style — and you apply this formatting all at once instead of needing to apply each formatting option individually. Pretty handy, huh?

Perhaps an example can help you understand paragraph styles better. Suppose that you're writing a paper containing numerous quotes and you want the quoted material to appear in italics and indented from both left and right margins. You could select each quote, click the Italic button on the status bar to add the italic attribute, and then open the Text Properties InfoBox and go to the Alignment tab, where you could click the appropriate button to indent the paragraph from both margins. Or you could do all that once, save the paragraph's formatting as a named style, and then apply that same formatting to each subsequent quote by simply clicking anywhere in the paragraph, clicking the Named Style button on the status bar, and then selecting the style name.

Actually, you've been using styles all along and you didn't even know what you were doing. (Okay, maybe you did, but you didn't get the information from us.) Every time you start a paragraph in Word Pro, that paragraph starts out with a certain paragraph style. So far, we've been using the default settings for a plain document; the default paragraph style is called *Default Text*. That means that, if you don't do anything to change the style, you're using the Default Text style for each paragraph you create. This style provides default values for all the text and paragraph formatting options Word Pro offers. You can override those settings by applying any other formatting that you want to a paragraph, but the paragraph style itself provides the starting point.

How do you know which paragraph style you're using? Just look at the status bar; the Named Styles button just to the right of the Attribute buttons displays the name of the current paragraph style.

In addition to the Default Text paragraph style, you may find that your Word Pro document contains predefined paragraph styles for headings, bulleted lists, numbered lists, and more. These styles greatly simplify the task of formatting your document.

To format a heading, for example, you may want to change the font and size, add the bold attribute to the text, and center-align the paragraph. Of course, you could do all that manually for each heading, but simply clicking the Named Styles button in the status bar (the button probably reads `Default Text` unless you've been playing with the styles while we weren't looking) and selecting the Heading style to make Word Pro apply all that formatting for you in a single stroke is much easier.

Whenever you create a new document, Word Pro bases that document on a specific SmartMaster template. (Even a plain document is based on a default template.) The SmartMaster includes a set of predefined paragraph styles you can use in your document. But you're not confined to those styles. You can redefine the styles and create new ones of your own.

You create new styles by example. Start by formatting a paragraph the way you want. Then right-click the paragraph and choose Named Styles⇨Create from the pop-up menu to open the Create Style dialog box.

Type in a name for your new style and, if you want, a description; then click OK. Word Pro adds the new style to the list that appears after you click the Named Style button in the status bar so that you can then apply that same new set of formatting to other paragraphs in your document.

To redefine an existing paragraph style, start by applying the style to a paragraph (or by selecting a paragraph that uses the style you want to change). Reformat the paragraph as needed and then right-click the paragraph and choose Named Styles⇨Redefine from the pop-up menu to record these changes.

Understanding SmartMasters

You don't need to know too much about SmartMasters to use them effectively in Word Pro. *SmartMasters* are simply templates that serve as patterns or molds for Word Pro documents. Every time you start a new document, Word Pro makes you choose a SmartMaster on which to base the document. (*Remember:* Even if you choose to create a plain document, Word Pro still bases that document on a default SmartMaster.)

At the very least, each SmartMaster contains a set of simple paragraph styles and settings such as page margins. The more elaborate SmartMasters also contain the skeleton of a document containing text, lines, and Click Here fields (fill-in-the-blanks) that enable you to get a head start on creating a finished document.

A simple memo SmartMaster, for example, may include the word *Memo* at the top of the page, plus the current date and all the normal To and From headers. If you start a new document based on that SmartMaster, all you need to do is just fill in the recipient's name, the subject, and the text of your memo to create a nicely formatted memo. You don't need to do any formatting to make the headers a different font or align the To and From names or add a line to separate the header area from the memo text. All of that is already taken care of by the SmartMaster. SmartMasters run the gamut from simple memos and letterheads to invoices, newsletters, and business cards.

Starting a new document based on a SmartMaster

To use a SmartMaster, you normally create a new document based on the SmartMaster of your choice. How do you start a new document by using a SmartMaster? Glad you asked. Just follow these handy steps:

1. **Choose File⇨New Document from the menu bar.**

   This action opens the New Document dialog box. To create a new document based on a SmartMaster you used recently, simply click the SmartMaster file name from the list in the Create from Recently Used SmartMaster tab of the New Document dialog box. Word Pro displays a preview of the SmartMaster in the right side of the dialog box. Otherwise, proceed to Step 2.

2. **Click the Create from any SmartMaster tab to display the SmartMaster selection options.**

3. **Choose a general category of SmartMaster from the Select a type of SmartMaster list on the left side of the dialog box; then select a variation or graphic treatment from the Select a look list box.**

   Word Pro displays a thumbnail sample of your selected SmartMaster on the right side of the dialog box.

4. **After you're satisfied with your selection, click OK.**

   Word Pro creates a new document based on the SmartMaster and opens that document in the workspace ready for you to begin work. Depending on the SmartMaster you choose, you may see a blank document with only a few default formatting options, such as the margins and font selection determined by the SmartMaster, or you may see a nearly complete document in which you can simply fill in a few blanks to produce the finished invoice or other document.

Working with styles in a SmartMaster

A SmartMaster is, above all, a collection of predefined paragraph styles. After you create a new document based on a SmartMaster, you can override and revise those styles with your own formatting choices. You should, however, keep a few of the following points in mind in dealing with styles and SmartMasters:

- ✔ If you modify a paragraph style in a document, the new style settings take precedence over those of the original SmartMaster.

- ✔ Modified paragraph styles affect only the current document. If you start a new document by using the same SmartMaster, the paragraph styles revert to their original settings.

- ✔ If you change a bunch of paragraph styles and other settings in a document, you may want to save the settings in a new SmartMaster so that you can use them in other documents. Choose File➪Save As to open the Save As dialog box and then select Lotus Word Pro SmartMaster from the Save as type list box. Give your SmartMaster a name and click Save. Now, whenever you choose File➪New Document from the menu bar, your newly created SmartMaster appears in the list of available SmartMasters along with all the others that came with Word Pro.

Chapter 6

Polishing Up Your Word Pro Document

· ·

· ·

*S*o you know how to do all sorts of stuff with words — put them in documents, save them, and change the way they look on the page. But what if you want to add some pretty pictures to your documents in the hope that no one notices how utterly boring and meaningless the words really are? Or add a table to clarify the meaning of a portion of text? (Meaning? What meaning?) And then comes the matter of *finding* all those words and making sure they're spelled correctly. If any of this seems relevant, you've come to the right chapter.

It's a Frame-Up!

Yeah, yeah. You want to learn how to put pretty pictures in your documents. So what's this "frame" stuff? In real life, you can unroll a poster and thumbtack it to the wall — no frame required (just some bandages, maybe). But in the world of Word Pro, the picture must go into a frame.

A *frame* is just a place to put stuff that's not part of the regular document text. After you have a frame, you can move or size the frame without affecting the layout of the rest of your document. And frames are good for more than just pictures — you can put charts (perhaps from 1-2-3 or Freelance), Approach data, or even text into frames. But why would you want to put text in a frame if you have a whole document for that purpose? Well, suppose that you're writing a company newsletter and you want to include a plea for help with the upcoming demonstration against management. And you want to be absolutely sure everyone sees the notice. Try putting the notice in a frame with a nice border — that sets that particular text off from the rest and helps ensure a higher level of participation in your demonstration (although management turnout may be rather sparse).

You can also use frames to link information from other SmartSuite 97 applications (or even — dare we say? — from non-SmartSuite 97 applications).

Creating a frame

Now that we've talked the concept of frames to death, shall we get to work and actually create one? Just follow these simple steps:

1. **Make sure that you're in Layout mode.**

   Choose View⇨Layout from the menu bar if you're not in Layout mode.

2. **Choose Create⇨Frame from the menu bar.**

   This action opens the Create Frame dialog box, as shown in Figure 6-1.

Figure 6-1:
The Create
Frame
dialog box.

3. **In the Width box, type or select a value to tell Word Pro how wide you want the frame.**

4. **In the Height box, perform the same action to tell Word Pro how tall you want the frame.**

   Don't worry too much about getting the dimensions exactly right — you can easily change them later. (And we even tell you how — also later, however.)

5. **Click OK.**

   You end up with an empty frame much like the one shown in Figure 6-2.

If you prefer a more visual approach, you can create a frame without entering any measurements. Just click the Create Frame SmartIcon (the one that looks like a little picture frame), or choose the Size & Place Frame Manually button after you're in the Create Frame dialog box (as described in the preceding steps). Your mouse pointer turns into a little box. Position the box on the page where you want one corner of the frame, press and hold the left mouse button, and drag the mouse until the box is the size you want; then release the mouse button. By using this technique, you still end up with an empty frame similar to the one shown in Figure 6-2.

Doing stuff to frames

In Figure 6-2, you see an empty box with a bunch of markers at the corners and in the middle of each side. You probably figured out that the empty box is the frame, but what are all those other things? Well, those little markers are called

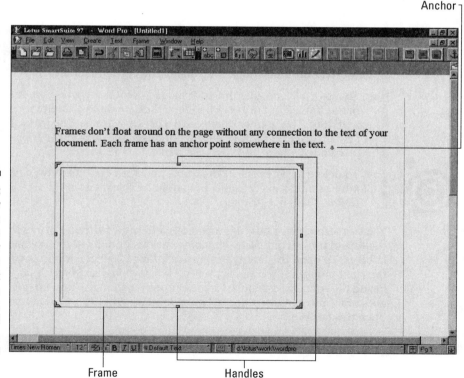

Figure 6-2:
You now have a frame in your Word Pro document and you can size, move, and put stuff in the frame.

handles. The visible handles tell you that this frame is selected; and, as you soon discover, you can also drag the handles somewhere else on-screen to change the size of the frame. A little anchor symbol gives the frame a home base in relation to the text on the page. The frame's position on the page is defined in relation to this anchor, which you can move around in your document as you do text. For example, the frame may fit flush with the left margin, one inch below the anchor. As you add or delete text ahead of the anchor, the anchor moves with the surrounding text, and Word Pro moves the frame automatically to maintain the same relative position one inch below the anchor — even if the anchor has moved to another page in your document.

The capability to select frames is important because you can't make changes to a frame unless you first select that frame. (You can find more information about selecting things in Word Pro in Chapter 4.) Here's some stuff you can do to a frame:

✔ To select a frame, click anywhere inside the frame. To deselect a frame, click anywhere outside the frame. (The handles disappear if you deselect a frame.) You must select frames before you can move, resize, delete, or modify them.

✔ To change the size of a frame, position your mouse pointer over one of the handles until the pointer turns into a double-headed arrow. Then drag the handle to make the frame larger or smaller. To change both the height and width at the same time, drag one of the corner handles.

✔ To move a frame, just put your mouse pointer anywhere on the outer edge of the frame (but *not* on a handle), click and hold the left mouse button, and drag. The pointer changes to a fist that "grabs" the frame to drag it. (Isn't that cute?) Just release the mouse button after the frame outline is positioned where you want the frame.

✔ To delete a frame, select the frame and then click its outer edge. The outer edge of the frame thickens to match the thickness of the handles. Press Delete. (Bye-bye, frame.)

You can also change how a frame looks and how the frame works in relation to the rest of the document by changing various options in the Frame Properties InfoBox. To open the Frame Properties InfoBox, select a frame and then click the right mouse button (an action that's also called a *right-click*) anywhere inside the frame and choose Frame Properties from the pop-up menu that appears. (You can also choose Frame➪Frame Properties from the menu bar to open this InfoBox.)

Changing the size and position options

After you first open the Frame Properties InfoBox, you normally see the Size and Margin tab, displaying the options shown in Figure 6-3.

Color, Pattern, and Line Style tab

Newspaper Columns tab

Size and Margin tab | Tab Settings, Alignment, Graphics Scaling, and Grid tab

Figure 6-3: The Size and Margin tab of the Frame Properties InfoBox.

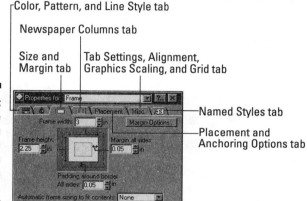

Named Styles tab

Placement and Anchoring Options tab

You can change the following size and margin settings:

- ✔ Adjust the size of the frame by entering numbers in the Frame width and/or Frame height boxes.

- ✔ Use the Margin all sides setting to tell Word Pro how much space to leave between the edge of the frame and whatever you put inside the frame.

- ✔ For more control over the margins, click the Margin Options button to open the Margin Options dialog box, where you can adjust the top, bottom, left, and right margins individually.

- ✔ Use the Padding around border setting to tell Word Pro how much space to leave between the frame and the surrounding text on the page.

- ✔ Select options from the Automatic Frame Sizing to Fit Contents drop-down list to instruct Word Pro to automatically resize the frame to fit a graphic or increase the height up or down to accommodate added text.

As with all Word Pro InfoBoxes, changes you make in the settings are immediately reflected in the frame displayed on the page, behind the InfoBox.

The Placement and Anchoring Options tab in the Frame Properties InfoBox offers the options shown in Figure 6-4.

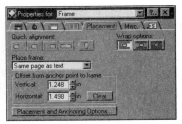

Figure 6-4:
The
Placement
and
Anchoring
Options tab
of the Frame
Properties
InfoBox.

You can change the following placement and anchoring settings:

✔ The five Quick alignment buttons enable you to align your frame with the page margins.

✔ The Wrap options buttons control how text on the page flows around the frame.

✔ The Place frame drop-down list enables you to tell Word Pro to put the frame in the same place on every page of your document, on left or right pages, or in various locations in relation to the location of the anchor. For example, the frame could be embedded in the text or positioned immediately after the paragraph containing the anchor.

✔ The Offset from anchor point to frame settings enable you to position the frame a specific distance from the anchor point in the text. You can even click the Placement and Anchoring Options button to open a dialog box in which you can exercise even more precise control. Usually, however, just using the mouse to move the frame to the position you want is much simpler.

Changing line and shadow settings

Unless you make any changes, a frame gets a simple border consisting of thin, solid lines on all sides. To make changes to frame borders, click the Color, Pattern, and Line Style tab in the Frame Properties InfoBox to access the options shown in Figure 6-5.

Look familiar? The options on this tab are nearly identical to those available for defining the border around a page. And you use them the same way. (Check out Chapter 5 for more information about lines around a page.) The best way to familiarize yourself with the various options is simply by trying them. As with all InfoBox options, the frame changes on-screen immediately to reflect any changes you make in the InfoBox settings, thus giving you instant feedback on the effect each setting has on the frame.

Figure 6-5:
The Color, Pattern, and Line Style tab of the Frame Properties InfoBox.

If you want a box without any borders, simply click the None button in the Lines around frame area.

Framing text and finishing up

If you plan to put text inside the frame, you may want to set some tab stops or divide the frame into columns. To define columns, click the Newspaper Columns tab in the Frame Properties InfoBox to access the options shown in Figure 6-6. The settings here work just like their counterparts in the Page Layout InfoBox described in Chapter 5. You select the number of columns and define the gutters (the space between the columns and any dividing line that should appear in that space); Word Pro takes care of the rest. By checking the Column Balance option, you can even tell Word Pro to automatically adjust the columns in the frame so that the columns are all the same length.

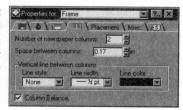

Figure 6-6:
You can add columns inside your frames by using these settings.

For placing tabs within a frame and adjusting other settings, click the Frame Properties InfoBox tab labeled Misc. Figure 6-7 shows the settings available on this tab.

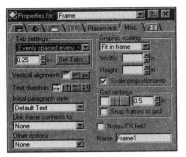

Figure 6-7:
The settings
on the Misc
tab enable
you to adjust
tab stops
and more.

You find a bunch of stuff in here, but most of the settings are rarely used. Here's a description of the settings you're likely to need:

✔ **Tab settings:** The default is None, but you can choose options from the drop-down list to set evenly spaced tabs or a single tab a fixed distance from the left or right edge of the frame. Click the Set Tabs button to open a dialog box in which you can set up custom tab settings.

✔ **Graphic scaling:** This area is where you tell Word Pro how to size any picture that you import into the frame. The drop-down list enables you to choose between maintaining the original size of the import, scaling the picture to fit in the frame, scaling the graphic to a certain percent of the original size, or scaling the imported picture to a custom size. Selecting the Scale Proportionately check box ensures that the picture isn't distorted by the resizing.

If you want to reuse your Frame Properties settings, click the Named Style tab on the far right. You can record the current settings by clicking the Create Style button and giving the style a name. Then that new style appears in the list of Frame styles. Just click a style name in the list to apply to the current frame the settings saved under that style name. If you want your current settings to become the default for any new frames you create in this document, make sure that you're using the Default Frame style, adjust the settings, and then click the Redefine Style button to update the style definition.

But enough talk about empty frames. Time to put something in them.

Putting stuff in frames

We start by putting some text inside a frame, because that action is the most straightforward one you can perform. And then we move on to the main attraction — pretty pictures.

Putting text in frames

Here's the deal: You're frantically trying to get out your year-end budget, but you just found out that you're missing some critical information. So, in your projected budget notice, you insert an APB (all points bulletin) for the missing data. Because getting the notice noticed is of prime importance, you put the notice in a frame to set its message off from the rest of the text. The result is as shown in Figure 6-8.

So how is this accomplished? Simple. To put text in a frame, simply follow these easy steps:

1. **Select the frame.**

   (You already know how to select a frame if you read this section on frames from the beginning. If not, meander back to the "Doing stuff to frames" section, earlier in this chapter.)

2. **Start typing.**

   After you select the frame, an insertion point appears inside the frame and you can type text inside the frame just as you can on the main page. If you type more words than can fit on one line, the text automatically wraps to stay within the frame.

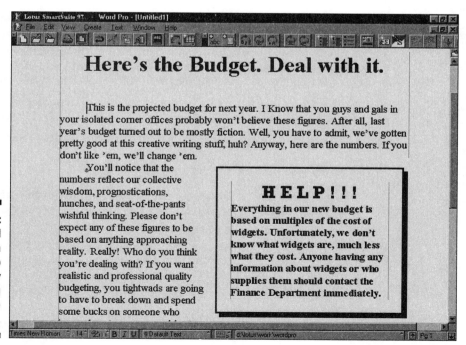

Figure 6-8: You can add extra emphasis to text by putting some inside a frame.

3. Format the text.

You can change the font or formatting by using any of the techniques we discuss in Chapter 4.

4. After you finish, click anywhere outside the frame.

Putting pictures in frames

Now that we've told you all about how to create frames, forget what we said. Yeah, you heard right. If you import a graphic image (picture) into a Word Pro document, you don't need to create the frame first — the frame is created automatically as you import the picture. But we really had a reason for going into all that frame stuff first — honest. Even though you don't need to actually go through the steps to create a frame, you still end up with a frame that you can move, delete, resize, and do all sorts of other things to. So everything you just read about frames is not for naught.

Where do you get pictures to put in your Word Pro documents? You have the following sources:

- ✔ Word Pro comes with a bunch of its own clip-art images you can use.
- ✔ You can use the graphics that come with some of the other SmartSuite 97 applications.
- ✔ You can import drawings or charts from Freelance Graphics or 1-2-3 into Word Pro documents.
- ✔ If you use other drawing programs such as CorelDRAW, Visio, or Adobe Illustrator, you can import their creations into Word Pro, too. (For some thoughts on how to work with files from other applications, see Chapter 26.)
- ✔ If you own or have access to a scanner, you can scan photographs or other images.
- ✔ You can buy commercial clip art and photographs from software stores.

To place a picture into your document, follow these steps:

1. If you already have a frame into which you want to put the picture, select the frame.

The frame you select should be empty. If the frame contains another picture, the new picture replaces the previous occupant of the frame. If your frame contains text, Word Pro creates a frame within a frame to hold the picture. If you don't want to create a frame ahead of time, just skip to Step 2. Word Pro automatically creates a frame as the program imports the picture.

2. Choose File⇨Import Picture from the menu bar.

This action opens the Import Picture dialog box, as shown in Figure 6-9.

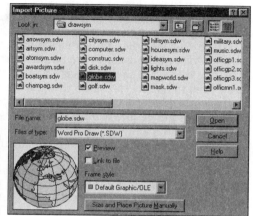

Figure 6-9:
The Import
Picture
dialog box.

3. Make a selection from the Files of type list.

This list displays all the different graphics file types that Word Pro supports. The pictures that come with Word Pro are in Word Pro Draw format (SDW).

4. If necessary, select the folder and/or drive containing the picture you want to import.

The current folder name appears in the Look in drop-down list box. (A *folder* is just another name for the directories you may be familiar with from DOS or earlier versions of Windows.) You can use standard Windows 95 navigation techniques to select a different folder or drive. If you're not familiar with these techniques, check out *Windows 95 For Dummies,* by Andy Rathbone (published by IDG Books Worldwide, Inc.).

5. Select the picture you want to use from the main list box in the middle of the dialog box.

If the Preview check box is selected (the default), you see a preview of the selected picture in the box in the lower-left corner of the Import Picture dialog box. This preview enables you to make sure that you selected the correct picture before importing the image into your Word Pro document.

6. Click Open to import the selected picture.

In Figure 6-10, we add a picture to our budget document.

You can move or resize the frame containing the picture. You can also move or resize a picture inside its frame. Selecting just the picture, however, can be a bit tricky. As you first select a frame containing a picture, you see the thick border appear around the frame, indicating that the frame itself is ready to be moved. You need to double-click the picture to get rid of the thick frame marker and show just the frame handles. Next, you must click the picture again to select the picture instead of the frame. After you select the picture, handles (small black boxes) appear around the picture. (The handles appear inside the frame and border. Sometimes they are hard to see because they are partially cropped by the frame and appear as thin lines instead of square boxes.) You can drag these handles to resize the picture within the frame the same way that you drag frame handles to resize the frame. Clicking and dragging the center of the picture instead of the handles moves the picture within the frame.

Moving or resizing a picture so that some of its handles are outside the frame (making the picture larger than the frame, for example) can result in some bizarre and difficult-to-control behavior. You're best off to just stick with moving and resizing the picture within the confines of the frame.

Figure 6-10:
For this picture, we created the frame first and modified its layout to get rid of the lines and shadow. Then we imported the lightbulb.

If you press Delete with the frame selected, both the frame *and* the picture go away. You can't just delete the frame and leave the picture. You can, however, achieve a no-frame effect by telling Word Pro not to display the lines in the frame. The techniques for performing this task are discussed in the section "Changing line and shadow settings," a little earlier in this chapter.

If you want to delete the picture and leave an empty frame, select the picture (as described in the preceding paragraphs) so that the handles appear around the picture inside the frame; then press the Delete key. That does the job. Given the hassle of selecting the picture inside the frame, however, you may find that just deleting the whole frame and then creating a new, empty frame is easier.

If your clicking finger's just too fast and you delete a frame and its contents without meaning to, just click the Undo SmartIcon right away (or choose Edit⇨Undo).

Printing documents containing lots of pictures can take a long time. You can speed up the printing process (which is especially useful for printing drafts) by telling Word Pro not to print the pictures. Just choose File⇨Print from the menu bar to open the Print dialog box, choose the Options button, and then choose Without pictures in the Print Options dialog box and click OK to close the dialog box. Finally, click the Print button in the Print dialog box to start printing.

Tabular, Dude!

In this section, we show you how to create a simple table. Tables are great for organizing text and numbers into rows and columns. In Chapter 5, we show you how to line up text by using tabs, but tables are easier to work with and offer a lot more formatting options.

Even though Word Pro enables you to perform calculations and other fancy stuff in tables, you're really better off doing that kind of stuff in 1-2-3 and then pasting or linking the 1-2-3 data into your Word Pro document. Part III covers 1-2-3, and Part VII tells you how to link data between applications. Check 'em out for pertinent info.

In case you're beginning to wonder why Word Pro even *has* a tables feature, however, let us hastily amend our preceding caveat. Word Pro tables are great for organizing text items into a tabular format. The tables even work well for small numeric tables.

To create a table in Word Pro, follow these steps:

1. **Choose Create⇨Table from the menu bar.**

    This action opens the Create Table dialog box, as shown in Figure 6-11.

Figure 6-11: Use the Create Table dialog box to create a table.

Create Table	
Table style:	OK
Default Table	Cancel
Description:	Help
Default Table Style	
Number of columns: 4	
Number of rows: 4	Size & Place Table Manually...

So that you can move the table freely within your document, put the table in a frame. Before you open the Create Table dialog box, create a frame and select that frame. As Word Pro creates the table, the program puts the table in the selected frame. You can then work with the table and its frame just as you can with any other frame and its contents.

2. **Type or select values in the Number of columns and Number of rows text boxes to tell Word Pro how many columns and rows you want and then click OK.**

Word Pro instantly displays the table on-screen.

Note: After you click OK in the Create Table dialog box, Word Pro actually adds a Table menu to its menu bar so that you can more easily work with tables. Considerate little program, isn't it?

Here are a few points to remember as you work with tables:

- ✔ To enter text in the table, just put your insertion point in one of the little boxes (called *cells*) and start typing.
- ✔ To move to the next cell, press Tab.
- ✔ If you're in the last cell of a row, pressing Tab takes you to the first cell of the next row.
- ✔ Press Shift+Tab to move backward a cell at a time.
- ✔ Press Tab in the last cell of the last row to create a new row.

That default table with single lines is pretty boring. Fortunately, Word Pro enables you to change the table's layout and formatting. To access Word Pro's table layout options, choose Table➪Table Properties from the menu bar to open the Table Properties InfoBox, as shown in Figure 6-12.

Figure 6-12: Use the Table Properties InfoBox to change a table's layout.

The options available in the Table Properties InfoBox are similar to the options available in the Frame Properties InfoBox (among others). You're probably getting the hang of these InfoBox settings by now. The main thing to remember about these settings is that they apply to the table as a whole.

To adjust the formatting of the cells, select the cells you want to format (by dragging the pointer across the cells — just as if you were selecting text), and either choose Table⇨Cell Properties or right-click a cell and choose Cell Properties from the pop-up menu. Either action opens the Table Cell Properties InfoBox, as shown in Figure 6-13.

Figure 6-13:
The Table Cell Properties InfoBox.

This InfoBox is where you adjust the settings for individual cells. For example, the table lines you see on-screen that separate the rows and columns aren't really lines. Well, they *are* lines, but they don't show up on the page if you print the table. The lines are just there to help you work with the table on-screen. If you actually want lines to appear in your finished table, click the Color, Pattern, and Line Style tab in the Cell Properties InfoBox and then click the second Lines around cells button. This option prints lines that resemble those on-screen. If you want lines around only certain sides of the cells, choose some of the other options.

The Number Format (#) tab of the Cell Properties InfoBox (as shown in Figure 6-14) is a little unusual. This tab enables you to configure cells to display numbers in consistent formats — automatically adding currency symbols and showing a certain number of decimal places and such. For example, if your cell contains the number 123, you could select Currency in the Format category list and U.S. dollar in the Current format list to instruct Word Pro to display the number as $123.00.

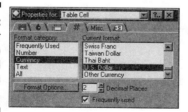

Figure 6-14:
The Number Format tab of the Cell Properties InfoBox.

You can add columns or rows to your table by choosing Table⇨Insert⇨Row/Column from the menu bar to open the Insert Row/Column dialog box, as shown in Figure 6-15. This dialog box enables you to add multiple rows or columns to your table.

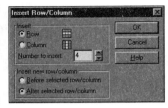

Figure 6-15:
The Insert
Row/
Column
dialog box.

Here's some other table stuff you can do:

✐ To insert a single row into the table, right-click a cell in the row below which you want to insert a new row and choose Insert a Row from the pop-up menu that appears.

✐ To insert a single column into the table, right-click a cell in the column to the left of which you want to insert a new column and choose Insert a Column from the pop-up menu. Word Pro adds the new column to the right of the column you clicked.

✐ To delete a row or column, right-click a cell in the row or column you want to delete and choose Delete Row/Column from the pop-up menu. Choose Row or Column in the dialog box that appears and click OK.

✐ To select the entire table, choose Table⇨Select⇨Entire Table from the menu bar.

✐ To change the width of a column by using the mouse, place your mouse pointer on the line that separates the two columns. After your mouse pointer turns into a two-headed arrow, drag the line in either direction to make the column wider or narrower.

Take a look at Figure 6-16 to see how a finished table can look in Word Pro after you create and pretty the thing up some. Impressive, huh?

Figure 6-16:
A finished
table that
explores
some of the
Word Pro
table cap-
abilities.

Preliminary Budget Forecast		
Category	**First Quarter**	**Second Quarter**
Whopee Cushions	$4,332.00	$7,598.00
Pencils	$122.00	$50.00
Erasers	$1,075.00	$922.00

Finding and Replacing Stuff

Suppose that you have a document full of text. Then you remember that premium widgets aren't premium widgets anymore — their name got changed to *plenipotentiary* widgets in the middle of the project. You know that you talked about those stupid widgets a lot, but you're not sure whether you used the new name throughout the document. You could laboriously read through the widget document, line by line, eyes slowly glazing over, or you could use the Word Pro Find and Replace feature — not only to find all the places where you mentioned the widgets, but also to replace any incorrect entries with the right text. Here's how to use Find and Replace:

1. **Choose Edit⇨Find & Replace Text from the menu bar (or press Ctrl+F).**

   You may expect this command to open a dialog box, but Word Pro has a surprise in store for you. The Find & Replace bar appears just below the menu bar and SmartIcon palette, as shown in Figure 6-17.

2. **Type the text you want to search for in the Find text box.**

3. **If you want to replace the text with something else, type the replacement text in the Replace with text box.**

Figure 6-18:
The Find &
Replace bar.

4. **Choose the Find button to locate the first place the search text occurs, or choose Replace All to automatically replace all occurrences of the search text with the replacement text.**

   If you choose Replace All, Word Pro goes through the document and does its thing without any input from you. Unless you're absolutely sure you want to replace every single occurrence of the search text, you're usually safer to choose Find. That way you get to make decisions about what to replace as you go along.

   In Figure 6-17, notice that the Find text is *premium widgets* instead of just *premium*. We chose to use both words because the word *premium* could easily be used in another context, and we wouldn't want to replace all occurrences of *premium* with *plenipotentiary*.

   If you choose Find, Word Pro stops at the first place it finds the search text. Click the Replace button to replace this instance of the search text and search for the next occurrence. Click Replace All to replace this and all other occurrences without further input from you.

5. Click the Done button to close the Find & Replace bar after you finish searching for text.

You can also use Find and Replace as a quickie way to delete text. Suppose that you find out that your boss, John Snowflake Adams, is terribly embarrassed by his middle name and begs you not to use it in the bio you just completed. Just do a search for *Snowflake*, don't put anything in the Replace with box, and choose Replace All. Word Pro replaces all occurrences of Snowflake with nothing. Now the only person left alive who knows John's middle name is you. Hmmm, with a little blackmail . . . er, that is, *subtle persuasion*, maybe you can finally get that corner office.

We've explained how to do a simple text search and replace. But hey, Word Pro doesn't stop there. You can narrow down the search specifications, you can tell Word Pro in which direction to search and what parts of the document to search, and you can even search for styles and text attributes such as bold and italic type.

For quick, routine control over the search, you can perform the following actions:

- ✔ Click the left- or right-arrow buttons to tell Word Pro in which direction to search — toward the beginning of the document or toward the end.

- ✔ Specify whether Word Pro should look for the search word as whole words only or for words that begin or end with or contain the search term. Make your selection in the drop-down list below the Find & Replace title.

To specify more elaborate search preferences, choose the Options button in the Find & Replace bar. This action opens the Find & Replace Text Options dialog box, as shown in Figure 6-18.

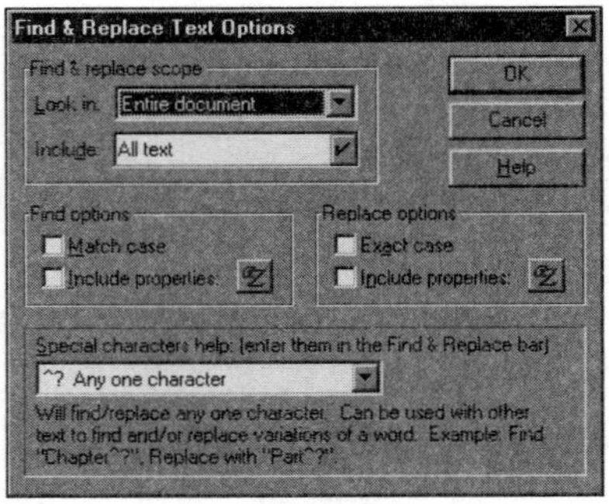

Figure 6-18:
The Find & Replace Text Options dialog box.

By using the options in this dialog box, you can perform the following search operations:

- ✔ Select Entire Document or Current Division (if you've divided your document into sections) in the Look in drop-down list box to tell Word Pro how much and what part of the document to search.

- ✔ Make selections in the Include drop-down list box to search all the text or just tables, headers, and so on.

- ✔ Select the Match case check box to find text that exactly matches the upper- and lowercase letters of your search word or phrase; otherwise, a search for *the* finds *the, The, THE,* and even *tHe* or *thE.* You can choose the counterpart to this option — Exact case — for replacement text.

- ✔ Select the Include properties check box to find the search text only if that text uses a specific font or type size or bold, italics, or another text attribute. If you choose this option, click the Text Properties button next to this option (the one marked with A-Z) and specify the text properties you want to match in the mini-InfoBox that appears. You can choose this option for both search and replacement text.

- ✔ Use the Special characters help drop-down list to find out how to specify special characters (such as tabs and returns) in the Find or Replace With boxes.

SmartCorrect Takes Shorthand

Do you repeatedly make common typographical errors, such as transposing characters (typing **teh** for *the* or **adn** for *and*)? If so, you're going to love the Word Pro *SmartCorrect* feature!

SmartCorrect watches as you type and, if the feature detects a common mistake, corrects the error automatically. But SmartCorrect can do more than just correct mistakes. The feature can also automatically expand abbreviations. You'd be amazed at how your typing speed picks up when you can type a few letters and have SmartCorrect replace them with an entire phrase. You may, for example, type **otoh** and have SmartCorrect replace this abbreviation with the full text *on the other hand.*

SmartCorrect works by keeping a list of mistakes and abbreviations as well as the corrected text with which to replace these errors (or their shorthand terms). SmartCorrect comes with a sizable list of common mistakes to seek out. To take full advantage of the SmartCorrect feature, however, you probably need to customize the list with your own entries.

Choose Edit⇨SmartCorrect to open the SmartCorrect dialog box, as shown in Figure 6-19. Here you can scroll through the list of SmartCorrect entries. After you click to highlight an entry, the replacement text appears to the side of the list.

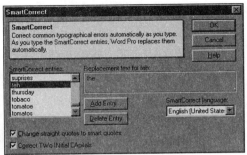

Figure 6-19:
The
SmartCorrect
dialog box.

You can change the SmartCorrect entries by performing the following actions:

- ✔ To delete an entry from the list, click that entry and then click the Delete Entry button.

- ✔ To add your own entry to the list, click the Add Entry button to open the Add SmartCorrect Entry Dialog box. Type the text you want to replace in the SmartCorrect Entry text box. Type the text you want to replace the original in the Replacement text box and click OK. Word Pro adds the entry to the SmartCorrect Entry list.

- ✔ Select the Change straight quotes to smart quotes check box to automatically replace straight quotes (") with typographically correct curved quotes (").

- ✔ Select the Correct TWo INitial CApitals check box to instruct SmartCorrect to correct this common typing error.

Spelling Words Right

All the SmartSuite 97 applications use the same dictionary for spell-checking purposes, and you use the same basic techniques to run a spell-check in each application. We describe spell-checking in SmartSuite 97 in general in Part I, but in this chapter, we cover some options that are unique to Word Pro.

Here's a quick reminder on how to start a spell-check: Click the Check Spelling SmartIcon (a little book marked with *ABC*) or choose Edit⇨Check Spelling from the menu bar. In other SmartSuite 97 programs, this command opens a dialog box, but in Word Pro, the same command opens the Spell Check bar, as shown in Figure 6-20.

The Spell Check bar may look different from the usual dialog box, but this feature works much the same as a dialog box. The bar arrangement just keeps a dialog box from covering up the text you're working with.

One interesting button on the Spell Check bar is SmartCorrect. Clicking this button adds the currently selected misspelled word (and its suggested replacement text) to the SmartCorrect Entry list. The next time you make that error, Word Pro corrects the error automatically; you don't need to use the Spell Check bar to make the correction.

Figure 6-20:
The Word
Pro Spell
Check bar.

Actually, the Spell Check feature is active all the time in Word Pro (or, at least, you can set the feature to remain active). Word Pro checks each word as you type and highlights any words the feature doesn't recognize. Choose View➪Show/Hide➪Misspelled Words to display the light blue highlights that mark misspelled words. Choose the same command again to suppress the highlights if you find them distracting.

Here, too, are a couple of points concerning the use of the status bar in spell-checking:

   ✓ Click the Check Spelling button on the status bar (it's in the middle and looks like a book marked with *ABC*) and then choose Show Misspelled Words or Hide Misspelled Words from the pop-up list to display or hide the highlighting that marks misspelled words. (Note that this button is the one on the status bar, *not* the Check Spelling SmartIcon.)

   ✓ Click a misspelled word and then click the Check Spelling button in the status bar for quick access to the basic Spell Check commands without opening the Spell Check bar. A pop-up menu appears displaying a list of options that vary depending on the circumstances. For example, for a simple misspelling, you see such commands as Add to Dictionary, Skip, and Replace, along with a list of suggested replacement words (one of which is highlighted).

After you open the Spell Check bar, Word Pro starts at your insertion point position and jumps to the next misspelled word. Click the Options button to give Word Pro specific spell-check instructions. The Spell Check Options dialog box opens, as shown in Figure 6-21. By using the various options in the Spell

Check Options dialog box, you can tell Word Pro to check or not check specific types of text and can identify the User Dictionary to use (which is the list of names and other words you previously identified as being spelled correctly).

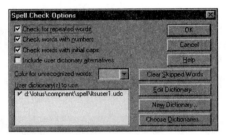

If you select Check for repeated words in this dialog box, the spell-check stops upon finding the same word twice in a row and asks what you want to do. You can either replace the word with something else or ignore the repeated word and move on. You may think that selecting the Check words with numbers check box is a good thing — and using this option usually is. After all, a slip of the finger can easily turn *steam* into *st3eam*. But what if your document contains a whole bunch of part numbers such as *CSP432a9z765?* If that's the case, you can save time and aggravation by turning off number checking.

Unless you have a particular reason not to, you should probably go ahead and select Check words with initial caps. With this option selected, Word Pro stops at every questionable word that begins with an uppercase letter (proper names, place names, product names, and so on). This stop-go procedure can become annoying, but we figure that spending a little extra time going over a handful of additional words is better than missing those few words that really are misspelled.

If you add words to your user dictionary during a spell-check (by clicking the Add To User Dictionary option on the Spell Check bar after Word Pro stops on a word), you can tell Word Pro to include words from your customized word list in the list of alternatives Word Pro gives you to choose from. (In other words, selecting the Include user dictionary alternatives check box in the Spell Check Options dialog box is usually a good idea.)

Make sure that you save your document after you run a spell-check. Until you do so, none of the changes made during the spell-check are safe and you could lose all the corrections if your system suffers a power surge or your dog chews through the power cord at that particular moment.

Using Thesaurus for the Perfect Phrase

Is that perfect word on the tip of your tongue but nowhere in sight of your typing fingers? Try Word Pro's thesaurus. (And no, you *didn't* see one of those in *Jurassic Park*!) Just use the closest word you can think of and have the thesaurus give you some help. To use the thesaurus, follow these steps:

1. **Place your insertion point in the word you want to check.**

2. **Choose Edit⇨Check Thesaurus from the menu bar.**

   Word Pro selects the word and opens the Thesaurus dialog box, as shown in Figure 6-22.

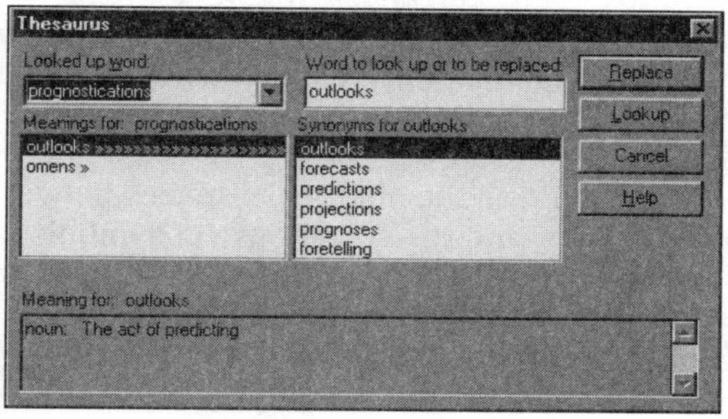

Figure 6-22:
Don't know
the right
word?
Thesaurus
to the
rescue.

3. **If the word you want appears in the Synonyms for list, select the word and choose Replace.**

4. **If none of the words work for you, try clicking a different word in the Meanings for list.**

   For each word in this list, you get a different set of synonyms; if you spot the one you want, select that word and choose Replace.

5. **If one of the words in the Synonyms for list is close but no cigar, try selecting that word and clicking Lookup.**

   Word Pro uses the selected word as a new jumping-off point and presents you with a new list of synonyms for that word.

6. **At any point, you can terminate the Thesaurus session without making any changes by clicking Cancel or pressing Esc.**

Fix Picky Details by Using Format Check and Grammar Check

In the old days of typewriters and monospaced fonts, the standard practice was to use two spaces following a period to separate sentences. Now, with modern proportional fonts in widespread use, the typesetting standard of one space to separate sentences is gaining acceptance. Most typing classes, however, still teach the old two-space technique and many people still hit two spaces after a period out of habit.

Luckily, we have the luxury of relying on an excellent team of copy editors to go over our manuscript and fix such details. If you don't have a copy editor who proofreads everything you write, you can enlist two Word Pro features — *Format Check* and *Grammar Check* — to help. These features aren't as good as a real human editor but can help you find and fix some annoying (and potentially embarrassing) mistakes.

Format Check looks for things such as the number of spaces between sentences, formatting of bulleted lists, and the correct use of symbols and special characters. To Format Check your document, choose Edit➪Check Format. The Format Check bar appears (and is similar in appearance to the Spell Check bar), and Word Pro locates the first suspected formatting error. As on the Spell Check bar, several buttons enable you to accept or reject Word Pro's suggestions. By using those buttons, you can perform the following actions:

- To accept the suggested formatting change, click Replace.

- To automatically accept the replacement for all occurrences of the same error, click Replace All of Rule.

- To proceed to the next suspected error without making any change, click Skip.

- To skip a suspected error and ignore all future occurrences in this document, click Skip All of Rule.

- If you're very daring, you can click Replace All to have Word Pro automatically make changes without requesting your acknowledgment. We don't recommend this option, however. Format Check is handy but is not ready to fly solo — the feature still needs some supervision.

The Word Pro Grammar Check feature does for grammar what Format Check does for formatting. The program includes a set of rules that the Grammar Check feature uses to analyze your sentences and suggest changes. To start a grammar check, choose Edit➪Check Grammar. Word Pro opens the Grammar Check bar, which looks and works essentially the same as the Format Check and Spell Check bars. The only significant difference is that the Grammar Check bar doesn't offer Replace All or Skip All buttons. This bar does, however, offer an Explain button that opens a message box containing an explanation of the grammar rule that applies to the highlighted error.

You may find Grammar Check useful at times, but you're probably just as well off spending the time carefully reading what you've written.

Keeping Track of Revisions

You compose a document. Next, you read through the document once to make sure that you typed what you intended; then you check the spelling, print the document, and send your masterpiece out. Ahh, don't you wish that life was as simple as that? In the real world, however, several other people usually need to review the document (and probably suggest changes) before your work is ready to go.

Fortunately, Word Pro includes some features to make collaborative editing a little easier (if not more fun). Word Pro can keep track of editing changes in a document. The program can show edits on-screen, with additions and deletions marked with distinctive colors and fonts. Then you can review the edits and decide whether to accept them or revert to the original text.

Marking edits

If you want Word Pro to keep track of editing changes as you make them and display those changes on-screen, choose Edit⇨Markup Edits to turn on the feature. While the feature is active, a check mark appears beside the command on the Edit menu. If you delete text, Word Pro changes that text's color and marks the deleted text with a strikethru line. If you add text, the additions appear in italics of a different color. If you want to disable the Markup Edits feature, simply choose the command again.

Reviewing marked edits

Before you begin reviewing marked edits, you need to prepare yourself for the task. Take a deep breath. Now imagine that your ego is a jacket. Remove the jacket and hang it outside in the hall. Leave the garment there until you finish reviewing the marked edits. (In extreme cases, removing the ego jacket may not be enough. You may need to don an imaginary asbestos suit as well.) There — now that you're adequately prepared, you can get started.

After your team members edit your document (using the Markup Edits feature, of course) you can review the changes they make and decide whether to accept or reject them (the edits, not your coworkers).

Open the document and choose Edit⇨Review Marked Edits. Word Pro opens the Review bar, as shown in Figure 6-23. You can move through the document, finding editing changes, by clicking Next Edit or Previous. (The Next Edit button is initially labeled Find Next.) After you locate a change, Word Pro shows who made the change and the date.

Figure 6-23:
The Review bar enables you to review marked edits.

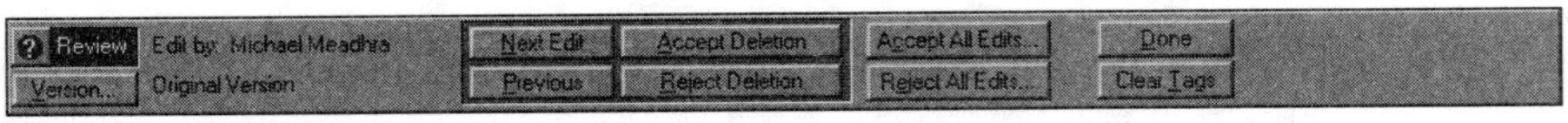

The buttons on the Review bar enable you to perform the following actions:

✔ Clicking the Version button opens the Version for File dialog box, where you can select a previous version of the document you're editing or create a new version of the document so that you can make changes freely in the new version and still go back to the previous version if you change your mind.

Oh, did you know that Word Pro can store more than one version of a document in a single file? Well, now you do.

✔ Click Accept Edit to make the suggested change and remove the editing markup.

Note: Depending on the kind of edit that is highlighted, the Accept Edit button may be labeled Accept Insertion, Accept Deletion, or something similar. The Reject Edit button changes in a similar manner.

✔ Click Reject Edit to revert to the original text and remove the suggested text.

✔ Click Accept All Edits to automatically accept all the suggested changes and remove the editing markups.

✔ Click Reject All Edits to automatically remove all the suggested changes and revert to the original text.

✔ Click Clear Tags to remove the editor's initials that Word Pro adds to the duplicate paragraphs that result from comparing two documents. (Comparing documents is a somewhat advanced feature of Word Pro. If you haven't used the Compare feature, the Clear Tags button doesn't do anything.)

✔ Click Done after you finish reviewing marked edits.

(You can retrieve your ego from the hall now.)

Chapter 7
Word Pro Final Touches and Shortcuts

*N*ot only can Word Pro create great-looking letters, but the program can also create form letters, follow commands automatically, and organize your files so that you can find those files again. Although none of the features described in this chapter are necessary to use Word Pro, these features can make Word Pro much easier to use. Unless you enjoy doing things the hard way, take a look at these fancy features that take the burden of writing off of you and put that weight on the computer, where the pesky thing so obviously belongs.

Hey, Babe, Wanna Merge?

Suppose that you want to type the same letter over and over again, except that you want to address each nearly identical letter to a different person. The hard way is to type each letter separately and hope you don't make a mistake. The easy way is to make some minimum wage coworker do the work for you so that you have someone to blame if something goes wrong. If neither approach is feasible, the computer solution is to make Word Pro type these letters for you automatically. To do so, you must create the following two separate documents:

↳ A form letter

↳ The merge document

The *form letter* contains the text you want to send to everyone. The text in a form letter never changes from one letter to another. To tell Word Pro where to plug in personalized information, you must create certain elements called *fields*. Often, these fields appear at the top of your letter, as in the following example:

<First_Name> <Last_Name>
<Address>
<City>, <State> <Zip>

Dear <Title> <Last_Name>,

Thank you for your recent inquiry on our latest best-seller, *Atom Bomb Testing For Dummies*. The book is being sent separately and you should receive your copy within one week from the receipt of this letter. We thank you for your business and hope that you may be interested in our other titles, such as *Chainsaws For Dummies, Artillery Spotting For Dummies,* and, of course, our perennial best-seller, *Tax Evasion For Dummies*.

In the preceding example, *<First_Name>* is a field because that information tells Word Pro: "Hey, this spot is where you insert a person's first name."

The *merge document* contains the information that you want inserted into a form letter, such as each person's name and address. For example, the Word Pro data file may contain the following information:

Mr. John Doe
123 Main Street
New York, NY 10012

Ms. Mary Jane
8763 Average Avenue
Fairmont, CO 30302

Word Pro actually stores the data in a funky, hard-to-read format with each record (address) on a single line and the fields separated by the tilde (~) character. But you don't need to worry about having to work with the merge data directly. Word Pro is the only one that needs to read this data. You can create and edit the data file by entering text in a dialog box.

If you tell Word Pro to create form letters for you, Word Pro grabs the document containing your merge data and plugs it into the gaps left vacant in your form letter to create a "personalized" letter, such as the following example:

John Doe
123 Main Street
New York, NY 10012

Dear Mr. Doe,

Thank you for your recent inquiry on our latest best-seller, *Atom Bomb Testing For Dummies*. The book is being sent separately and you should receive your copy within one week from the receipt of this letter. We thank you for your business and hope that you may be interested in our other titles, such as *Chainsaws For Dummies, Artillery Spotting For Dummies,* and our perennial best-seller, *Tax Evasion For Dummies.*

Creating a form letter from scratch

To create both a form letter and merge data file from scratch, open a plain, blank document in Word Pro and follow these steps:

1. **Choose Text ⇨Merge⇨Letter from the menu bar.**

   The Mail Merge Assistant dialog box appears, as shown in Figure 7-1.

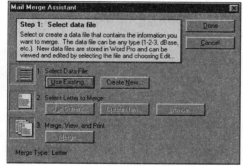

Figure 7-1:
The Mail Merge Assistant dialog box.

The first step is to specify a data file to use.

2. **Click the Create New button to begin the process of creating a data file.**

   The Create Data File dialog box appears, as shown in Figure 7-2.

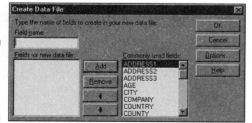

Figure 7-2:
The Create Data File dialog box.

3. **Type a field name (such as First Name or City) in the Field name text box and then click Add to add the field to the Fields for new data file list.**

   Repeat this step for each field that you want to create.

You can save some typing by selecting a field name from the Commonly used fields list and then clicking Add to add this field name to the Fields for new data file list.

4. **Arrange the fields in the Fields for new data file list in a convenient order by clicking a field name and then clicking the up- or down-arrow buttons to move the field name up or down in the list.**

5. **After the list of field names is complete, click OK.**

Word Pro displays an Edit Data File dialog box, as shown in Figure 7-3, showing the fields you created accompanied by empty text boxes in which to type your merge data.

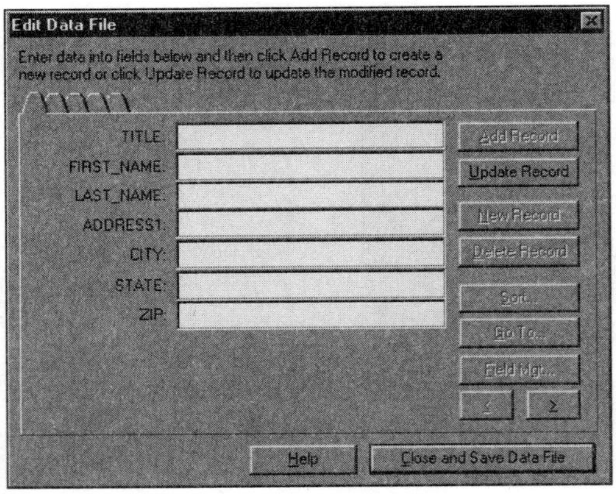

Figure 7-3:
The Edit
Data File
dialog box.

6. **Click any field text box and then type the appropriate data in the field text box; click Add Record after you finish adding data for one record.**

Repeat this step for all the field text boxes for the merge data you want to create.

7. **Click the Close and Save Data File button after you finish creating your merge data.**

Word Pro displays a dialog box asking if you want to save your newly created merge data.

8. **Choose Yes.**

A Save As dialog box appears.

9. **Type a name for your file and click Save.**

The Mail Merge Assistant dialog box reappears. The icon beside Step 1 in this dialog box displays a check mark to indicate that the step is complete and the options in Step 2 are now available.

10. **Click Use Current to tell Word Pro that you want to create your form letter in the current (blank) document.**

    Word Pro displays your blank current document in the workspace and opens the *Merge bar* across the top, just below the menu bar and SmartIcon palette, as shown in Figure 7-4.

Figure 7-4:
The Merge bar.

11. **Type your form letter; whenever you want Word Pro to insert data stored in your merge data file, click the field name in the Merge bar's list and then click Insert Field.**

    Figure 7-5 shows one possible result.

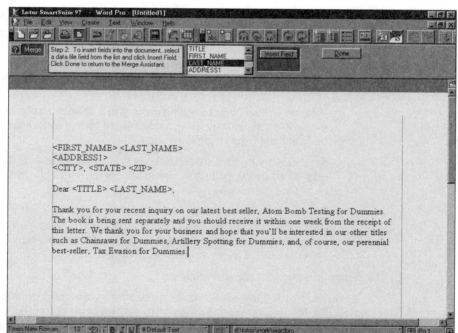

Figure 7-5:
A typical form letter.

12. **After you finish creating your form letter, click the Done button in the Merge bar.**

The Mail Merge Assistant dialog box reappears with the Step 2 icon checked off and Step 3, Merge, View and Print, available.

13. **Click Merge.**

The Merge, View and Print dialog box appears, as shown in Figure 7-6. You can choose the following options for what items to print and how Word Pro prints the merge letters:

Figure 7-6:
The Merge,
View and
Print dialog
box.

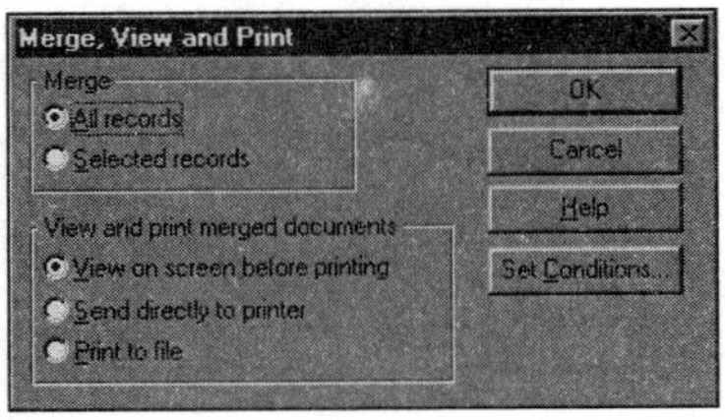

- *All records* prints a merge letter for each record in the merge data file.

- *Selected records* enables you to specify what records to use for merge letters. Click the *Set Conditions* button to open a dialog box where you can specify the selection criteria (such as State=CA) for which records to print by making selections from a set of drop-down list boxes.

- *View on screen before printing* gives you a chance to view your form letters before printing so you don't print lots of form letters only to find that the formatting is wrong.

- *Send directly to printer* does exactly what you think — this option tells Word Pro to print the merge letters immediately without previewing each one on-screen first.

- *Print to file* does not print your form letters but saves the letters as a Word Pro document. If you choose this option, type a filename for your document in the Save As dialog box that appears. You can then skip the rest of these steps. You're done!

14. **Turn on your printer and click OK.**

If you select the View on screen before printing option in the preceding step (highly recommended), Word Pro displays on-screen the first form letter with all the merged data in place. The Merge bar appears across the top of the workspace with a different set of buttons than those you use to create a form letter. The following buttons in the Merge bar enable you to preview the form letters and control printing:

- *Print and View Next* prints the current form letter and then displays the next variation with new data in place.

- *Skip and View Next* discards the current version of the form letter and displays the letter with data from the next merge data record.

- *Print All* automatically prints all the form letters — one for each selected record in the merge data file — without previewing each one on-screen.

If you select Send Directly to Printer, Word Pro cheerfully prints out your form letters with your merge data typed in the fields that you specified without your previewing the letters first.

15. Choose File⇨Save to save your form letter.

A Save As dialog box appears.

16. Type the filename for your form letter and click Save.

If your merge document is missing data, such as someone's last name or address, guess what? Word Pro cheerfully shoves a blank space in the form letter where the last name or address is supposed to go. Before printing a lot of form letters, first use the View on screen before printing option of the Merge, View and Print dialog box to view your completed form letters.

If you save your form letter, you can always open the letter later to make changes. Until you specify otherwise, Word Pro assumes that you always want to merge your form letter with the last merge document you used with that particular form letter.

To edit information stored in a merge document (to update the names and addresses, for example), follow these steps:

1. Open the form letter document you want to edit.

2. Choose Text⇨Merge⇨Letter to open the Mail Merge Assistant dialog box.

(Refer back to Figure 7-1 if you don't recall what this dialog box looks like.)

3. Click the Use Existing button to open the Browse dialog box; then locate and select the merge data file you want to edit and click Open.

4. Click the Edit button in the Mail Merge Assistant dialog box to open the Edit Data File dialog box.

Note: The Edit button appears after you select a Word Pro merge data file.

(Refer back to Figure 7-3 if you don't recall what the Edit Data File dialog box looks like.)

5. **Click the Delete Record or New Record button to delete or add a new record; to edit a record, click a tab or use the arrow buttons in the lower-right corner of the dialog box to select the record, type your changes, and then click the Update Record button.**

6. **Click Close and Save Data File after you're done.**

   A dialog box appears asking if you want to save your changes in the file.

7. **Click Yes.**

   The Mail Merge Assistant dialog box reappears. At this point, you can click Done to close the dialog box, or you can continue with the process of creating a merge letter, as described in Steps 10–16 of the steps on creating a form letter from scratch, a bit earlier in this section.

Creating a form letter by using an Approach database

If you have information stored in an Approach database using the dBASE format, you can merge the data into a Word Pro form letter. To link a Word Pro form letter to an Approach database, follow these steps:

1. **Open an existing form letter document or a blank document.**

2. **Choose Text⇨Merge⇨Letter to open the Mail Merge Assistant dialog box.**

   (Refer to Figure 7-1 if you don't recall what this dialog box looks like.)

3. **Click the Use Existing button beside the Step 1 icon to open the Browse dialog box.**

4. **Click the Files of type list box and select dBASE/ASCII (*.DBF).**

5. **Click the name of the Approach database file that you want to use from the list of files and then click Open.**

   Note: You may first need to change drives or folders to find the database you want.

   The File Type dialog box may appear. If it does, select dBASE/ASCII from the list to confirm the file type and click OK.

   The Import dialog box appears.

6. **Click the Entire file radio button and then click OK.**

   The Mail Merge Assistant dialog box reappears with the Step 1 icon checked off.

7. **Follow Steps 10 through 16 of the first set of steps in the section "Creating a form letter from scratch," earlier in this chapter.**

Automating Word Pro

If you need to type long, repetitive blocks of text often, what can you do? After forcing a subordinate to perform this dirty work, the next best solution is to create a *script* — a prerecorded set of instructions for Word Pro that you can use to execute several actions with a single command. A script tells Word Pro, "Remember what I just typed. Then, when I tell you, retype everything that I told you to remember." By using scripts, you can make Word Pro type entire paragraphs of text with just a few clicks of a mouse button.

For those power users out there, scripts can do a lot more than type words or phrases. In fact, scripts can perform any Word Pro command that you want. As a general rule, if you can perform an action in the program, a Word Pro script can perform that action, too.

Any typos you make while recording a script Word Pro stores in that script. Word Pro has no way of knowing whether you've made a mistake, so while recording a script, be very careful — or you may record your errors as well as what you want recorded.

Scripts are not always known by that name. Some programs (including Word Pro's predecessor, Ami Pro) call these handy keystroke savers *macros*. The name itself doesn't really matter; the terms are interchangeable but the function is the same.

Recording a script

One way to create a script is by typing script commands and text into a script editor dialog box. But that's an exercise best left to the programmer types. For the rest of us, the easiest way to create a script is to tell Word Pro to "watch me and record what I do." Then, later, Word Pro can repeat the sequence of keystrokes and menu choices on command. To record a script this way, follow these steps:

1. **Move the cursor to the place in your document where you want your script to begin.**

2. **Choose Edit⇨Script & Macros⇨Record Script.**

   The Record Script dialog box appears, as shown in Figure 7-7.

3. **Click the Into this file radio button, type a name for your script in the text box (no spaces allowed), and click OK.**

   For some reason, Word Pro insists on naming the first script in each file *Main*. The program ignores anything you enter as the script name for the first script. If you record additional scripts, you can name those anything you like (as long as you avoid spaces).

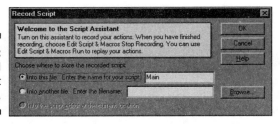

Figure 7-7:
The Record
Script
dialog box.

The Recording message appears in the status bar where the document file name (among other information) usually appears.

4. Take whatever actions you want Word Pro to record.

You can type text, choose menu commands, and make selections in dialog boxes. You can't use the mouse to make text selections, however, or to copy and move things while you're recording a script.

5. Choose Edit⇨Script & Macros⇨Stop Recording to stop recording your script.

You can also stop recording a script by clicking the Document Information button in the status bar — the one that currently reads Recording.

After you stop recording a script, Word Pro opens the very complicated-looking Scripts For window. You can edit your script here if you are so inclined (and have a degree in computer programming). Fortunately, the typical recorded script requires no editing.

6. Choose File⇨Save Scripts from the menu bar in the Scripts For window and confirm the action by clicking OK in the dialog box that appears.

Word Pro saves your document file and the scripts along with the file.

7. Click the Close (X) button to close the Scripts For window.

That's the entire procedure — you just recorded a script. The script is saved along with your document and is available to play back the actions you recorded at any time you're working in the document. In fact, you can even play scripts stored in other documents, as you discover in the following section.

Playing a script

After you create a script that records some tedious chore in Word Pro, you can play that script back to automate the task as often as you like. To play a script, follow these steps:

1. Place the cursor at the point in your document where you want your script to begin.

2. Choose Edit⇨Script & Macros⇨Run.

The Run Script dialog box appears, as shown in Figure 7-8.

3. Select the Word Pro file containing the script you want to run.

Click the Run script saved in the current file radio button to use a script recorded in the current document.

To use a script saved in another file, click the Run script saved in another file radio button and then click Browse to open the Browse dialog box. Locate and select the file containing the script you want to run and click Open to return to the Run Script dialog box. Word Pro automatically enters the filename in the Run script saved in another file box.

4. Select the name of the script you want to run from the drop-down list next to the Run script saved in the current file radio button.

This step applies only if, in Step 3, you chose to run a script from the current file. If you chose to run a script from another file instead, you can specify the filename, but not the script name. Word Pro runs the script named Main from the specified file. You can't choose any other scripts from that other file.

5. Click OK.

Word Pro plays the script, recreating the keystrokes and other actions you recorded earlier.

Fill in the blanks with Click Here blocks

Scripts provide one kind of automation in Word Pro documents. SmartMaster templates can automate the preparation of entire documents by enabling you to create a new document that already contains much of the text and layout information. Most of the SmartMaster templates that come with Word Pro use Click Here blocks as placeholders for the information you must add as you finish up a new document based on the SmartMaster. You've seen them (and probably used them) if you've tried out many of the Word Pro SmartMasters. (If you haven't checked out Word Pro's assortment of SmartMasters, now would be a good time to do so.) To use a Click Here block, you just click the Click Here prompt on-screen and, as prompted, fill in the blank with the information requested to complete the document.

You may think that creating the Click Here prompts in SmartMasters takes special programming skills, but if you do, you're wrong. You can create Click Here blocks in your own document and save the document as a SmartMaster. Then you (or your associates) can use your SmartMaster as the basis for new Word Pro documents, complete with the fill-in-the-blanks features of the slick, professionally designed SmartMasters.

To prepare your own SmartMaster template, start by creating a normal Word Pro document, complete with the text and formatting that is to remain the same in all the documents based on the template. For the areas that are to change in each document, you can add Click Here blocks to serve as placeholders for the type the user must fill in. To create a Click Here block, follow these steps:

1. **Position the insertion point at the location in your document where you want the Click Here block.**

2. **Choose Create⇨Click Here Block from the menu bar.**

   The Create Click Here Block dialog box appears, as shown in Figure 7-9.

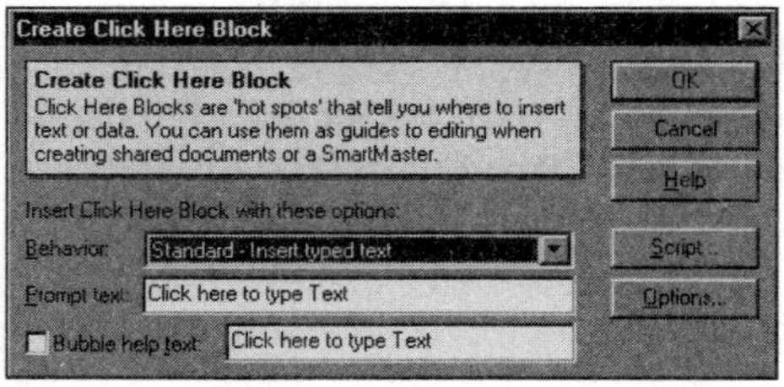

Figure 7-9:
The Create Click Here Block dialog box.

3. **Specify what the Click Here block needs to do by making a selection from the Behavior drop-down list box.**

   Normally, you want to stick with the default selection: Standard - Insert typed text. You can also use Click Here blocks, however, to create tables, pictures, charts, and more.

4. **In the Prompt Text box, type the prompt that you want to appear in the document (assuming that you want something more enlightening than the default prompt text supplied by Word Pro).**

   If you selected the Standard - Insert typed text behavior and want a separate Bubble Help prompt, select the Bubble Help Text check box option and enter the appropriate text for the prompt in the accompanying text box. The text you enter appears in one of those cartoon-like bubbles after you point to the finished Click Here block for a few seconds.

5. **Click OK.**

   Word Pro creates the Click Here block in your document.

6. Select the Click Here block (by dragging the pointer across the prompt text) and add any formatting you want the final text to have.

(See Chapter 5 for the scoop on formatting.)

If you click the Click Here block, Word Pro deletes the prompt text and, in its place, enters the text you type or inserts a chart or takes some other action (depending on the kind of Click Here block you create).

You can add other Click Here blocks to your document as needed.

Although you could use Click Here blocks in a regular Word Pro document, you're most likely to use them in creating your own SmartMaster templates. To save a document as a SmartMaster template, follow these steps:

1. Choose File⇨Save As to open the Save As dialog box.

2. In the Save As Type list, select Lotus WordPro SmartMaster (*.MWP).

3. Type a name in the File Name box.

You can find your new SmartMaster more easily if you save the file in the same folder as all the other Word Pro SmartMasters — usually C:\LOTUS\SMASTERS\WORDPRO. Select that folder in the Save In list box.

4. Click Save.

Word Pro opens the Save As SmartMaster Options dialog box where you can select some optional features for the SmartMaster file. For example, you can instruct Word Pro to update the preview image for the SmartMaster or automatically adapt the SmartMaster settings to match the user's page settings or document language settings whenever creating a new document based on the SmartMaster.

5. Check the appropriate options in the Save As SmartMaster Options dialog box and then click OK button.

Word Pro saves the document as a SmartMaster. In the future, you can use your newly created SmartMaster as a template for new documents, just as you use any other SmartMaster.

Getting Info about Documents

If you happen to be working in an oppressive office environment that absolutely requires you to know the last time a document was created and modified, along with the length of time used to edit that document, you're going to love Word Pro's document information feature.

The whole purpose of the document information feature is to show you the history behind a document, along with its size, word count, page length, and any comment you care to add about your document.

To display the document information, open a document and then choose File⇨Document Properties⇨Document. A Document Properties dialog box appears, as shown in Figure 7-10.

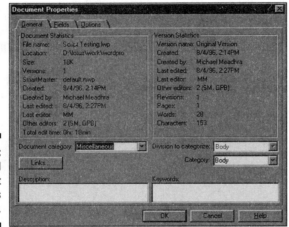

Figure 7-10:
A typical
Document
Properties
dialog box.

The Word Pro document information screen is a handy way to track time spent on projects if you need to bill by the hour or need to know how many times someone has revised a document. Feel free to explore this screen if you're so inclined.

Part III
Spreadsheets As Easy As, Well — 1-2-3!

In this part . . .

Time to put away your abacus. Whether you're scared or excited by the prospect of diving into the numbers-oriented world of spreadsheets, this part should allay your fears and heighten your excitement. Get ready to discover what all the spreadsheet fuss is about. These chapters describe what spreadsheets are good for and how they can make your life easier — or at least less dependent on your pocket calculator. And, thank goodness, you don't even need an MBA to put 1-2-3 to work. In fact, if you understand fourth-grade math (or know some patient fourth-graders who can help you), you're all set.

Chapter 8

Boot Camp for 1-2-3 (a.k.a. Basic Training by the Numbers)

In This Chapter

▶ Hey, Mr. Wizard, what's a spreadsheet?

▶ Starting 1-2-3

▶ Entering labels and values

▶ Makin' copies

▶ Doing the math — calculating in 1-2-3

▶ Naming ranges

▶ Saving your worksheet

▶ Printing your worksheet

*A*re you tired of scribbling numbers on scraps of paper and then finding that not enough light is left for your solar calculator to calculate? If you're ready to move from that trusty old pocket calculator to the brave new world of computer number crunching, you should find this transition as easy as 1-2-3. NOT! But never fear. Although Lotus 1-2-3 may not be quite as easy as . . . er, well, 1-2-3, we intend in this part to make finding your way through the thicket of spreadsheet technobabble as painless as possible. So relax. After all, we haven't lied to you yet, have we?

Hey, Mr. Wizard, What's a Spreadsheet?

Spreadsheet. To the nontechnophile, the term may conjure up images of freshly washed bed linens drying on a clothesline or perhaps a bed turned back all comfy and inviting. Well, computer spreadsheet programs aren't nearly so romantic. They are, however, more practical if you want to put a bunch of numbers and text in neat rows and columns. Spreadsheets can even calculate the numbers and turn them into dazzling charts and graphs.

Think of a spreadsheet as the electronic equivalent of an accountant's ledger paper — the stuff with the grid lines that help line up all the rows and columns of numbers. And 1-2-3 enables you to create multiple worksheets in a file, so using the program is like having a whole ledger book (which 1-2-3 calls a *workbook*) in one file.

An electronic workbook actually contains thousands of rows and columns. If you just *must* know the nitty-gritty details, each spreadsheet page in a Lotus 1-2-3 workbook has a total of 8,192 rows and 256 columns, and a workbook can contain up to 256 worksheets.

By the way, even though the terms *spreadsheet* and *worksheet* are often used interchangeably, *spreadsheet* usually refers to the computer program, and *worksheet* refers to the actual document you create by using the spreadsheet program. Clear? Well, sorta?

Okay, we hear you asking: "But what are these spreadsheet things really good for? You know, for *humans*, not you techno-dweebs." All right, the following are just a few examples of what spreadsheets such as 1-2-3 are commonly used for:

- ✔ **Creating budgets.** This use is probably the most common spreadsheet task. Whether you're putting together a household budget that reflects some reasonable facsimile of reality (and that you can actually stick to this time) or a multiyear budget for a multibillion dollar, multinational corporation, a spreadsheet makes its creation easy. Well, at least a spreadsheet makes entering and calculating the numbers easy. Picking the *right* numbers . . . that's another matter.

- ✔ **Figuring out loan payments** (or how long you're going to need to pay off that loan). With 1-2-3's financial functions, tasks such as this one are a piece of cake.

- ✔ **Creating financial statements.** You can bet that 1-2-3 doesn't look like an accountant's ledger for nothing. (Or does it . . .?) You can create any sort of financial statement or accounting document you can imagine. Even if you can't imagine one, 1-2-3 can probably create it anyway.

- ✔ **Performing statistical analyses.** You can use 1-2-3 to find, for example, the average, maximum, and minimum price for a gallon of gas.

Although 1-2-3 can create and manage lists of data, such as to-do lists, lists of appointments, and so on, you are usually better off turning to more specialized database tools for these types of tasks. Fortunately, you have two terrific database tools available to you right here in SmartSuite 97: Approach and Organizer, which are covered in later parts of the book. You also soon discover that 1-2-3 provides a dizzying variety of options for turning your numbers into persuasive charts and graphs (a.k.a. *pictures*). A picture is, after all, worth a thousand words (in the immortal words of someone or other). But keep in mind that SmartSuite 97 also includes Freelance Graphics, which is specifically designed for creating charts. Explore both tools before deciding which is best for a particular job.

Lotus 1-2-3 is rooted in laziness

Laziness is oft said to be the true mother of invention. This adage was proven correct again in 1978, when a couple of Harvard Business School students, Dan Bricklin and Bob Frankston, with too much homework and too little time (what with all their parties and carousing and all), decided to put their newfangled personal computers to work to ease their burdens.

Most of their homework time was spent recalculating all the formulas in huge financial models as assumptions changed. Even with pocket calculators, the job was tedious and time-consuming. Perhaps, they reasoned, they could write some software to turn their computers into big ol'

calculators. Yeah, they thought, *that's* the ticket! So the two created the first spreadsheet, called *VisiCalc*, which was short for "visible calculator." Most computer historians credit VisiCalc with starting the personal computer revolution (or at least kicking it into high gear).

A few years later, one of Dan and Bob's employees, Mitch Kapor — who had created a graphics program to work with VisiCalc, called VisiTrend/Plot (you gotta love that name) — decided to go off and start his own software company. The company . . . Lotus. The product . . . 1-2-3. And that's how the story all began. . . .

Starting 1-2-3

Wouldn't life be easy if you had only one way to start 1-2-3? No such luck. As with just about everything else in SmartSuite 97, you have myriad ways to kick off 1-2-3. The good news is that starting 1-2-3 works just the same as does starting any of the other SmartSuite 97 programs. Following are a few options for bringing 1-2-3 to life:

- ✔ If SuiteStart is running, click the 1-2-3 icon in the taskbar's system tray. The icon is easy to spot — it's the one that reads 1-2-3 (of course).

- ✔ If SmartCenter is running, open the SmartSuite drawer by clicking the drawer front, click the Lotus Applications folder, and then double-click the 1-2-3 icon. If neither SuiteStart or SmartCenter is running — why the heck not? Check out Chapter 2 for details on getting SmartCenter running.

- ✔ Click the Start button in the Windows 95 taskbar, point to Programs, point to Lotus SmartSuite, and then choose Lotus 1-2-3 97.

Friendly ol' 1-2-3 starts and greets you with the Welcome to 1-2-3 dialog box (unless you previously told 1-2-3 not to bother you with the welcome stuff anymore). From here, you get to make another choice. (Oh boy! *More* choices, you mumble sarcastically.) You get to decide whether to create a new workbook or work on an existing workbook file. The dialog box displays several recently used files. To open one of them, simply click the filename and then click OK. To open a file that isn't on the list, click the Browse for More Workbooks button to open the Browse dialog box, from which you can locate a file anywhere on your disk or network.

To start creating a new worksheet, just click the Create a New Workbook Using a SmartMaster tab to have 1-2-3 display the next page of the dialog box containing — you guessed it! — still more choices (see Figure 8-1).

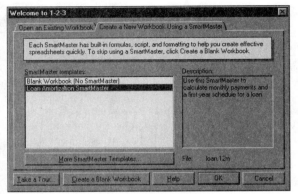

Figure 8-1:
The Welcome to 1-2-3 dialog box with a SmartMaster highlighted. Notice the SmartMaster Description area of the dialog box.

To create a plain worksheet, you can take a shortcut and just click the Create a Blank Workbook button. To create a worksheet based on a SmartMaster template, such as the Loan Amortization SmartMaster, click the SmartMaster you want in the SmartMaster Templates list and then click OK. SmartMasters are great, by the way, and come complete with all the formulas and formatting already in place — all you need to do is supply the numbers, and you end up with a completed worksheet in no time.

You can skip the Welcome to 1-2-3 dialog box if you want. If you decide to bypass the Welcome dialog box, 1-2-3 whisks you straight to a new 1-2-3 workbook. To disable the Welcome to 1-2-3 dialog box, choose File⇨User Setup⇨ 1-2-3 Preferences to open the 1-2-3 Preferences dialog box. In the Startup area of the General tab, click the Show Welcome Dialog check box (so that the option's *not* checked) and then click OK.

You can click the Start Tutorial button in the Welcome dialog box to see a short tutorial on some of 1-2-3's primary features. If you have some free time, running through this tutorial isn't a bad idea.

After you wade through these choices, you reach the initial 1-2-3 screen, which contains a blank worksheet just waiting for you to fill it in, as shown in Figure 8-2. The worksheet includes the following elements:

Cell pointer

Worksheet tab

Selection Indicator   @Function Selector button

SmartIcon   Navigator button | Mouse pointer Columns   Edit line   Worksheet window

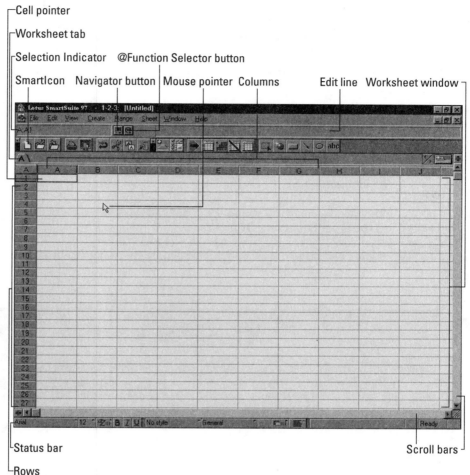

Figure 8-2:
The initial
1-2-3 screen
with a blank
worksheet
awaiting
your input.

Status bar

Rows

Scroll bars

- ✔ The area of the window containing all the cells is called the *Worksheet window*.

- ✔ The worksheet is made up of vertical *columns* (which are lettered A, B, C, and so on) and horizontal *rows* (which are numbered 1, 2, 3, and so on).

- ✔ The intersection of a column and a row is called a *cell*. Cells are where information — numbers, text, and formulas — is entered.

- ✔ The *Selection Indicator* displays the address of the current cell (the one the cell pointer is on). A cell's address is its column letter followed by its row number. For example, the cell in the first row of column A is cell A1.

- ✔ The *cell pointer* is the rectangle that surrounds the current cell.

- ✔ The *Navigator* button enables you to move to a named range or other named object in a file. A *named range* is simply a group of cells to which you assign a more meaningful name. *Objects* are items such as charts or graphics.

- ✔ The *@Function Selector* enables you to insert one of 1-2-3's zillions of functions. *Functions* are predefined procedures for various types of calculations.

- ✔ The *Edit line* shows the contents — if any — of the current cell (the one surrounded by the cell pointer, remember?).

- ✔ The *Worksheet tab* shows which worksheet you're currently working with. If you see multiple worksheet tabs, you have multiple worksheets in the workbook file.

The menus, SmartIcons, and scroll bars all work the same as these features do in the other SmartSuite 97 programs.

If you need more details about SmartIcons, check out Chapter 1.

Classic, dude

Some people just don't want to do things the new way. New Coke bombed, classic cars are all the rage, and classical music (not to mention classic rock) has certainly had a resurgence lately. If you like doing things the old (comfortable?) way and you're familiar with an older, DOS version of 1-2-3, you may be pleased to know that you can use 1-2-3 97 just as though nothing's changed — almost.

Just press the slash key (/) to display the Classic 1-2-3 menu. These menus are just like the ones in 1-2-3 Release 3.1 for DOS. If your 1-2-3 experience takes you back even farther than 3.1, you still find these menus remarkably similar to the menus in the very oldest releases.

We recommend that you not rely on the Classic menus too much or for too long. You're going to need to bite the bullet sometime and get up to speed with the Windows 95 ways of doing things — the way all the other SmartSuite 97 programs, as well as other Windows programs, work.

If you inadvertently summon the Classic menu and want to get out of the old thing, press the Esc key. If you find yourself knee-deep in Classic menus — several levels in — you can press Esc several times to get out or just press Ctrl+Break. The Break key is the one on your keyboard (usually near the top right somewhere) that has the words Pause and Break printed on it.

If you aren't sure what a particular SmartIcon button does, just point to the icon for a few seconds with the mouse pointer (without clicking) to display the button's Bubble Help description.

Getting Around

Before you can enter anything in your worksheet, you need to move the _cell pointer_ to the cell into which you want to enter data. If the cell pointer is close to the cell you want to get to, moving to the target cell is simple — just click the cell that you want to go to or use the arrow keys to reposition the cell pointer. If the distances are greater, however, you may want to use more efficient alternative modes of transportation.

If you're creating a new worksheet, and want to start working in the upper-left corner of the worksheet after starting 1-2-3, you don't need to go anywhere. You're already there. That's the default location of the cell pointer in a new, blank worksheet. After you start working with larger worksheets that span distances far greater than what you can see on a single screen, however, you need to know how to get from one location in the worksheet to another.

Correctly addressing 1-2-3

Even Carl Sagan may have trouble navigating the _bill_-ions and billions of cells in a 1-2-3 file. Okay, 1-2-3 files don't really have billions of cells, but they do have millions. And that's plenty mind-boggling for pea-brained authors such as us. Good news! Each cell has its own address to help you keep track of that particular cell. A cell's _address_ is its column letter followed by its row number. So the address of the cell at the intersection of column C and row 12 is C12. Simple. But wait! If you're using several worksheets in a workbook file, each cell address also includes the sheet letter followed by a colon. The sheets are lettered A, B, C, and so on. So the address of cell C12 in sheet D is D:C12.

If you use multiple worksheets in your workbook files, you can give them names that are more meaningful than the letters 1-2-3 assigns them. (Gee, you'd be hard put to come up with _less_ meaningful names.) Just double-click the sheet tab. 1-2-3 enlarges the tab and creates a text box where you can type the name you want to assign that sheet (and then press Enter). You can use up to 15 characters for each sheet name.

You don't need to worry about the sheet letter if you're working with a single-sheet workbook or just moving around in the current worksheet.

You can always figure out what the current cell or range is — and locate the cell pointer — by looking at the Selection Indicator area (at the left end of the line just below the menu bar). This area shows you either the worksheet name, cell address, or the name of the range in which the cell pointer is located. (Range names are covered in the section "Naming Ranges," later in this chapter.)

Beam me up — or over

After you know where you want to go in a 1-2-3 file, getting there is a piece of cake. Our pal 1-2-3 provides a veritable plethora of navigation shortcuts for both keyboard peckers and mousers.

If you know the cell address or range name you want to move to, you can use the Go To command or the Navigator button. Choose Edit⇨Go To (or press Ctrl+G) to display the Go To dialog box, as shown in Figure 8-3.

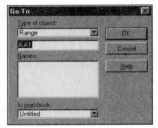

Figure 8-3:
The Go To dialog box enables you to go to a single cell or a multi-cell range.

To jump to a specific cell, just type its address in the text box below the Type of Object drop-down list box and press Enter. If you have named ranges in your worksheet, these ranges are listed in the Names list box in the Go To dialog box. You can double-click the one you want. 1-2-3 highlights the entire range and positions the cell pointer in the first cell of the range.

The *Navigator button* is another quick way to move to and select a named range. Click the Navigator button (located just to the right of the Selection Indicator area on the Edit line) to display a drop-down list of named ranges. Then click the named range that you want to select. 1-2-3 highlights the range and moves the cell pointer into the first cell of the range just as if you had chosen the range in the Go To dialog box.

For more random roaming, use scroll bars or one of the keyboard shortcuts, as described in the following list:

> ✔ Press the Tab key to move one column to the right.
>
> ✔ Press Shift+Tab to move one column to the left.
>
> ✔ Press Page Down to move down a screenful of rows.
>
> ✔ Press Page Up to move up a screenful of rows.

Use the scroll bars to scroll vast distances. Using the scroll bars doesn't move the cell pointer, just the portion of the worksheet that's visible in the worksheet window.

You can move to the beginning of a worksheet simply by tapping the Home key. If you want to move to the last cell containing data in the worksheet, press End, Home. (That's the End key followed by the Home key.)

Entering Labels and Values

Entering data into the cells of a worksheet is pretty straightforward. Just move the cell pointer to the desired location and start typing. Sound simple? It is.

Of course, 1-2-3 really understands only two kinds of information: *labels,* which are any sort of text entry, and *values*, which are any number or formula. Why the brain trust at Lotus came up with the terms *labels* and *values* instead of just calling these info types *text* and *numbers* is anybody's guess. You just have to deal with their terms.

Before you make a cell entry, 1-2-3 should be in *Ready mode*. How can you tell that 1-2-3 is in Ready mode? Take a look at the *Mode indicator* at the right side of the status bar — that's down in the lower-right corner of the screen. If 1-2-3's in Ready mode, that's just how that area of the status bar reads (refer back to Figure 8-2).

Just follow these easy steps for making any cell entry:

1. **Move the cell pointer to the cell into which you want to enter data by using any of the techniques described in the preceding section.**

   Make sure that the Mode indicator on the status bar tells you that 1-2-3 is in Ready mode. If the Mode indicator doesn't read Ready, clicking another cell or pressing the Enter key should solve the problem.

2. **Start typing whatever you want in the cell.**

   As soon as you start typing, the Mode indicator changes to either *Label* or *Value mode*, depending on the first letter of your entry. If your entry begins with a letter, 1-2-3 swings into Label mode. If your entry starts with a number or any character that could start a formula, 1-2-3 switches to Value mode. Formulas are covered in the section "Doing the Math — the Formula for Calculating in 1-2-3," later in this chapter.

3. **Confirm the entry by pressing Enter or moving the cell pointer to another cell.**

   If you decide you don't want your new cell entry after all, you can instead press the Esc key.

After making a cell entry, remember that you can easily replace the cell's contents by creating another entry right over the unwanted one. If you just want to blast a cell's contents out of existence, however, press Delete. Poof! (But make sure that your cell pointer is in the cell that contains what you want to delete before you make the entry go poof.)

The instant you start typing, whatever was in the cell vanishes. Omigosh! You can avert disaster by pressing Esc before confirming the new entry. If you're too late for that and you haven't made another entry since confirming the new one, choose Edit➪Undo . . . or just click the Undo SmartIcon — the one that looks like a curved arrow. (Remember that you can locate the SmartIcon you're looking for by reading the icon descriptions in the little balloons that appear after you position the mouse pointer over them.)

After making some entries, you may notice that your labels start at the left edge of the cell and expand to the right while values start out at the right and expand to the left. Nope, you didn't do anything wrong — those Lotus wizards just decided that most folks would want their labels left-aligned and their values right-aligned. The alignment for both labels and values can be changed, of course. The steps for changing alignment are spelled out in Chapter 9.

Don't worry if some of your entries seem to be chopped off in the middle. The entries didn't really change; they are all still right where you typed them. This abbreviated appearance is just something 1-2-3 does with entries if the program can't fit an entry in the cell. The following chapter gives you the lowdown on formatting your worksheets, including how to adjust column widths to make everything in a cell fit like a glove.

Makin' Copies

Most of what you learned about copying (and moving) data in Word Pro applies to 1-2-3. (Check out Chapter 4 for more information about copying and moving in Word Pro.) You can cut or copy selected cells to the Clipboard and then paste them to new locations, or you can drag a selection to another location. You must position the pointer over the edge of a selection before the pointer changes to a hand, indicating that you can drag the selection, but other than that, dragging in 1-2-3 works just as that feature does in Word Pro.

In addition to the basic stuff, 1-2-3 actually adds intelligence to some of its copy procedures (they don't call the thing *Smart*Suite 97 for nuthin'). If you type **January** in cell B1, for example, you probably don't want to put *January* in C1, D1 and E1. Sure would be great if 1-2-3 knew that you wanted *February*, *March*, and *April* in those other cells. Well, guess what? The program does just that. Yippee!

To get 1-2-3 to do its smart copying, position the mouse pointer in the lower-right corner of the cell you want to copy. You know the pointer's in the right spot if it has two little extra arrows pointing down and two more pointing to the right. After you see these arrows, you can drag down, to the right, or both.

Drag down to *increment* down the column or to the right to *increment* across the row. (*Incrementing* just means increasing the cell value by a specified amount.) If you enter **Monday** in a cell, for example, incrementing enters Tuesday, Wednesday, Thursday, and so on in the succeeding cells. You can make 1-2-3 increment numbers and days of the week as well as months.

Copying *formulas*, however, is an entirely different animal. Check out how to perform this action in the section "Copying formulas," later in this chapter.

Doing the Math — the Formula for Calculating in 1-2-3

If you view 1-2-3 as a really expensive pocket calculator — except that the program doesn't fit in your pocket — you're partly correct. Math is at the heart of 1-2-3. If not for its math capabilities, 1-2-3 wouldn't have much of a reason to exist. Oh sure, you can do zillions of things with 1-2-3 that don't involve those nasty, nerve-wracking calculations. But you know that their number-crunching capabilities are what make spreadsheet programs sizzle.

Unfortunately, 1-2-3 can't read your mind. So you must tell the program what numbers you want to crunch and how you want to crunch those numbers. You perform this task by entering a *formula* into a particular cell. A formula is nothing more than a mathematical equation that usually uses cell addresses — for example, B5 + B6 or B5 – B2.

Suppose that you want to find the answer to the burning question "What is 2×2?" You can go to any cell and type **2*2**. (The asterisk is the symbol for multiplication in 1-2-3.) As soon as you confirm the cell entry, 1-2-3 dutifully answers 4. Cool! And typing **4/2** (4 divided by 2) returns the answer 2. For addition and subtraction, you use the plain old plus and minus signs (+ and –).

By the way, after 1-2-3 completes its calculations, the answers appear in the cell that contains the formula. If you enter a formula in cell B3, the answer appears in B3. (The formula appears in the Edit line in case you need to refer to it or edit the formula.)

As swell as 1-2-3's capability to perform these math tricks is, its real math power comes from its capability to reference other cells in the worksheet that contain values. So, instead of entering **2*2** in a cell, you can enter a formula in cell B5 that multiplies B3 times B4. That way, if you change the values in B3 or B4, the result in B5 (the formula cell) is automatically updated.

This formula may come in handy, for example, in a weekly report worksheet that figures out how much money your company made in the sale of various products. Suppose that you sold eight of an item for $50 each. If you multiplied 8 by $50, you'd get the correct answer, but the formula would change every week based on which items you sold. If the formula referred to the cells that contain the quantity and the price, however, you'd always have the correct answer no matter how much you changed the numbers.

To create a formula in B5 that multiplies B3 by B4, follow these steps:

1. **Move to cell B5 and type + (the plus sign).**

   As far as 1-2-3 is concerned, formulas are just regular old values. If you start by typing B3, 1-2-3 thinks you are entering a label instead of a value. Starting with the + puts 1-2-3 in Value mode.

2. **Type** B3 **or click cell B3.**

   Clicking cells as references is often easier than typing the cell names.

3. **Type * (the asterisk).**

4. **Type** B4 **or click cell B4.**

5. **Press Enter or click the Confirm button.**

   The result of the formula instantly appears in B5. The formula in the *Contents area* of the Edit line should appear as follows: +B3*B4. The Contents area is on the Edit line — which itself is just below the menu bar — to the right of the Confirm button.

The way 1-2-3 normally displays information, you can't see which cells contain formulas and which contain only numbers. The Contents area of the Edit line is the giveaway. If the cell pointer is positioned on a cell containing a formula, the Edit line displays the formula in all its gory . . . er, *glorious* detail.

If you want 1-2-3 to indicate which cells contain formulas, you can tell the program to display a small green dot in the lower left corner of those cells. Choose View⇨Set View Preferences to open the Workbook Properties dialog box. On the View tab, select the Formula markers check box and click OK.

While you're looking for dots in cells, you may notice a small red dot in the upper-left corner of a cell. That indicates that someone attached a comment to the cell. You can use comments to make notes about your assumptions, the source of your numbers, or anything you like. To create a comment, right-click the cell and choose Cell Comment from the pop-up menu that appears. This action opens the Range Properties InfoBox with the Comment tab selected. Just type your comment into the Cell Comment text box and then click the Close button to close the InfoBox. 1-2-3 marks the cell with a red dot to indicate that this cell now has a comment attached. To read a comment, open the InfoBox just like you did to create the comment in the first place.

Be very careful not to delete cells that contain formulas — doing so can really ruin your day. (If you do accidentally wipe out a formula, click the Undo button before doing anything else. The day is saved.)

Entering formulas incorrectly is all too easy (for us, at least), so proofreading your worksheet to see whether the numbers make sense is very important. If you have a formula that should be multiplying 5 by 100 and the answer you get is 48,673, something is obviously wrong.

Copying formulas

If you're going to use the same formula to calculate several different values in your spreadsheet, you don't need to keep typing that formula over and over. Instead, just copy your formula from one cell to another.

The procedure for copying formulas is generally the same as for copying any other sort of data. If you copy formulas, however, 1-2-3 understands that you normally want the copies to be relative to their new location.

Suppose, for example, that the numbers in B3 are the number of hours your employees worked last month and that the numbers in B4 are their wages in dollars per hour. The formula in B5 to calculate how much they earned is +B3*B4. If you copy the formula to cell C5, you'd want it to change to +C3*C4. Good news. That's exactly what 1-2-3 does.

Yes, 1-2-3 uses *relative referencing*, so as you copy a formula, 1-2-3 copies the *logic* of the formula rather than the formula itself. The logic that 1-2-3 uses as you copy +B3*B4 from B5 to C5 is "Multiply the contents of the cell two rows up by the contents of the cell one row up." (Pretty logical, huh?)

Doing the math II — functional literacy

Four-function math got you down? Having a hard time using addition, subtraction, multiplication, and division to create formulas for statistical analysis? Looking for easier ways to get the answers you need from your worksheet data?

Feeling tired, irritable, and bloated? Take heart — 1-2-3 *functions* can solve most of your problems. We know that we don't feel as tired, irritable, and bloated since we started using functions.

Our friend 1-2-3 provides *functions* to solve virtually any math or data problem you can imagine. Functions are like preconstructed formulas that you can use simply by inserting their names into a cell in your worksheet. Want to find an investment's internal rate of return or future value? Use a function. Want to find the largest or smallest value in a range? Well, 1-2-3 has functions for that, too. Functions even exist for simple little things such as adding up a range of cells.

The reason to use functions instead of creating your own formulas is to make your life easier. We know that some folks like doing things the hard way. Not us. If an easier way is available, let us at it.

To use a function, start by typing the at symbol (@). Then type the function name — for example, **SUM**. Don't put a space between @ and the function name. Finally, in parentheses, enter the values, *operators* (the math symbols), and cell references that you want the function to work on. (All the stuff in parentheses is called the function's *arguments*.)

Better yet, you can just click the @ button on the Edit line (the @Function Selector button, remember?) to open a drop-down list of some of the more common 1-2-3 functions. If the function you need isn't in the list, click List All to display the @Function List dialog box, as shown in Figure 8-4. Just select All @functions from the Category list, select the function you want from the @Functions list, and that function appears on the Edit line. Look, Ma, no typing!

Figure 8-4:
The
@Function
List dialog
box enables
you to scroll
through a
zillion
functions.

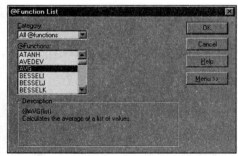

The All @Functions list is a long list. If you select a more limited category, such as Financial or Engineering, from the Categories list box, you don't need to wade through so many @Functions to find the one you want.

Suppose, for example, that you want to find the average value of a range of cells. One of 1-2-3's functions is @AVG, which finds averages (what else?). To create a formula by using @AVG, follow these steps:

1. **Click the cell that is to contain the formula (the one in which the answer is to appear).**

2. **Click the @Function Selector button on the Edit line to display the list of common functions and then click** AVG **in the list.**

   @AVG(list) appears in the formula cell and on the contents portion of the Edit line with the *list* placeholder highlighted. The range of cells for which you want to average the contents replaces the word *list* after the formula is completed.

3. **Point to the first cell in the range you want to average, press and hold the left mouse button, and then drag until the entire range is selected.**

   The first and last cell addresses of the range, separated by two periods, replace the word *list* in the parentheses. If the range is C3 through C22, for example, the formula appears as @AVG(C3..C22).

   Note: The two dots between the first and last cells of a range indicate that all the cells from the first to the last are included.

4. **Press Enter or click the Confirm button on the Edit line to complete the formula using the @AVG function.**

   The answer appears instantly in the cell you clicked in Step 1.

If you need additional help with a particular function's usage and *syntax* (its correct construction), the function Help screens are particularly useful. Suppose that you want to use the @AVG function to find the average value in a range, but you don't know exactly how to use this function. Just type **@AVG** in a cell and press F1. An @Function Help screen appears to enlighten you, as shown in Figure 8-5.

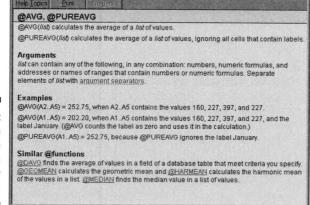

Figure 8-5:
@Function
Help
screens are
actually
helpful.

If the functions on the @Function Selector list aren't the ones you normally use, you can modify the choices to suit you. Click the Menu button in the @Function List dialog box to expand the dialog box to include additional buttons and list boxes. In the @Functions list, click the function you want to add to the @Functions Selector button menu, and then click the >> (Add) button. To remove a function, click the function in the Current menu list and then click the << (Remove) button.

That's SUM function

Creating a formula to add a row or column of numbers is easy enough. You want to add B2 and B3? No sweat. The formula is +B2+B3. But suppose you want to add all the cells in the range B2 through B10. Start sweating. The formula would look like this: +B2+B3+B4+B5+B6+B7+B8+B9+B10. Yech!

The easy way around this mess is to use the SUM function. In fact, 1-2-3 makes using the SUM function completely automatic. Just move the cell pointer to the cell directly below a column of numbers you want to sum or to the right of a row of cells you want to sum and click the SUM SmartIcon button — the one that appears to be adding 1+2. (The button's description, seen in the Bubble Help description after you pause the mouse pointer on the SmartIcon, is Sum values above or to the left.) That's all you do! Using the SUM function can be just that easy.

Look at the Contents area of the Edit line to see that the function is entered just as though you typed the thing yourself.

One situation in which you may *not* want to use the SUM SmartIcon to enter the SUM function automatically is if the range you want to sum isn't adjacent to the formula cell — the cell where you want the answer to appear. In that case, you can enter the @SUM function manually, just as you can any other function, by typing the @SUM function into the formula cell and entering the range of cells you want to sum between the parentheses.

Here's a slick way to enter @SUM functions even more easily. Go to the cell at the bottom of a column of numbers (or several adjacent columns of numbers) and then move one cell to the left. Type **Total** into that cell and press Enter. Magically, 1-2-3 sums each column of numbers for you. Can you beat that? Sometimes 1-2-3 can read your mind. Oh, by the way, the same trick works with rows of numbers. The cells where the sums appear must be to the right of the numbers, and the word *Total* goes in the cell above.

Naming Ranges

Assigning names can make finding portions of a large worksheet much easier. Figuring out where your budget's 1995 income area is located, for example, is a whole lot easier if the section of the worksheet is called *Income 95* instead of *F22 through J43*.

To assign a range name, follow these steps:

1. **Select the range of cells you want to name by dragging the mouse over them while holding the left mouse button.**

   The address of the range is displayed in the Selection area of the Edit line.

2. **With the mouse pointer anywhere in the selected range, right-click to display the selection's pop-up menu and choose Na_me.**

   The Name dialog box appears, displaying any range names that are already assigned.

3. **Type a name (up to 15 characters) for the selected range and then click OK.**

You can use the Navigator button to jump to a named range. Click the Navigator button on the Edit line and then click the range name you want to go to in the list that 1-2-3 opens. You see the entire range selected.

In using functions, you usually find that named ranges are far easier to use and far more understandable than are ordinary cell references. If the cells containing your company's 1995 income are in the range F22 through J43, for example, you could name the range Income 95. (Hmmm, where have we heard that before . . .?) Then, instead of a hard-to-understand formula such as @SUM(F22..J43), you could simply use @SUM(Income 95).

Printing Your Worksheet

Prognosticators have been hailing the coming paperless office for years. Is the great event here yet? We don't think so. And until it arrives, you need to get your worksheets on paper.

Fortunately, 1-2-3 97 makes the printing process more painless (or at least less painful) than did any of the earlier releases of 1-2-3.

To print a worksheet, make sure that your printer is turned on, is on-line, and has paper loaded. Then follow these steps:

1. **Click the Print Preview SmartIcon button or choose File➪Preview & Page Setup.**

1-2-3 opens a Print Preview window beside the window containing your worksheet. The Preview & Page Setup InfoBox also appears, as shown in Figure 8-6.

Now the fun begins.

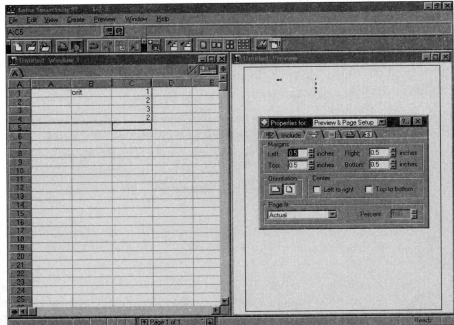

Figure 8-6:
The 1-2-3
Print
Preview
window is
interactive.

2. **Change the options in the various tabs of the InfoBox and edit your worksheet as desired.**

   You see those changes reflected in the Print Preview window instantly.

3. **After the Print Preview looks the way you want, click the Print SmartIcon or choose File⇨Print.**

   The Print dialog box appears.

4. **Click the Current sheet, Entire workbook, or Selected Range option button.**

   The Selected Range option makes sense only if you selected a range before opening the Print dialog box.

5. **Click Print.**

   Your masterpiece should start spewing from your printer momentarily.

You find more information on 1-2-3 printing options in the next couple of chapters.

Chapter 9
I Feel Pretty (Adding Style to Your Worksheet)

- -

In This Chapter

▶ Formatting numbers

▶ Aligning cell entries

▶ Using fonts to spruce things up

▶ Changing column widths and row heights

▶ Adding lines and borders

▶ Using gallery styles

- -

Dahling, you look mahvelous! If that's not the reaction your 1-2-3 worksheets are getting, time to get with the program. You can pour hours of blood, sweat, and tears into creating an accurate and informative worksheet, but if the thing doesn't *look* good, who cares? Who's even going to read your masterpiece? Not us. Figure 9-1 shows a dull, drab, unformatted worksheet. Pretty uninspiring, huh? Figure 9-2, however, is the same worksheet with some nifty formatting added. Ah, that's better.

Changing various formatting attributes (how text and numbers are displayed) can change a dull, lifeless worksheet into a powerful persuader. And persuasion, after all, is often what worksheets are designed for. You want your boss to approve your budget proposals, and a beautiful worksheet gives the boss the impression that you gave your work more thought. You *did* give the budget work *some* thought, didn't you?

A	A	B	C	D	E	F	G	H	I
1		January	February	March	Totals				
2	Classes	16500	17800	18300	52600				
3	Textbook Sales	4500	5000	5500	15000				
4	Total Income	21000	22800	23800	67600				
5									
6	Rent	1400	1400	1400	4200				
7	Salaries	3500	3500	3500	10500				
8	Materials	1100	1250	1300	3650				
9	Total Expenses	6000	6150	6200	18350				
10									

Figure 9-1: An icky old unformatted worksheet that wouldn't even get a CPA excited.

	January	February	March	Totals
Classes	16500	17800	18300	**$52,600**
Textbook Sales	4500	5000	5500	**$15,000**
Total Income	**21000**	**22800**	**23800**	**$67,600**
Rent	1400	1400	1400	**$4,200**
Salaries	3500	3500	3500	**$10,500**
Materials	1100	1250	1300	**$3,650**
Total Expenses	**$6,000**	**$6,150**	**$6,200**	**$18,350**

Figure 9-2: Wow! The same worksheet with pizzazz! What a difference a bit of formatting can make.

Formatting Numbers

Why can't 1-2-3 just leave my numbers the way I enter them? Seems to me that, if I enter **300.50**, that's just how the number should look in the cell. But noooooo! Headstrong 1-2-3 decides that I don't really need that last zero and drops the extra digit — without even asking! And suppose I enter **1,000,000,000**. Well, 1-2-3 changes *that* to `1.0E+009`. What's 1-2-3 up to? Generally speaking, the problem is *General formatting.*

Unless instructed otherwise, 1-2-3 uses its General formatting rules to mess up. . . er, display your numeric entries. Trailing decimal places that don't fit in the column are arbitrarily discarded as cavalierly as a recruit's hair at Marine boot camp. Numbers that are too big to fit in the column are changed to the indecipherable *Scientific Notation (Exponential) format*, such as 1.2E+008. Ouch! Our brains hurt from even looking at numbers formatted like that.

Contrary to what you may be thinking, General formatting's mission isn't to mess up your worksheets but to try to make big numbers fit in little columns. Ignoring leading and trailing zeros, dropping trailing decimal places that don't fit, converting huge numbers to scientific notation — all of these tricks are among 1-2-3's efforts to make big numbers fit into narrow columns. And 1-2-3's default column width is only nine characters. Without 1-2-3's heroic measures to scrunch your numbers, you'd often have to take heroic measures of your own just to keep your numbers visible.

If you're worried about how all this number scrunching may affect calculations, don't give the idea a second thought. No matter how your numbers are formatted, 1-2-3 stores the actual number. Formatting affects only how the numbers appear on your computer screen.

If you don't want General formatting making decisions for you, be specific. Either enter numbers in a way that enables 1-2-3 to figure out your formatting intention (see the accompanying section, "Formatting automatically — sometimes"), or choose the number formatting you want, as discussed in the section "Changing Number Formats," later in this chapter.

Formatting automatically — sometimes

Now, 1-2-3 really does have *some* smarts in the area of formatting numbers. The program tries to figure out by the way you enter your numbers how you really want those numbers to look. If you enter **$100.00**, for example, 1-2-3 automatically applies the *U.S. Dollar format* so that the number appears exactly the way you entered it. 1-2-3 even retains the dollar formatting if you enter a different number in the cell. Enter **200** in the cell, and the number's formatted as $200.00.

So how far do the 1-2-3 mind-reading powers go? The following are some examples of numbers on which 1-2-3 can perform its automatic formatting wizardry:

- *Numbers with comma separators.* Enter **1,000** and 1-2-3 applies the comma format and displays the number just as you entered it.

- *Numbers entered as percentages with a percent sign* are formatted as percents. Enter **10%** and that's just what 1-2-3 displays. (Of course, 1-2-3 records the value as 0.1.)

- *Numbers entered as dates.* You can enter dates by using just about any of the 1-2-3 date formats. All the following are acceptable date formats: 22-Apr-97, 22-Apr, Apr-97, and 4/22/97. Well, 1-2-3 alters some of these entries just a bit. For example, 4/22/97 is formatted as 04/22/97.

- *Numbers entered as times.* As with dates, you can enter times in a variety of formats: 1:42, 1:42 PM, 13:42, and just about any other time format that makes sense are acceptable to 1-2-3.

If you're concerned about the actual number 1-2-3 stores, place the cell pointer in the cell in question and take a gander at the Edit line. The real number — the one 1-2-3 uses for calculations — appears there. For example, 1-2-3 stores 1,000.00 as 1000 and stores 10% as 0.1.

Dates and times are the exceptions to the previous rule. If you format dates and times as dates and times, that's how they appear on the Edit line as well as in the cells. 1-2-3, however, stores dates and times as serial numbers. For dates, the numbers represent the number of days after (or before) January 1, 1900. For example, 1/1/97 automatically appears in the cell *and on the Edit line* as 01/01/97. The number 1-2-3 actually uses for calculations, however, is 35431 — 35431 days past January 1, 1900.

After 1-2-3 automatically changes the formatting of a cell or range of cells, the name of the new formatting style appears in the Number format button in the middle of the status bar.

Some date formats just don't work at all. For example, 12/6 looks like 12 divided by 6 to 1-2-3. If you use the slash (/) in dates, make sure that you include the month, day, *and year* so that 1-2-3 doesn't get confused. After you format a cell as a date, however, you can safely enter 12/6 without 1-2-3 arguing about whether the thing's a date or a division formula.

Changing number formats

So now you know what 1-2-3 does with your numeric entries. But what if you're tired of 1-2-3 pushing you around, and you want to change the formatting of one or more cells? No problem. To change number formatting, follow these steps:

1. **Move the cell pointer to the cell you want to format, or select the range you want to format.**

2. **Click the Number format button in the middle of the status bar.**

   A pop-up list of number formats appears, as shown in Figure 9-3.

3. **Click the number format in the list that you want to use.**

   1-2-3 instantly formats the contents of the cell or range with the style you select.

4. **If the number format is one that enables you to choose the number of decimal places, click the Decimal button in the status bar (the box just to the right of the Number format button) and choose a number from 0 to 15.**

   Note: The Decimal button is available only if you choose a number format that supports decimals (Comma, or a currency format, for example). Otherwise, the button appears as a blank box.

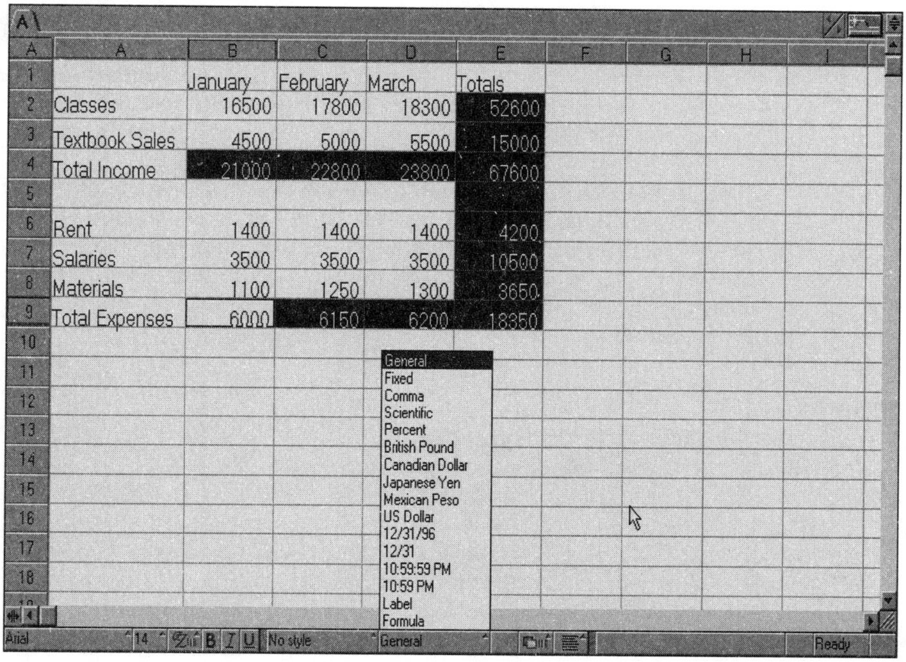

Figure 9-3:
All the number formats are visible in the status bar's pop-up Format list.

Another way to change number formats is by right-clicking the selection and choosing Range Properties from the pop-up menu that appears. The Range Properties InfoBox appears. Click the Number Format (#) tab and then select a format from the list boxes. The worksheet changes immediately to reflect your selections. The status bar method is faster, however, so why bother with the dialog box?

Line 'em Up — Aligning Your Cell Entries

You've probably figured out by now that text entries align to the left edge of the cell and number entries align to the right. Why? To quote Tevye in *Fiddler on the Roof*, "Tradition." That's the way the alignment was done in the very first spreadsheet — VisiCalc — so that *must* be the right way to set up alignments.

Don't be a slave to convention. Be bold and daring. No real reason exists to keep text and numbers in their default alignment. In fact, more often than not, having text and numbers more in alignment with each other makes more sense, stylistically speaking. You have no right or wrong way to align your entries. Just do what looks best.

To align the contents of a cell or range of cells to the left, right, or center, the easiest way is to use another of those slick little status bar buttons. The *Alignment button* (the third button to the right of the Number format button) gives you a choice of five standard alignments: left, right, centered, evenly spaced, and the default left-aligned text with right-aligned numbers.

If you want to get a little fancier and experiment with some of the other alignment possibilities, however, right-click the selected cells and choose Range Properties from the pop-up menu. This action opens the Range Properties InfoBox. Click the Alignment tab and make your choices from the options shown in Figure 9-4. (For some really wild effects, check out the options in the Orientation drop-down list box.)

Figure 9-4:
The Alignment tab of the Range Properties InfoBox.

Figure 9-5 shows examples of some of the more — and less — popular alignment options. The following paragraphs describe a few of the more — and less — useful alignment options.

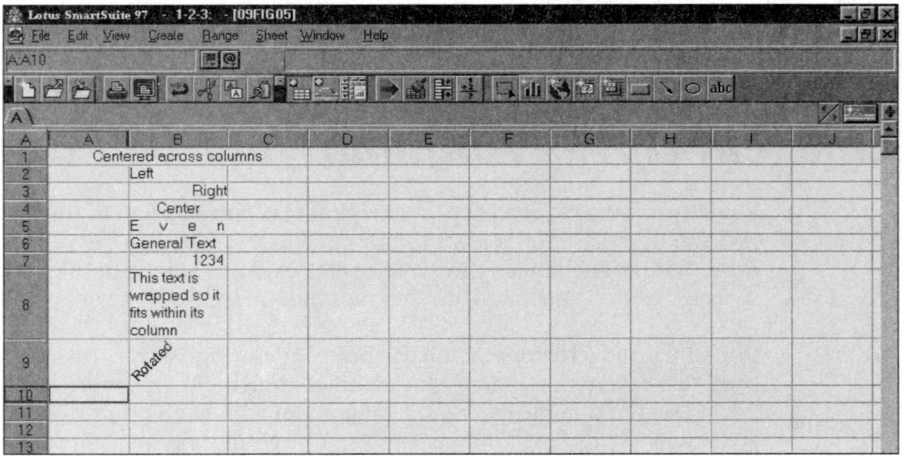

Figure 9-5:
Alignment chaos.

Centering a label entry across several columns is a snap if you use the Align across Columns check box on the Alignment tab of the Range Properties InfoBox. Suppose that you want to center an entry in row 1 of columns A through D. Make the entry in A1 and then select A1 through D1. Right-click the selection and choose Range Properties to open the InfoBox and then click the Alignment tab. Then click the Center alignment option button and the Align across columns check box and — *voilà!*

To make a multiword cell entry that spills into the next column fit into its own column, click the Wrap text in cell check box in the Alignment tab of the InfoBox. The row height adjusts to accommodate the text. (Using the Wrap Text in Cell option is a much easier way to enter column headings than is entering each word in its own row.)

Sometimes, *rotating* a cell entry provides just the effect you need. To change the orientation of a cell's contents, choose one of the options in the Orientation drop-down list on the Alignment tab of the InfoBox. If, for example, you choose the Angled Orientation option, another drop-down list box appears from which you can specify the number of degrees of rotation or accept the default 45-degree angle.

The Evenly Spaced option, found in both the Alignment selector and the Alignment tab of the InfoBox, enables you to spread out all the letters of an entry so that the letters are evenly spaced across the cell. (Seems like kind of a dumb idea to us, but you can use that option if you really want.)

Using Fonts to Spruce Things Up

Nothing does more to add pizzazz to your worksheet and ensure that your readers perceive your work the way you intended than using the right fonts. (A *font*, if you don't know by now, is a typeface in a particular size.)

To change fonts, select the cell or range of cells to which you want to apply the new font and then right-click the selected cells; choose Range Properties from the pop-up menu that appears. After the Range Properties InfoBox appears, click the Font, Attribute and Color tab, as shown in Figure 9-6.

Figure 9-6:
The Font, Attribute and Color tab of the Range Properties InfoBox.

You can also choose fonts from the Font and Point size buttons at the left end of the status bar. The Font button displays the name of the typeface — such as Arial or Times New Roman — in the active cell. The Point size button displays a number — such as 10 or 12 — indicating the size of the font. Using the InfoBox is a better method, however, because all the font selection options are right there together — you don't need to keep opening selector menus to try different combinations of fonts, sizes, and attributes.

Click the name of the font you want in the Font name list of the Range Properties InfoBox and then select a point size from the Size list. If you like, you can also apply attributes from the Attributes list and select a color from the Text color drop-down list.

The status bar includes buttons for the **bold**, *italic*, and <u>underline</u> attributes. To apply any of these attributes, select the cell or range to which you want to apply the attribute and then click the appropriate button. You can reverse an attribute by clicking the button again. If, for example, you click the Bold button to make a cell's contents bold, you can "unbold" the contents by clicking the Bold button again.

You can also change the color of your font by clicking the Text colors button (located between the Point size and Bold buttons) in the status bar and choosing the desired color from the color palette that appears. Remember, however, that your worksheet doesn't print in color unless you have a color printer.

Changing Column Widths and Row Heights

The 1-2-3 default column width is nine characters. That's a fine number to use as a default but is often too small to fit the wider entries you need to make and wastes space if you have a column of only one or two character entries. Fortunately, changing column widths is easier than changing your socks — and certainly easier than learning Spanish.

Although you can specify a new column width in characters, you can more easily make the change visually by dragging with the mouse. Just move the mouse pointer to the right border (next to the column letter) of the column for which you want to change the width. Click and hold the left mouse button. The mouse pointer assumes the shape of a double-headed horizontal arrow. Drag right to increase or left to decrease the column's width. As you drag, a vertical guide line helps you see your new column width and a small box pops up to display the number of (standard-width) characters the column holds at that width. After you release the mouse button to set the new column width, all the columns to the right shift left or right to accommodate the revised column.

We are the world — so give global formatting a chance, man

If you know in advance that you want a particular font, color, number format, column width, or alignment for most of the entries in a worksheet, you can make your life easier by changing the default for these formatting options.

Choose Sheet⇨Sheet Properties from the menu bar to open the Sheet Properties InfoBox, and then specify the desired format changes you want to make on the various tabs.

You rarely need to change row heights, as 1-2-3 automatically adjusts row heights to accommodate their contents. If you change to a larger-sized font or rotate the text in a cell, the row height increases to fit the font size.

If you do need to adjust a row's height for some reason, click the mouse pointer over the row border, just below the row number, so that the pointer assumes the shape of a double-headed vertical arrow. Hold down the left mouse button and drag down to increase row height or up to decrease row height. 1-2-3 moves all the rows below to make room. Simple, no?

If you want to change the column width of several columns at the same time, select the columns and perform the column-width changing procedure just described. Ta daaa! All the selected columns change to the new width. (You can select multiple columns simply by dragging the mouse over the column letters you want to select.)

If you feel you simply must tell 1-2-3 in more precise terms how wide a column needs to be, right-click the column (or selected range of columns) you want to change and choose Range Properties from the pop-up menu to open the Range Properties InfoBox. Click the Basics tab and, in the Column area, click the Width radio button and enter the number of characters your new column width can hold in the adjacent list box. The Basics tab also contains options for automatically adjusting the selected columns to fit the widest entry (the button beside the Width list box), resetting them to the worksheet default columns widths, hiding the column, and forcing a page break at the column, plus similar options for row heights.

A slick way to quickly adjust column widths to accommodate the largest entry, without resorting to the Range Properties InfoBox, is to double-click the mouse on the right border of the column, right next to the column letter. 1-2-3 adjusts the column width automatically.

Adding Lines, Borders, and Frames

The *grid lines* that normally appear on-screen help you see just where the cells are. Usually, you don't print the grid lines (although you can if you want). But 1-2-3 enables you to add all sorts of lines to your worksheet — and have plenty of control over how the lines look. Adding lines or borders can greatly enhance the appearance of your worksheet, as you can see in the example in Figure 9-7.

	January	February	March	Totals
Classes	16500	17800	18300	52600
Textbook Sales	4500	5000	5500	15000
Total Income	21000	22800	23800	67600
Rent	1400	1400	1400	4200
Salaries	3500	3500	3500	10500
Materials	1100	1250	1300	3650
Total Expenses	6000	6150	6200	18350

To add lines, borders, or frames, follow these steps:

1. **Select the cell or range of cells that you want to format with lines, borders, or frames.**

   Remember that you select cells by dragging the mouse over them while holding down the left mouse button.

2. **Right-click the selection and choose <u>R</u>ange Properties from the pop-up menu to open the Range Properties InfoBox; then click the Color, Pattern, and Line Style tab.**

   The Color, Pattern, and Line Style tab of the Range Properties InfoBox is shown in Figure 9-8. By using the Border options, you can choose which sides of the selected cells get borders and the style and color of the border lines. You can fill a cell or range of cells with a color and/or pattern by making selections in the Interior area of the dialog box.

3. **In the Border area, click the button to designate where to apply borders and, if you like, choose a Line St<u>y</u>le and a Li<u>n</u>e Color from the drop-down palettes.**

4. **If you want to add a designer frame, click the Designer frame check box and choose a Frame style and Frame color from the drop-down palettes.**

   You can see the effect of your selections immediately.

Figure 9-8:
The Color,
Pattern, and
Line Style
tab of the
Range
Properties
InfoBox
gives you
myriad
options for
changing
your
worksheet's
appearance.

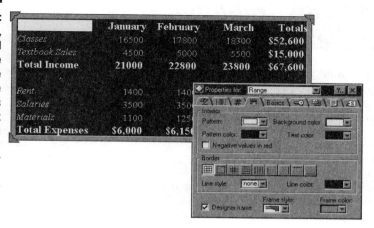

You can more easily determine what your lines, borders, and frames are going to look like on the printed page by getting rid of the grid lines that normally appear on-screen. To make these grid lines disappear, choose View⇨Set View Preferences, click the View tab in the Workbook Properties dialog box, and then deselect the Grid lines check box. This procedure affects only the display, not how the worksheet prints. If, on the other hand, you want the grid lines to print, choose File⇨Preview & Page Setup, click the Include tab in the Preview & Page Setup InfoBox, scroll down the Show list box, and click Sheet grid lines so that a check mark appears beside the option.

To remove lines from a selected range of cells, just select None in the Line style drop-down list in the Border area of the Color, Pattern, and Line Style tab of the Range Properties InfoBox. And deselect the Designer frame check box, too.

Note: If the Line style list box is blank in the Color, Pattern, and Line Style tab of the Range Properties InfoBox, the selected range contains mixed line types. In other words, the lines in the selection aren't consistent — for example, some may be single lines and others may be double lines. You can still make a selection from the drop-down list if you want to override the previous settings for the entire selection.

Pictures at an Exhibition — Using Gallery Styles

So you want your worksheets to look really cool? You want to be a graphic designer, but you don't have the talent or skill? Never fear, 1-2-3's Gallery styles can save you.

The *Gallery styles* are sets of professionally designed worksheet formatting combinations that you can slap right on top of your existing worksheet. No fuss, no muss. To use any of these nifty styles, just select the range you want formatted, open the Range Properties InfoBox (by right-clicking the selected range and choosing Range Properties from the pop-up menu), click the Styles tab, and then click the Style Gallery button to display the Style Gallery dialog box, as shown in Figure 9-9.

Figure 9-9:
The Style
Gallery
dialog box.

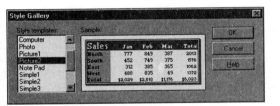

As you highlight the various names in the Style templates list in this dialog box, the Sample area displays an example of a worksheet with that style applied. After settling on a design template, just click OK.

The range you select to format with Gallery styles is usually the range you intend to print. Of course, you may need to experiment to get the effect just right.

If you change your mind after applying a Gallery style, choose Edit⇨Undo SetGalleryStyle. Remember, however, that Undo works only right after you apply the Gallery style. If you want to get rid of the Gallery style later (after you perform other activities), you must choose Edit⇨Clear to open the Clear dialog box and then select the Styles and Number Format and Borders check boxes (don't forget to deselect the Contents check box) before clicking OK to eliminate all styles from a selected range.

If you want to use a different Gallery style than the one you picked, select the range again and choose the new template from the Gallery dialog box.

Chapter 10

Charting Your Course

· ·

· ·

*E*xplaining things and persuading others that you're headed in the right direction is usually easier if you chart your course. And because, as we all know by now, a picture is worth a thousand words (at least), using charts can make you seem that much more convincing (or at least more verbose). Of course, the idea that people with a lot to say *must* know what they're talking about is a given . . . right?

Figure 10-1 shows some dreary old sales numbers on the left side of the worksheet. Yawn. The same numbers, however, are represented by an attention-grabbing chart on the right side of the worksheet. See the difference?

Figure 10-1:
Sleep-inducing numbers are magically transformed into a really cool chart.

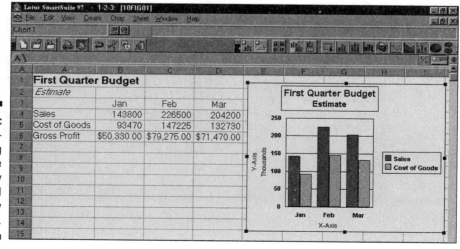

Chart Chat

Thankfully, 1-2-3 enables you to create gorgeous charts (or ugly ones — the choice is yours) to graphically represent the numbers in your worksheets. As with every other aspect of 1-2-3, you may find the vast number of charting options available to you somewhat overwhelming. But take heart — after you enter your data in a worksheet, creating a chart is just a matter of telling 1-2-3 which information you want to use, what type of chart you want, and where you want to put the chart. You don't even need to know much charting lingo to create charts, although familiarity with a few terms and what goes into a typical chart does help keep you on the right track. Check out Figure 10-2 to see the parts of a typical 1-2-3 chart.

All charts contain at least one data series. A *data series* is just a set of values for a particular category. Sales figures, for example, comprise one data series. The figures for the Cost of Goods are another data series. Each data series is represented on a chart by a line, bar, dot, or pie slice.

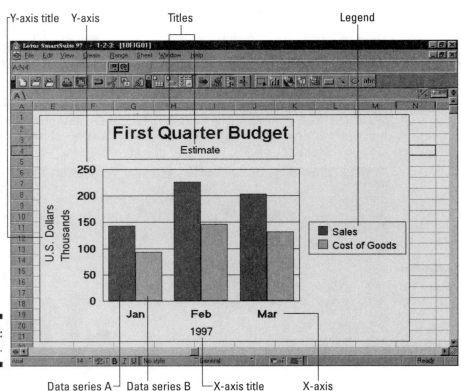

Figure 10-2: Chart parts.

Most charts have an x-axis and a y-axis. Don't get freaked out by the terminology — the *x-axis* is the chart's horizontal plane, and the *y-axis* is the vertical plane. (I hope that's plane . . . er, plain enough.) The way most data is set up in a worksheet is that the x-axis (sometimes called the *category* axis) plots the data series over time. The y-axis (sometimes called the *value* axis) plots the amount of the numbers.

Keep in mind, too, the following points in considering charts:

- You can create 1-2-3 charts most easily if you enter your data in normal table format, using contiguous rows and columns. Don't insert any blank rows or columns into the table.

- Charts are based on numbers stored in your worksheet. If you change any of those numbers, 1-2-3 automatically updates the chart to reflect the new numbers.

- Although you have no practical limit to the number of data series you can include in a 1-2-3 chart (well, okay, maybe a couple dozen), you're better off keeping this number to a minimum to avoid creating a chart that's chaotic and confusing. The practical minimum varies, too, depending upon the chart type. A bar chart, such as the sample shown in Figure 10-2, may start to look crowded with six or seven data series. See the section "Choosing the Chart Type That Makes Your Point," later in this chapter, for some insight into other chart types.

- 1-2-3 stores — and displays — your charts right on the worksheet. You can have as many charts on your worksheet as good taste (or printer memory) dictates. See the section "Printing Charts," later in this chapter, for information on resolving printer problems.

- You can change, customize, and fiddle with every part of a chart until its appearance suits you perfectly.

- You can use the data in 1-2-3 to create charts in other SmartSuite 97 programs, such as Freelance or Approach. You discover, as you explore all the SmartSuite 97 programs, that no one *right* program exists for creating charts. (Chapter 3, however, provides some hints on how to choose the right program for the job.)

Creating Charts, Quick and Dirty

Nothing is easier than creating a chart in 1-2-3. Okay, maybe getting someone else to provide the charts is easier, but we digress. Here are the steps for creating a quick and dirty chart from the data in a worksheet. (You find out how to clean up the chart in the section "Editing Charts," later in this chapter.)

1. **Select from your worksheet the data you want to chart.**

   The selection needs to include all the values and labels you want in your chart. In the example shown in Figure 10-3, we selected all the data in the worksheet. (Remember that you select cells by dragging the mouse over the cells while holding down the left mouse button. You can also select entire columns by clicking the column letter or rows by clicking the row number.)

2. **Click the Create a Chart SmartIcon — the one near the middle of the second palette of SmartIcons, displaying a picture of a bar chart; you can also choose Create➪Chart.**

   After you click the Create a Chart SmartIcon, the mouse pointer turns into a crosshair pointer. The title bar displays the message `Click where you want to display the chart`.

   Note: If you click the Create a Chart button without first selecting the chart data, 1-2-3 displays the Chart Assistant dialog box, from which you can specify the data range and then continue on to Step 3.

Figure 10-3: After selecting the data, you need to define where you want the chart.

3. **Move the mouse pointer to the point in the worksheet where you want the location of the upper-left corner of the new chart, and then click the mouse button.**

   As soon as you click the mouse button, the new chart appears on-screen.

If you don't want to use 1-2-3's default chart size, you can create the chart by dragging the mouse to specify the size of the chart. Just position the mouse where you want one corner of the chart, press and hold the left mouse button, and then drag diagonally until the outline is the desired size. After you release the mouse button, the chart appears. Cool!

Whenever 1-2-3 creates a default chart, the program makes the following assumptions — some of which may accidentally (er, actually) be correct:

✔ 1-2-3 always creates a bar chart. We describe how to change to other chart types in the section "Choosing the Chart Type That Makes Your Point," later in this chapter.

✔ 1-2-3 assumes that any text in the upper-left cells of the selected data is the chart title (or titles).

✔ 1-2-3 uses the first column for x-axis labels — if the column contains labels. If the first column contains values, 1-2-3 treats the contents of this column as chart data and inserts placeholders for the x-axis labels.

✔ 1-2-3 automatically figures out how large the y-axis needs to be to accommodate the values you're charting and adds labels, if necessary, to indicate the magnitude of these values.

✔ 1-2-3 inserts placeholder x-axis and y-axis titles.

As soon as 1-2-3 creates the chart, the program also selects the chart — and selection handles (those little black squares at the corners and in the middle of each side of the chart box) appear around the chart. You can manipulate the various elements of the chart by double-clicking the element and then making the appropriate choices in the InfoBox for that element's properties. (See the section "Editing Charts," later in the chapter, for more details.)

✔ After you (or 1-2-3) select a chart, the chart's name appears in the selection indicator (the left end of the Edit line). The default chart names are CHART 1, CHART 2, and so on. You can change the default name of a selected chart to something more meaningful. You may, for example, name a pie chart comparing costs for your restaurant's hamburger ingredients *Cow Pie*. To change a chart name, double-click the chart background and click the Basics tab in the Chart Properties InfoBox. Then enter the new name in the Chart name text box.

Note: Identifying the *chart background* can be a little tricky. Basically, the background is anything inside the chart that isn't something else, such as a title, legend, plot area, bar, and so on. The tricky part is that the *plot area* of the chart is its own element and some other chart elements are bigger than you may think. The title, for example, usually encompasses a good-sized block of space above the plotting area, even though the text may not occupy all that space. Selecting the chart background, however, is not such a difficult issue. Clicking anywhere in the chart creates selection handles. If the handles appear around the title or some other element, instead of the entire chart, you know that you selected the wrong thing. If you do happen to double-click the wrong chart element and open its InfoBox instead of the Chart Properties InfoBox — no problem. Just select Chart from the drop-down list in the title bar of the InfoBox to display the correct set of options.

✔ Changing a chart's name (the one that appears in the Selection Indicator and on the Basics tab of the Chart Properties InfoBox) doesn't change the chart's title — just the name 1-2-3 uses to refer to the chart.

✔ Notice that, after you (or 1-2-3) select a chart, a Chart menu (which has commands for working with charts) replaces the Range menu (which includes commands for manipulating data ranges) and the default Chart SmartIcon palette replaces the default Worksheet palette.

Editing Charts

You soon discover that 1-2-3 gives you endless options for changing your charts. Charts consist of many elements that can be selected and manipulated individually. As a general rule, to manipulate a particular chart element, you can double-click the element to display an InfoBox relevant to that particular element. You can also right-click an element to display the object's pop-up menu and choose (Element) Properties from the menu to open the InfoBox, but double-clicking is faster and works on almost every chart element. (By the way, double-clicking some other frequently formatted objects in this, and other, SmartSuite 97 programs opens the related InfoBox, but switching to text editing mode is a more common result of double-clicking something.)

The following are some examples of chart elements that you can easily change:

✔ **Chart titles in the chart data range:** For the chart titles, 1-2-3 uses the contents of the labels in the upper-left cells of the chart data range. You can edit chart titles by editing the contents of those cells. As soon as you change the contents of the cells, the titles in the chart change.

✔ **Custom chart titles:** If you don't want to use the contents of the cells as the chart titles, you can edit the titles by double-clicking one of the chart titles to display the Title Properties InfoBox and then clicking the Options tab. Type new text into the Line 1, Line 2, and Line 3 text boxes and deselect the Cell check box next to each text box. You can also have 1-2-3 use the contents of other cells for the titles by selecting the Cell check boxes and entering the appropriate cell addresses in the text boxes. Clicking the button that appears between the checked Cell check box and the text box for a title line enables you to select a cell simply by clicking that cell instead of typing the cell address into the text box.

✔ **Legends:** To change the text for the legend, you must do things just a bit differently. If you double-click the text of the legend, you open the Legend Properties InfoBox, in which you can control the positioning of the legend and the formatting of the text and such — but not the text of the legend itself. You need to double-click the color key box in the legend or one of the bars (or lines, or whatever) of the data series to open the Series Properties InfoBox; then click the Options tab of that InfoBox. Near the bottom of this tab is where you find the Legend Label text box. Select the Cell check box and enter into the text box the cell address of the cell containing the legend text. Or you can deselect the Cell check box and type your new text for the legend into the text box.

✔ **Chart size and position:** You don't need to settle for the default chart size or the position you originally chose. You can select the chart and then just drag the entire chart to a new location. (Just make sure that you click and drag the chart background and not one of the chart elements or you move the chart element instead of the chart.) You can resize the chart by first positioning the mouse pointer over one of the chart's corner selection handles so that the pointer turns into a four-headed arrow. Press the left mouse button and drag the mouse until the dotted box that appears is the desired size; then release the mouse button.

✔ **It's outta here:** To delete a chart, or any chart element, select the chart or element and press Delete.

Try double-clicking various chart elements to see what happens. You are likely to stumble upon all sorts of unexpected editing options. Sometimes just poking around — especially with visual objects such as charts — is the best way to learn. Explore. Have fun. (Really.)

Printing Charts

Great news! You don't need to know anything special to print charts. Because charts sit right on your worksheet, just include the chart in the range you want to print and let 'er rip. Check back to Chapter 8 for specific printing instructions.

If you want to print only the chart, select the chart and then choose File⇨Print. 1-2-3 automatically chooses the Selected Chart option button in the Print area of the Print dialog box. Just click the Print button, and the chart prints.

Note: Of course, the beautiful color charts you see on-screen don't print in color unless you own a color printer.

Choosing the Chart Type That Makes Your Point

Good ol' 1-2-3 enables you to create all kinds of different types of charts, from bar charts to pie charts to amazing 3D charts that really impress your boss. Changing the chart type is a snap. Just select the chart and then click the SmartIcon that displays the picture of the kind of chart you want. The Default Chart SmartIcon palette includes buttons for some of the most popular chart types.

If you can't find a SmartIcon for the chart type you're thinking of, that doesn't mean 1-2-3 can't create that kind of chart. Just click the Select a Chart Type SmartIcon (the one with a picture of four chart types) to open the Chart Properties InfoBox with the Type tab displayed, as shown in Figure 10-4.

Figure 10-4: The Type tab enables you to choose from 12 chart types.

You can choose a basic chart type from the Chart type list on the left. Then you can select from a variety of styles within each chart type by clicking one of the option buttons for the chart type. The available options are represented by buttons on the right. Figure 10-4 shows the Line chart styles.

As described earlier, the default chart type is a standard bar chart. You can, however, present your data by using any of about a zillion different chart types. Yes, 1-2-3 doesn't give you a mind-boggling variety of chart types just for fun. Okay, they're a bunch of fun-loving guys and gals out there in Lotus land, but sometimes they do things for a reason.

In this case, the reason is that some chart types are better than others for presenting some types of data. This book isn't big enough to describe all the nuances of all the various chart types, but here are some basic rules of thumb for the common chart types:

- *Bar charts*, the 1-2-3 default chart type, often are used for comparing two or more related data series at a specific point in time or a small amount of data over time. The bar chart works for the example back in Figure 10-1 because we were creating two data series (sales versus cost of goods) over time (a three-month period).

- *Pie charts* are great for displaying proportional relationships among data items, such as the share that each month's sales contributes to the sales for the quarter. Pie charts' primary limitation is that they can display only one data series, so a pie chart wouldn't work for the example in Figure 10-1.

- *Line charts* are used to emphasize the continuity of data over time. These charts are also a good choice for showing trends. They are especially useful for showing large sets of data, such as monthly sales of a product over a five-year period.

- *Area charts* are essentially line charts with the spaces between the lines filled in. You use area charts for the same kinds of data for which you use line charts. The only difference is aesthetic.

You can also choose among several mixed charts, which combine line and bar charts for data that could benefit from both chart types.

Many of the chart types, including several of the SmartIcon chart type options, are available in a 3D style. 3D just gives you a different look. Use 3D if you like it.

No hard and fast rules exist about which chart type is best to use in each situation. What we provide here are just general guidelines. Experiment to find the chart type that conveys your message the way that you — or your boss — want it conveyed.

Chapter 11

Final Touches and Shortcuts
for 1-2-3

In This Chapter

▶ Enhancing worksheets and charts by using the 1-2-3 drawing tools

▶ Using spell-check

▶ Automating tasks by using scripts

*A*s if doing calculations, formatting worksheets, and creating dazzling charts weren't enough, 1-2-3 packs enough other features into the program to make you think you may never discover everything 1-2-3 has to offer, let alone figure out how to use all its features. Relax! You don't *need* to know everything possible about 1-2-3 to use the program effectively. In fact, you can do scads more with 1-2-3 than we have room to cover in this book. This chapter, however, introduces you to some of the niftier things hiding under 1-2-3's hood.

Enhancing Worksheets and Charts by Using the 1-2-3 Drawing Tools

Do you have a hankering to express your artistic creativity but don't think a spreadsheet program is the best place to express yourself? Well, you're right. But you can still do some pretty fancy doodling in 1-2-3. In addition to all its standard spreadsheet text, number, formula, and charting capabilities, 1-2-3 includes a bunch of neat drawing tools to give you something to do if you don't want to concentrate on your real work — I mean, er, if you want to *enhance* your worksheets and charts. Yeah — that's the ticket! *Enhancement.* A wonderful concept . . . .

Figure 11-1 shows you just one example of some of the things you can do by using 1-2-3's drawing tools, even if — as is sadly true of your authors — you have no artistic talent whatsoever.

Arrows SmartIcon   Ellipses SmartIcon ⌐ Text Block SmartIcon

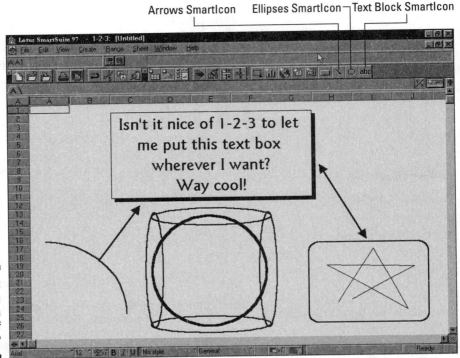

Figure 11-1:
Aren't you
just drawn
to this stuff
(ahem)?

Almost all the major SmartSuite 97 programs have pretty much the same drawing capabilities — and drawing in all those programs works pretty much the same way. So you don't need to use a specific SmartSuite 97 program just to do some doodling. If you're in Word Pro, draw in Word Pro; if you're in Freelance Graphics, draw in Freelance. You get the idea. (Organizer, however, doesn't "do" drawings. I guess Lotus figures that, if you really want to get organized, you shouldn't be wasting your time doodling.)

Common SmartIcon palettes provide buttons for several of the more common drawing objects, including arrows, ellipses, and text blocks. These drawing SmartIcons are shown in Figure 11-1.

In addition, after you select any drawn object, 1-2-3 displays the default Arrange SmartIcon palette, which includes buttons for manipulating selected objects in the following ways:

✔ *Flipping objects.* To flip an object horizontally, click the Flip Selected Objects Left-Right SmartIcon. To flip an object vertically, click the Flip Selected Objects Top-Bottom SmartIcon.

✔ *Sending objects to the back or bringing them forward.* To bring selected objects forward, click the Bring Selected Objects to the Front SmartIcon. To send selected objects to the back, click the Send Selected Objects to the Back SmartIcon. Keep in mind that you can't send an object behind a cell's contents. All drawing objects float on top of the worksheet. You can only send objects behind other objects. On the left side of the worksheet shown in Figure 11-2, for example, notice that the ellipse is behind the rectangle. On the right side, the ellipse is in front of the rectangle.

✔ *Grouping or ungrouping selected objects.* To group selected objects so that you can size, move, and otherwise manipulate the objects as a group, click the Group or Ungroup Selected Objects SmartIcon. If you find that you need to manipulate one of the objects in a group independently, click the Group or Ungroup Selected Objects SmartIcon again to ungroup the objects for individual attention.

All the drawing tools that aren't available from the SmartIcon palettes are conveniently available from a secondary Drawing menu. Choose Create⇨ Drawing to display this Drawing menu, as shown in Figure 11-3.

You can use all the drawing options to annotate and add emphasis to worksheet data and charts. You can also use these options to create your own drawings for any purpose you can imagine. Your options are limitless.

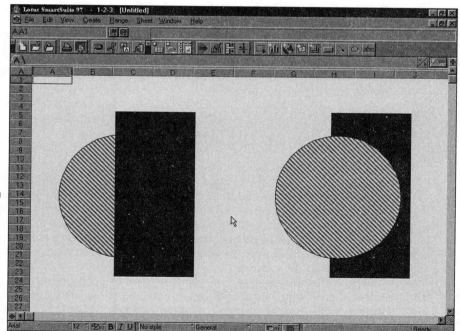

Figure 11-2: Front-to-back and back-to-front placement of selected objects.

Figure 11-3:
Yet more
drawing
options are
available on
the Drawing
menu.

Moving and resizing objects

To move a drawn object (or a group of objects), click to select the object. Then position the mouse pointer over the object (but not over a sizing handle). After the pointer changes into a hand, you can drag the object to a new location on-screen.

To change the size of an object, you must first select that object. Then position the mouse pointer over one of the selection handles (after which the pointer changes into a double-headed or four-headed arrow) and drag the handle toward the center of the object to make the object smaller or drag away from the center to make the object larger. Dragging a corner handle changes the size of the object proportionally. Dragging a side handle enables you to change the height or width of the object without affecting the other dimension. (Remember that the selection handles are those little squares that surround a selected object.)

Changing an object's attributes

You can also change a drawn object's attributes, such as line widths, interior patterns, and colors. You change these attributes in — you guessed it! — the Draw Object Properties InfoBox. You open this InfoBox by double-clicking the object, by right-clicking the object and choosing Drawing Properties from the pop-up menu, or by selecting the object and choosing Drawing⇨Drawing Properties from the menu bar. After the InfoBox opens, click the Color, Pattern, and Line Style tab to access the options shown in Figure 11-4.

The available options vary depending on the particular object you want to manipulate. If, for example, you select a text block (which you use to add to worksheets any text elements you don't want constrained to a range of cells), you see the version of the Color, Pattern, and Line Style tab shown in Figure 11-4.

Figure 11-4:
The Color,
Pattern, and
Line Style
tab of the
Draw Object
Properties
InfoBox for
a text block.

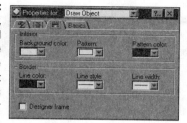

This version includes options for designer frames, borders, interior patterns, and so on. If you select an arrow, you lose the borders and some other options on the Color, Pattern, and Line Style tab, but you gain options that enable you to put an arrowhead at either end of the line — or both ends — as shown in Figure 11-5. If you select a text object, the Draw Object Properties InfoBox includes a Font, Attribute, and Color tab and an Alignment tab as well.

Figure 11-5:
The Color,
Pattern, and
Line Style
tab of the
Draw Object
Properties
InfoBox for
an arrow.

So why draw?

Some legitimate uses exist for using drawing tools in worksheets — not that playing around isn't legitimate, of course. One of the more common uses for spreadsheet drawings is to emphasize and call attention to the portions of the worksheet or chart to which you want the reader to pay special attention. You may, for example, draw an arrow to point to an important number or chart element. Figure 11-6 shows a chart on a worksheet with some drawing enhancements.

Be careful not to go overboard placing drawing objects on your worksheet. A few objects, tastefully placed, can enhance your message and help get your point across. Too many just add clutter and distract from your message.

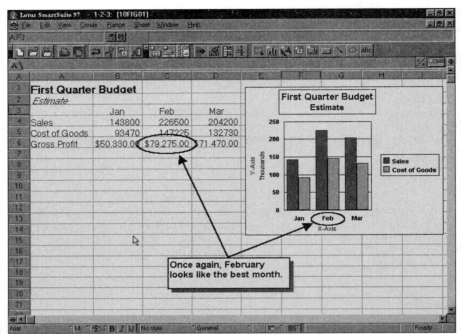

Figure 11-6:
Oh, so that's
the point.

Using Spell-Check

If you thought spell-checking was just for word processing, think again. If you read the preceding part of this book on Word Pro, you see how to use the spell-checker to help rid your word processing documents of misspellings and typos. The idea is for your readers to think that you know what you're talking about — that you actually put some thought into the document (and, of course, you *did* — right?). Well, that readers of your worksheets think you know what you're talking about with your figures and charts is just as important — and maybe more so. After all, if the boss thinks the worksheet is sloppy and therefore doesn't approve your budget proposal, you're sunk.

Fortunately, spell-checking 1-2-3 worksheets is just about as easy as spell-checking word processing documents. The only difference is that 1-2-3 doesn't highlight misspelled words for you before you start the spelling checker, as Word Pro does (sigh). To start spell-checking your worksheet, you must choose Edit⇨Check Spelling. The Check Spelling dialog box appears, as shown in Figure 11-7.

Figure 11-7:
1-2-3's
Check
Spelling
dialog box.

To begin checking all the worksheets in the entire file, make sure that you have Current Workbook selected in the dialog box's Look in drop-down list box and then click Start. To check just the current worksheet, select Current sheet in the drop-down list. You can also check a selected range or all linked workbooks.

After you begin spell-checking, you use the Check Spelling dialog box pretty much as you use the Spell Check bar in Word Pro. (See Chapters 1 and 6, respectively, for more information on using the SmartSuite 97 Spell Check feature in general and for Word Pro.) The Spell Checker finds a misspelled word and offers suggested replacements. Then you click buttons to skip the word, skip all occurrences of the word, replace the word, replace all misspelled words automatically, or add the word to your user dictionary.

You may want to keep the following things in mind while spell-checking 1-2-3 worksheets:

✔ If you know you want to spell-check just a certain range, select that range before you open the Check Spelling dialog box. Then select Selected range in the Look in drop-down list box.

✔ As discussed in Chapter 1, all the major SmartSuite 97 programs share the same main and supplemental dictionaries. If you add words to the spelling dictionary in Word Pro, you don't need to add the same words again in 1-2-3. Check out Chapter 1 for more details on spell-checking.

Automating Tasks by Using Scripts

If you want to really save time and effort, *scripts* are the way to go. The concepts for 1-2-3 scripts — what they can do for you — are the same as for Word Pro scripts, as discussed in Chapter 7. If you're tired of typing the same text or commands over and over again, make a script and be done with it.

So you're wondering why you'd go to the trouble of creating a 1-2-3 script? For any repetitive task that requires more than a few keystrokes or mouse clicks, whether entering your company's name and address, as shown in the example later in this section, or printing complex accounting reports on a weekly basis, a script can cut the task down to size.

1-2-3 actually offers two forms of automation: macros and scripts. Macros and scripts perform similar functions. Each feature gives you a means to define a series of commands and then have 1-2-3 execute those commands automatically. The older-style macros record the commands right on your worksheet. (If you're familiar with macros from previous versions of 1-2-3, you can continue to use your knowledge, and many of your macros, in 1-2-3 97.) The newer-style scripts are discreetly hidden out of sight but still available. Both scripts and macros enable you to do some pretty amazing things — provided you have (or are willing to pick up) some programming skills. Scripts are the more powerful of the two, because the LotusScript language enables programmers to do things outside of 1-2-3, such as have 1-2-3 exchange data with other Windows programs.

Scripts and macros are powerful tools in the hands of programmers. But you don't need to be a programmer to create and use scripts. Creating simple scripts to automate typing and formatting is pretty simple and straightforward. 1-2-3 "watches" what you do and records your actions. Then, if you want to repeat the same actions again, you just play back the recording. Even if you're scared to delve too deeply into the inner workings of 1-2-3, try out at least a couple of simple scripts. Your efforts are sure to be greatly rewarded.

Remember: Recording a script is like turning on a tape recorder and then playing the recording back. After you turn on 1-2-3's recorder, your actions are recorded in a *Script Editor* in a form that 1-2-3 understands. After you're done recording, you simply save the contents of the Script Editor. The following steps tell you how to record a 1-2-3 script:

1. **Open the worksheet in which you want to record the script, and move to the location where you intend to perform the actions you want 1-2-3 to record as a script.**

   Make sure that you select an appropriate cell *before* you start recording your script. You don't want to click a cell to get things going after you start recording the script or you include that cell address in the script. Normally, you don't want your scripts tied to a particular cell address. That way you can use the script anywhere you want in your worksheet.

2. **Choose Edit⇨Scripts & Macros⇨Record Script.**

   The Record Script dialog box appears, as shown in Figure 11-8.

Figure 11-8:
The Record
Script
dialog box.

Record Script	☒
Script name:	Record
	Cancel
Record script into:	
Script Library ▼	Help

3. **Type a name (with no spaces) for your script in the Script Name text box and select the workbook's file name from from the Record script into drop-down list box; then click OK.**

   The tape recorder turns on, and 1-2-3 displays the message Rec at the right side of the status bar — and even displays a floating palette of buttons so that you can stop or pause the recording.

4. **Carry out the actions that you want your script to record.**

   If you want the script to record your company's name and address, enter these items as you want them to appear. You may, for example, decide to enter the name in one cell and the address in the cell below the name.

5. **Choose Edit⇨Script & Macros⇨Stop Recording or click the Stop button (the red one marked with a square) to stop recording your script.**

   After you stop recording a script, 1-2-3 opens the Scripts for window. You can edit your script here if you're so inclined (and have a degree in computer programming). Fortunately, the typical recorded script requires no editing.

6. **Choose File⇨Save Scripts from the menu bar in the Scripts for window and confirm the action by clicking OK in the dialog box that appears.**

   1-2-3 saves your document file and the script at the same time.

7. **Click the Close (X) button to close the Scripts for window.**

   You're done. You recorded a script. Now you can play the script back to repeat the recorded actions any time you like.

Run, Script, Run!

If you need to run a script you recorded, nothing could be simpler. (Well, almost nothing.) Just follow these steps:

1. **Select the cell in your worksheet where you want your script to begin running.**

2. **Choose Edit⇨Script & Macros⇨Run.**

   The Run Script dialog box appears, as shown in Figure 11-9.

3. **Select the Script radio button and then select the filename in the From drop-down list box.**

   Be sure you select the filename where you recorded your script, as described in the steps in the preceding section.

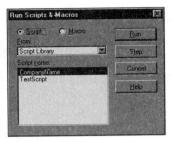

Figure 11-9:
The Run
Scripts &
Macros
dialog box.

4. **Select the name of the script you want to run from the Script name list box and click Run.**

   1-2-3 plays back the keystrokes and other actions you recorded earlier.

And that's that. As is true of everything else in SmartSuite 97, working in 1-2-3 is as easy as . . . oh, you know!

Lots more stuff is available in 1-2-3 than we can possibly cover in this book. We hope that this part of the book provides enough information to get you started in the program. If you want to know more, however, check out *Lotus 1-2-3 97 For Windows For Dummies,* by John Walkenbach (published by IDG Books Worldwide, Inc.).

Part IV

Caution —
Database
Approaching

"I STARTED DESIGNING DATABASE SOFTWARE SYSTEMS AFTER SEEING HOW EASY IT WAS TO DESIGN OFFICE FURNITURE."

In this part . . .

This truly is the information age. Trying to manage and keep up with the tons of information that companies — and even individuals — constantly accumulate is a Herculean task. Good news. By using Approach, you don't need to be Hercules to wrestle mountains of data into submission. If you possess just enough strength to tickle your computer keyboard's ivories (and, of course, the smarts to read this part), you can get your data under control in no time.

Chapter 12

Boot Camp for Approach

· ·

In This Chapter

▶ What's a database (and why should I care)?

▶ The need for planning

▶ Getting started with Approach

▶ Putting data in

▶ Printing data out

▶ Custom-tailoring your own database

· ·

*A*s part of your wonderful SmartSuite 97 package, Lotus includes a database called Approach. Although Word Pro is great for writing letters to people you may not want to call and 1-2-3 is great for calculating future profits you may never see, Approach is handy for storing information you don't want to lose, such as phone numbers for hot dates, addresses of people you're blackmailing, or names of corrupt politicians who owe you a favor.

Lotus Organizer (included in your SmartSuite 97 package and discussed in Chapters 22 through 24) is also technically a database. Organizer is specifically designed for storing certain kinds of information, such as appointments, records of calls, and names and addresses. Approach, on the other hand, is better for creating custom databases to store more esoteric information. For example, Approach can store the names of all the wines stored in your wine cellar, credit card numbers of customers ordering products from you, financial values of all your business assets, or serial numbers of all the counterfeit money you've created by using your desktop publishing program.

Because you can design your own databases in Approach, it's a far more flexible, powerful, and (unfortunately) confusing program than Organizer.

Getting to First Base — Databases Defined

Telling you that Approach is a *database* is useless if you don't have the slightest clue what a database is. Even if you're not familiar with the idea of a computer database, you've probably used a paper database at one time or another. A telephone book, a restaurant menu, and a library card catalog are all examples of paper databases because they contain information that's useful to keep.

Approach is nothing more than a program to help you store information in your computer so you can get it back out again. To give the illusion of organization, every Approach database consists of the following three parts (see Figure 12-1):

- ✔ Files
- ✔ Records
- ✔ Fields

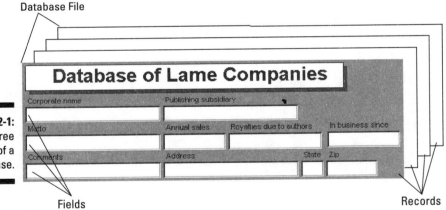

Database File

Figure 12-1:
The three
parts of a
database.

Fields

Records

Fields organize your information into categories, such as name, address, and telephone number. *Records* consist of one or more related fields. In a telephone book, each person's name, address, and telephone number together make up one record. *Database files* consist of one or more records. From a computer's point of view, a telephone book is considered a file.

Planning Your Database

You can just take information and dump the data into your database. Unfortunately, this approach is much like dumping your laundry on the floor and then wondering why finding a matching pair of socks takes so long. Before you can store any information into an Approach database, you must decide what type of information you want to store. Do you want to store names and addresses, telephone numbers and dates, or serial numbers and salaries?

No matter what you want to save, a database enables you to store a variety of information. For example, the Internal Revenue Service stores names and addresses of potential tax cheats (unless they're prominent politicians, of course); the Central Intelligence Agency stores personality profiles of suspected terrorists; and the National Security Agency stores signatures (specific noises) of Russian submarines.

To help you plan your database, try designing that database on paper first. If you want to create a database to track business contacts, for example, write down all the information you want to save, such as the person's name, company name, telephone number, e-mail address, and fax number. By first designing your database on paper, you can see how useful your completed database is going to be.

Starting Approach

Before you can store any information in an Approach database, you must start the program. Depending on how you like using your computer, you can start Approach in any of the following ways:

✔ The simplest way to start Approach is to click its SuiteStart icon in the taskbar's system tray. The Approach icon has a blue diamond background behind what looks like an upright paper clip with a paper airplane glued to the front, giving the thing an A-shape. (If you put the cursor over this icon, you see a big, obnoxious yellow Help bubble that reads: `Lotus Approach.`)

✔ If SmartCenter is running, you can click the SmartSuite drawer to open the drawer, click the Lotus Applications folder, and then double-click the Approach icon.

✔ The other (just slightly more complicated) way to start Approach is through the Windows 95 Start menu. Just click the Start button, point to Programs, point to Lotus SmartSuite, and finally choose Lotus Approach 97 from the cascading menus.

The moment you start Approach, the program displays a Welcome to Lotus Approach dialog box (see Figure 12-2). At this point, Approach is asking you: "Hey, do you want to use an existing database or create a new one of your own?" You can build a database from scratch, as explained in the section "Designing Your Own Database," later in this chapter. Approach, however, has a couple of ways to get you up and running a database quickly: by loading an existing database and by creating a new database using a SmartMaster.

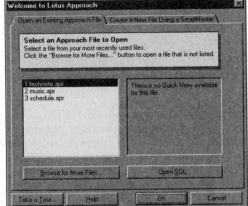

Figure 12-2:
The
Welcome
to Lotus
Approach
dialog box.

Loading an existing database

If you know you want to load an existing database rather than create a new database from scratch, you can perform the following steps:

1. **Click the Open An Existing Approach File tab in the Welcome to Lotus Approach dialog box.**

   A list of existing files appears on the left side of the dialog box.

2. **If the file you want to use appears in the list box, select the file and click OK.**

   If you want to use a different existing database file, click the Browse For More Files button to open the Open dialog box. Choose the database file you want to open from the list box and click Open.

Creating a new database with a SmartMaster

If you don't have an existing database with which to work, Approach enables you to create a new database quite easily. Approach contains more than 50 different database templates — called *SmartMasters* — that you can use as the basis of a new database. The SmartMasters are predesigned databases, complete with all the fields and forms you need. All you need to do is enter your data. You can create a new database using a SmartMaster right from the Welcome to Lotus Approach dialog box by following these steps:

1. **Click the Create a New File Using a SmartMaster tab.**

2. **Select from the list the SmartMaster you want to use and click OK.**

   Approach provides both database templates and applications from which to choose. (You can choose to list Applications or Templates in the SmartMaster Types drop-down list box.) If you want to create your own database from scratch, select Blank Database. A New dialog box appears.

3. **Type the name of your new database in the File name text box and click Create.**

Getting to know Approach is easier if you start out working with an existing database or one based on a SmartMaster template. The Customers or Customer Contacts templates are good choices for your initial explorations, because these templates contain a variety of fields that nearly everyone can relate to.

Note: Approach includes more than 50 SmartMaster *templates* and more than a dozen SmartMaster *applications*. Both templates and applications are predesigned databases that you use as the basis for new database files into which you add your own data. The difference between templates and applications is that applications have a slick point-and-click interface that guides you through your work with the database.

Entering Data

After you create a database file, Approach gives you two ways to enter data into a database file:

- ✔ In the Form view
- ✔ In the Worksheet view

As you may expect, *Form view* mimics the appearance of an actual paper form. Form view enables you to see all your defined fields at the same time (see Figure 12-3). The advantage of Form view is that this view enables you to see the field contents (the categories of information) for one record at a time.

Form tab

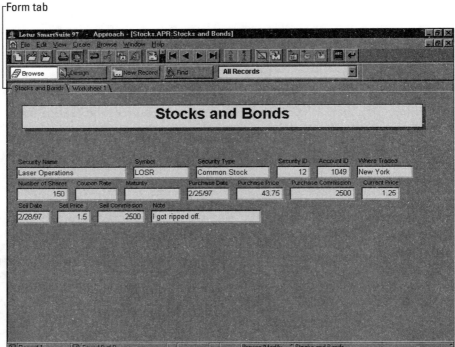

Figure 12-3:
The Form
view of an
Approach
database.

Worksheet view, on the other hand, displays your fields as headings in a spreadsheet (see Figure 12-4). The Worksheet view arranges fields in columns and each record appears on a separate row. The advantage of Worksheet view is that this view enables you to see a good chunk of the information stored in your entire database (although seeing the information individual records contain is difficult).

To switch between Form and Worksheet views, just click the tab that appears in the upper-left corner of the screen. (Because you can create multiple views and give them different names, the trick is to remember what name you give each form and worksheet view so that you click the correct tab.)

Field   Worksheet tab   Blank row

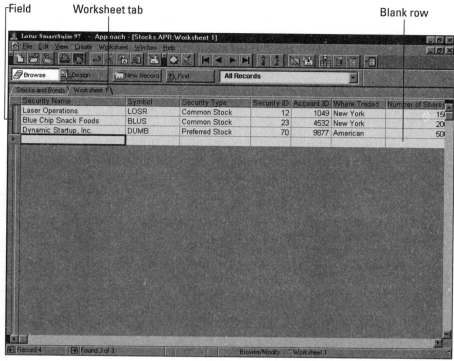

Figure 12-4:
A
Worksheet
view
showing
fields
displayed as
columns
and records
as rows.

To choose a field to enter data, Approach gives you the following two choices:

✔ Click the field in which you want to enter data (the easy way).

✔ Press Tab or Shift+Tab until the cursor moves to the field in which you want to enter data (the hard, clumsy way).

Entering data in Form view

Form view is most convenient if you're entering data for the first time. To enter data in Form view, follow these steps:

1. **Click the Form tab of your worksheet (displayed in the upper-left corner) to switch to Form view.**

   Remember that the tab may be labeled with the name of the form instead of the word *Form*. For example, in Figures 12-3 and 12-4, the form tab is labeled Stocks and Bonds.

2. **Choose Browse⇨New Record from the menu bar, click the New Record button, or press Ctrl+N.**

   Approach creates an empty record.

3. **Click a field in the empty record and type the information you want to store.**

   Repeat this step as needed to fill in the form.

   If you prefer to keep your hands on the keyboard, you can move to the next field by pressing Tab instead of clicking the field with the mouse pointer.

4. **After you get to the last field on the form, press Tab.**

   Approach creates another empty record for you to fill.

Entering data in Worksheet view

Worksheet view is most convenient if you are editing data. To enter data in Worksheet view, follow these steps:

1. **Click the Worksheet tab to switch to Worksheet view.**

2. **Choose Worksheet⇨Records⇨New, click the New Record button, or press Ctrl+N.**

   Approach creates an empty record at the bottom of the worksheet. (If you have lots of data, you may need to scroll down to the bottom of the worksheet to see this empty record.)

3. **Click a field in the empty record and type the information you want to store.**

   Repeat this step as needed to fill in the record.

4. **After you get to the last field on the row, press Tab.**

   Approach creates another empty record.

   Note: Because Approach automatically creates a new, blank record after you complete data entry into the preceding row, you always have a blank row at the end of your database. That's normal. You don't need to worry about that empty record in your database.

As you type your data into a database, Approach automatically saves your work as you go along. That way you don't need to keep telling Approach to save your data. The only time you must periodically save your work is if you're designing a Form or Worksheet view. To save a Form or Worksheet view, choose File⇨Save Approach File or press Ctrl+S.

Printing Your Database

After storing vital information in a database, you may want to print it so you can view the entire database contents on paper. Approach enables you to print in either Form view or Worksheet view. (You can also create and print reports, but that's the topic of another chapter — Chapter 16 to be exact.) Before you print your database, you can save paper by using the Print Preview feature. If the preview looks good, you can print your database.

To see a preview of what your document is going to look like after you print the file, follow these steps:

1. **Click the Form tab to see what your forms are going to look like, or click the Worksheet tab to see what your worksheets are going to look like.**

 2. **Click the Print Preview SmartIcon (which looks like a piece of paper in a computer monitor), choose File⇨Print Preview, or press Ctrl+Shift+B.**

Approach displays the preview screen of your form or worksheet (see Figure 12-5).

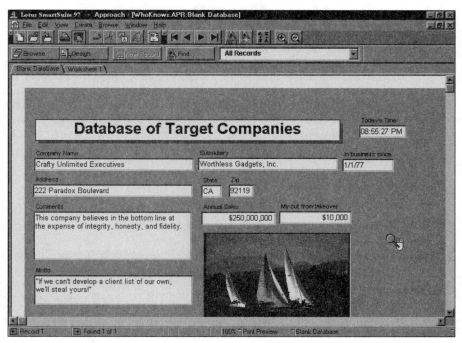

Figure 12-5:
A typical print preview of a Form view.

3. **Browse through your database to see what different records look like before printing.**

4. **To exit Print Preview, click the Print Preview SmartIcon, choose File⇨Print Preview, or just press Ctrl+Shift+B.**

To print a database, follow these steps:

1. **Click the Form tab (to print the Form view) or click the Worksheet tab (to print the Worksheet view).**

 2. **Click the Print SmartIcon (which looks like a printer), choose File⇨Print, or just press Ctrl+P.**

A Print dialog box appears.

3. **Click Print to print.**

If you want, you can adjust settings in the dialog box to print different portions of your database instead of the default current record (for forms) or all records (for Worksheet view) before you click Print.

Designing Your Own Database

The section "Starting Approach," earlier in this chapter, teaches you the two easy ways to begin using an Approach database — loading an existing database and creating a new database by using one of Approach's samples. But what if you don't find what you're really looking for among the sample templates? No problem: You can create your own database from scratch. Creating your own database is slower and clumsier than using one of the sample templates but enables you to create custom databases to store exactly the type of information you want.

To create your own database, you need to define two parts:

✔ The file format for your database

✔ The fields in which to store the actual information in your database

Choosing a database file format is like choosing whether to store your clothes in the closet or in a dresser. What you choose doesn't really matter as long as you're happy with your decision. Usually, you're better off sticking with Approach's default setting (the dBASE IV.DBF format) unless you have a specific need for another file format.

After you decide which database file format to use, the next step is to make fields that actually store your data. A *field* divides your information into categories such as names, addresses, and phone numbers. In defining the fields that make up your database, you can exercise real control over what kind of information your database contains and how that information is organized. Approach gives you lots of options. You can create database fields, define what kind of data each field contains, determine the lengths of the fields, and much more.

How do you want to save your data?

Whenever you create a database file, Approach gives you a choice about whether you want to store your data in one of a long list of file formats. For example, the formats you're most likely to use are Paradox (with a file extension of DB), Access (MDB), dBASE (DBF), or FoxPro (DBF) file formats. Although Approach couldn't care less which file format you choose, you may want to store your data in a certain file format so that other people using a different program can access the file.

Why does Approach offer so many different database file formats from which to choose? If you need to share data with people who use dBASE, save your database files in a dBASE (DBF) file format. If you need to share data with people who use Paradox, save your database files in Paradox (DB) files. By giving you so many choices for storing data, Approach tries to make sure that you can share your data with practically anyone.

Unless you specify otherwise, Approach stores your data in the dBASE IV (DBF) file format.

Making sure that you get the right data

Database fields can hold any type of information such as names, addresses, phone numbers, ages, or marital status. Inevitably someone thinks he's being clever by typing in nonsensical information in a database field, such as typing **Yes** in the following database field:

Sex: ____

Besides revealing a lack of imagination and creativity, typing the wrong data in a database field can mess up the integrity of your database. After all, if you create a database to hold names and addresses, but some jerk types in phone numbers and ages, your database is next to worthless.

To ensure that fields actually contain the type of information they're designed to hold, Approach enables you to define the names of fields and the type of data that field is supposed to store. Fields can store the following eight different types of data:

✔ *Text fields* typically contain information such as names, addresses, and phone numbers.

✔ *Numeric fields* typically contain information such as ages, salaries, and quantities.

✔ *Memo fields* typically contain supplementary information such as brief notes or comments that you want to add. In a personnel database, a memo field may contain information such as "Unreliable worker" or "Groom him for a management position because he owes me money."

✔ *Boolean fields* contain information such as Yes, No, Y, N, 1, or 0. Boolean fields can be used for storing information such as "Yes! I want a free trial subscription to *The Weekly World News*."

✔ *Date fields* contain (surprise!) dates in a variety of formats, such as July 4, 1997; 7-4-97; or 7/4/97.

✔ *Time fields* contain (another surprise) time in a variety of formats, such as 5:34 PM or 17:34.

✔ *Picture fields* contain pictures. In a personnel database, a picture field may contain actual digitized photographs of each employee.

✔ *Calculated fields* contain formulas that calculate a result. A calculated field may be used to add up the number of vacation days someone has, based on the number of years they've been employed.

See Figure 12-6 for examples of different types of database fields.

Okay, now that you've got an idea of the kinds of database fields you can define in Approach, see how you can use that information to create fields in a database.

Making your own fields of dreams

Assuming that none of the Approach SmartMasters exactly meet your needs for a new database, you can define your own database structure by creating the fields you do need to meet your particular needs. In the name of freedom, Approach provides two ways to define the fields of a database:

✔ Create them yourself (the hard way).

✔ Modify a predefined database template that Approach has already created (the easy way).

Text fields   Numeric field   Time field   Date field

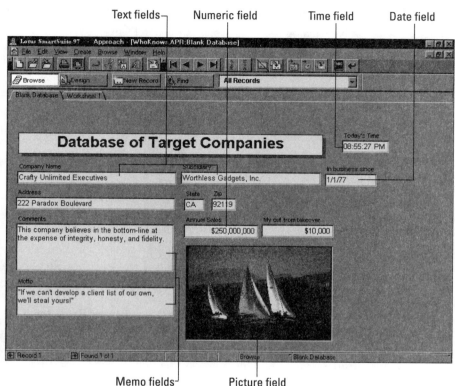

Memo fields   Picture field

If, for example, you raise show dogs and want a database to store their names, medical records, and ancestry, you aren't going to find a SmartMaster with the correct fields predefined for you. So you have two choices: You can use a predefined database template and modify that template, or you can just create your own database from scratch. The method you choose depends on how easily you can modify a predefined database template to do what you want.

Creating fields from a template

Just as in high school, the easiest way to do anything is to copy from somebody else and pass the work off as your own. Because Approach has predefined more than 50 database templates already, using one of these templates is a lot easier than creating your own. To create fields by using one of Approach's predefined templates, follow these steps:

1. Choose File⇨New (or click the Create a New Database File SmartIcon).

A New dialog box appears, as shown in Figure 12-7.

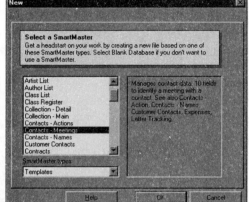

Figure 12-7:
A list of
available
templates
on which to
base your
database.

2. Choose Templates from the SmartMaster types drop-down list and then select from the list the SmartMaster template you want to use.

Do not choose the Blank Database SmartMaster. If you insist on starting from scratch, read the following section.

3. Click OK.

A different New dialog box appears. This one is similar to the Save Approach File As dialog box.

4. In the Create Type drop-down list, select the file format you want Approach to use for your database.

5. Type a name for your database file (such as Friends) **in the File name text box, and click OK.**

Approach displays your newly created database as Form 1. You can now modify the form to your own requirements. (You can read more about how to do that in Chapter 13.)

Creating fields from scratch

Creating database fields from scratch isn't necessarily hard, just a bit more time-consuming and troublesome than using one of Approach's templates — kind of like buying ingredients at a supermarket and then mixing them up yourself instead of going to a restaurant and ordering a gourmet meal.

To create database fields from scratch, perform the following steps:

1. **Choose File⇨New (or click the Create a New Database File SmartIcon).**

   A New dialog box appears. (Refer back to Figure 12-7.)

2. **Choose Blank Database from the SmartMaster list.**

3. **Click OK.**

   A different New dialog box appears. This one is similar to the Save Approach File As dialog box.

4. **In the Create type drop-down list, select the file format you want Approach to use for your database.**

5. **Type the name you want for your new database in the File name text box and then click Create.**

   A Creating New Database dialog box appears, as shown in Figure 12-8.

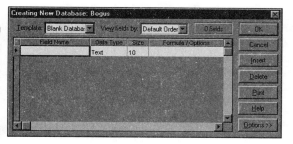

Figure 12-8: The Creating New Database dialog box.

You're not too late — you can still choose to use a template instead of creating fields from scratch. Just select a template from the Template drop-down list and click OK to fill the Creating New Database dialog box with fields from the template.

3. **Type the name of your field under the Field Name category and press Tab.**

   The names of your fields can be as logical or irrational as you like. You can name your field *NAME* and store people's names in the field, for example, or you can name your field *SDIOEK* and store addresses. Approach doesn't care what you name your field, so use any name you want. Just pick a name that makes clear what kind of information the data field contains — otherwise, you (and anyone who uses your database) may have a hard time entering and looking up stuff later.

4. **Click the Data Type list box and choose a data type (such as Text, Numeric, and so on) and press Tab.**

5. Type a size for your field in the Size text box and press Tab.

Make sure that the size you choose for your field is large enough to hold the longest block of data for that field. If you know that somebody has a last name of 10 letters, for example, make sure that you specify a Last Name field that can contain 10 or more characters. (*Note:* Some fields, such as Date, Time, and Boolean, don't enable you to choose a size.)

6. Repeat Steps 3 through 5 for each field that you want to create and then click OK after you're done.

Your new database is complete and ready for you to begin entering data!

Chapter 13

Designing Database Forms That Work

*F*orms are nothing more than windows that enable you to look at one record stored in your database. (If you need to look at two or more records simultaneously, you must switch to the Worksheet view.) As you create a database, Approach creates one form for you automatically. Because Approach is just a dumb computer program, however, the forms Approach creates are functional but visually dull.

Fortunately, you can modify forms or create new forms altogether. By creating or modifying forms, you can create your own unique views of your database records that look pretty or display only certain information. You may, for example, have a personnel database that lists your coworkers' names, addresses, ages, and salaries. You probably don't want to give your coworkers access to everyone's salary, so you can create a form that displays everything except the salaries.

Creating a New Form

Every time you create a database, Approach creates one form with all your database fields on it. You can create as many forms as you like, however, to give you different views of the data stored in your database. To create a form, follow these steps:

1. **Choose Create⇨Form.**

   A Form Assistant dialog box appears with its Layout tab open, as shown in Figure 13-1.

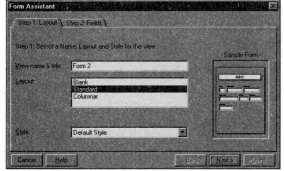

Figure 13-1:
The Form
Assistant
dialog box.

2. **Click the View name & title text box and type a name for your form.**

   If you don't choose a name, Approach gives your form a boring name such as Form 2 or Form 3. (Nothing exciting such as "Fred" or "Zon.")

3. **Click the Style drop-down list box and select from the list the style you want to use.**

   The style you choose simply affects the appearance of your form for aesthetic purposes.

4. **Select the layout you want to use from the Layout list box.**

   Blank creates a form without any database fields on it. *Standard* creates a form with all database fields arranged in rows. *Columnar* creates a form with all database fields arranged in columns.

5. **Click the Next button.**

   The Form Assistant dialog box displays Step 2 of your available options, the Fields tab, as shown in Figure 13-2.

6. **Click each field displayed in the Fields list that you want to add to your new form and click Add.**

   As a shortcut, you can select two or more fields by holding down the Ctrl key and clicking each field that you want to add. After you click Add, the field names appear in the Fields to place on view list.

7. **After you finish selecting fields to add to the form, click Done.**

   Approach displays your newly created form.

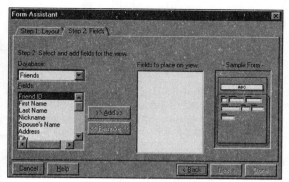

Figure 13-2:
The Form
Assistant
dialog box,
displaying
Step 2 of
your
options.

Note: In case you're wondering, you can also delete a form, thereby destroying all your hard work in creating the form in the first place. To delete a form, you must switch to Design view by pressing Ctrl+D and then choose Form⇨Delete Form from the menu bar.

Editing a Form's Design

After you create a form, you can use the form right away or pretty the form up a bit so that the poor thing looks less like an eyesore. Any design changes you make to a form affect only its appearance and not its function (much like bad sports teams that get new uniforms).

Approach offers two views for displaying your form: the *Browse view* and the *Design view*. The Browse view enables you to see what your form looks like and to add data if you want. The Design view enables you to change the appearance of your form. In Design view, Approach enables you to change the form's name, the form's border, and the form's background color.

You can switch between Browse view and Design view by choosing a menu command, pressing a shortcut key, or clicking a button in the Action bar. (The Action bar is located just below the SmartIcons. If the Action bar isn't showing, choose View⇨Show Action Bar.) To switch views, use one of the following methods:

    ✔ Choose View⇨Design or View⇨Browse & Data Entry.

    ✔ Press Ctrl+D (for Design view) or Ctrl+B (for Browse view).

    ✔ Click the Design or Browse buttons on the Action bar.

Changing the form's name

The form's name normally appears in three places, as shown in Figure 13-3: on the *form* itself, as a *tab* at the top of the form, and on the *status bar.*

You can name a form anything you want (including four-letter words, if you're so inclined), but you should choose a name that identifies the main purpose of the form. If a form displays only telephone numbers, for example, you may want to name the form PHONES.

To change the form name that appears on the form, follow these steps:

1. **Click the Design button on the Action bar to switch to Design view.**

   Approach displays your form on a grid.

2. **Click the form name text object that appears on the form.**

   Small black handles appear around the corners of the form name text object (that's the big Form 2 in Figure 13-3), and the pointer turns into a hand.

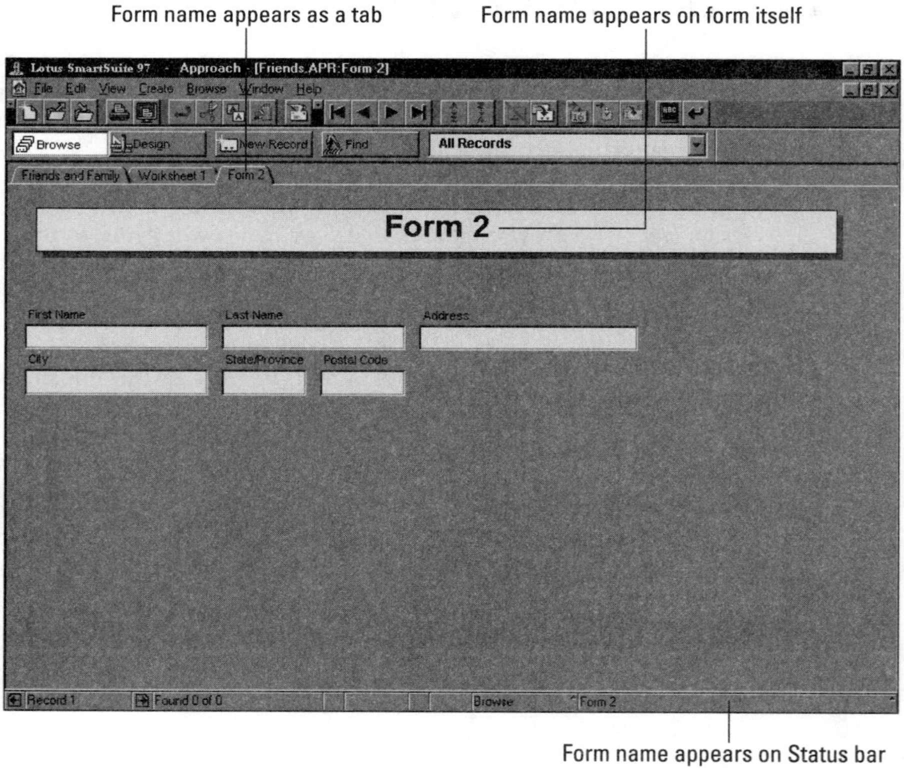

Form name appears as a tab   Form name appears on form itself

Figure 13-3:
The three
places
where a
form's name
appears.

Form name appears on Status bar

3. **Move the pointer hand over the form name text object and click.**

   The pointer turns to an I-beam and a text editing cursor (a blinking vertical line) appears.

4. **Press Backspace or Delete to erase the current form name, and then type a new name.**

5. **Click anywhere on the form outside the form name you just typed.**

The form's name is changed on the form itself. To change the form name that appears as a tab and in the status bar, follow these steps:

1. **Click the Design button on the Action bar to switch to Design view (if you're not already there).**

   Approach displays your form on a grid.

2. **Choose Form⇨Form Properties from the menu bar; press Alt+Enter; click the Show InfoBox SmartIcon; or right-click anywhere on the form and choose Form Properties from the pop-up menu.**

   A Form Properties InfoBox appears, as shown in Figure 13-4.

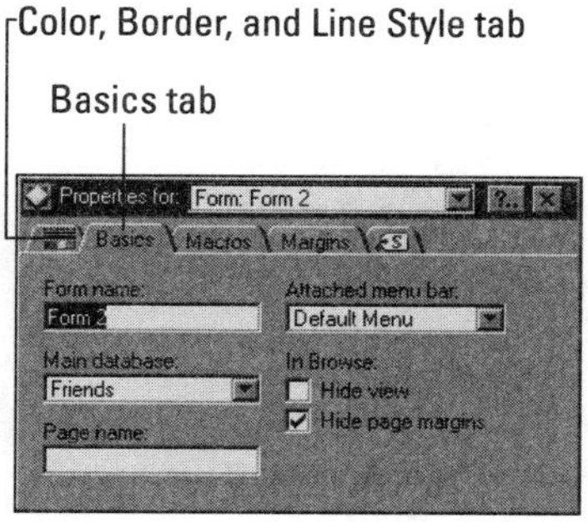

Color, Border, and Line Style tab

Basics tab

Figure 13-4:
A Form
Properties
InfoBox.

3. **Click the Form name text box in the Basics tab and type a new name for your form.**

   As soon as you move the insertion point to another InfoBox option, Approach changes the name of the form.

4. **Click the InfoBox's Close (X) button to remove the box from sight.**

Changing the border and background color

Approach also enables you to modify the following properties of your form's border: the border *width*, the border *color*, the border *frame*, and the border *location*.

To change the form's border and background color, follow these steps:

1. **Click the Design button in the Action bar.**

   Approach displays your form on a grid.

2. **Open the form's InfoBox by clicking the Show InfoBox SmartIcon, choosing Form⇨Form Properties, pressing Alt+Enter, or right-clicking the form and choosing Form Properties from the pop-up menu.**

   A Form Properties InfoBox appears.

3. **Click the Color, Border, and Line Style tab.**

   The Color, Border, and Line Style options appear in the InfoBox, as shown in Figure 13-5.

Figure 13-5: The Color, Border, and Line Style options in the Form Properties InfoBox.

4. **Click the Width drop-down list box in the Border area and select a width from the list.**

5. **Click the Color drop-down list box and select a color.**

   If you choose a width that's too small, you may barely be able to see your border. If you choose a width that's too wide, your border may look obnoxious. You may need to experiment with different widths and colors to get the right look.

6. **Click the Fill Color drop-down list box in the Effects area and select a background color for your form.**

7. **Click the Style drop-down list box and select a border style.**

8. **Make sure that a check appears in each Border area check box (Left, Right, Top, or Bottom) where you want a border to appear on the form.**

   As you make changes in the InfoBox settings, Approach updates the form to show the results of your selections. You can continue to refine your selections to achieve the effect you desire.

9. **After you're through adjusting the form's border and background color, click the InfoBox's Close (X) button to close the InfoBox.**

Changing the Form Layout

As you create a form, Approach throws your database fields on the form into neat, organized rows or columns. To further customize your form, you can move database fields around, change their sizes, or change the color, font, or border of the database field.

Moving and resizing a database field

Changing the position of your database fields on a form doesn't affect your data. The whole purpose of changing the layout of your fields is to keep yourself amused and your users happy by creating pretty forms that make your database more interesting to use.

To move a database field, follow these steps:

1. **Click the Design button in the Action bar.**

   Approach displays your form on a grid.

2. **Click the database field you want to move.**

   Black handles appear around your chosen database field, and the pointer turns into a hand.

3. **Press and hold the mouse button and drag the mouse.**

   As you drag the mouse, a box appears to show you the new location of your database field, as shown in Figure 13-6.

4. **Release the mouse button after the database field is where you want it.**

To resize a database field, follow these steps:

Gray box   Hand pointer

Figure 13-6:
Moving a
database
field.

Form 2

To resize a database field, follow these steps:

1. **Click the Design button in the Action bar.**

   Approach displays your form on a grid.

2. **Click the database field you want to resize.**

   Black handles again appear around your chosen database field, and the pointer turns into a hand.

3. **Move the pointer over one of the handles at the corner of the database field until the pointer turns into a double arrow.**

4. **Press and hold the mouse button and drag the mouse.**

   As you drag the mouse, a gray box appears to show you the new size of your database field.

5. **Release the mouse button after the database field is the size you want.**

Changing the font, color, and border of a database field

Approach gives you a wide variety of options for modifying the appearance of your database fields. The more bizarre your database fields are, however, the more confusing the form may appear to the user. Generally, you're better off not getting too wild with fluorescent colors and unusual fonts, or your database fields may look more like graffiti than a useful database that normal people want to use.

Modifying the appearance of a database field changes only the way the field looks; the modifications don't change the actual data stored in your database.

1. **Click the Design button in the Action bar.**

   Approach displays your form on a grid.

2. **Click the database field you want to modify.**

3. **Open the field's InfoBox by clicking the Show InfoBox SmartIcon, choosing Field Object⇨Object Properties, and pressing Alt+Enter, or right-clicking the form and choosing Field Properties from the pop-up menu.**

   A Field Properties InfoBox appears.

4. **Click the Color, Border, and Line Style tab.**

   The Color, Border, and Line Style options appear.

5. **Click the Style drop-down list box and select a frame or border to use for your field.**

6. **Click the Width drop-down list box and select a width.**

7. **Click the Color drop-down list box and select a color.**

   Remember: Gaudy colors may look nice if your border is narrow, but the same colors can look disastrous if your border is too wide.

8. **Click the Fill color drop-down list box and select a background color for your database field.**

9. **Click the Shadow color drop-down list box and choose a color.**

10. **Make sure that a check appears in each check box of the Borders area (Left, Right, Top, or Bottom) where you want a border to appear on a field.**

11. **Click the Font, Attributes, and Color tab and then select the Label radio button to access the options shown in Figure 13-7.**

12. **Select a font from the Font name list box.**

13. **Select the type size for your label from the Size list box.**

14. **Click the desired font styles (Bold, Italics, or Underline) in the Attributes list box.**

Figure 13-7: The Label options in a Field Properties InfoBox.

15. **Click the Alignment buttons to choose Left, Center, or Right alignment for the label text.**

16. **Click the Label text text box and type a new label name.**

17. **Click the Label position drop-down list box and select a position (such as Above, Below, and so on) for your label.**

    The label position is in relationship to the field itself, not the form as a whole.

18. **Click the Text color drop-down list box and select a color for the label.**

    Remember that colors make your database field easier or harder to see. If you're color-blind, you may want to skip this step altogether.

19. **Click the Text relief drop-down list box and choose a text relief style.**

    You can use the text relief option to make your text appear normal, appear as raised letters, or appear as if someone chiseled the text into your form. Try the different options and see what you like.

20. **Click the InfoBox's Close (X) button to close the InfoBox.**

Hey! Just look at those snazzy fields on that attractive database form. But do you have enough fields? Too many? Read on.

Adding and Removing Fields

As you create a new form, Approach enables you to choose which fields to display on your form. But people, being the forgetful, imperfect creatures that we are, may later decide to add a new database field or delete an existing database field.

To add an existing database field to a form, follow these steps:

1. **Click the Design button in the Action bar.**

    Approach displays your form on a grid.

2. **Choose Form⇨Add field.**

    The Add Field dialog box appears, as shown in Figure 13-10.

3. **Click the database field listed in the Add Field dialog box that you want to add to your form and then press and hold the mouse button.**

4. **Drag the mouse pointer across the form.**

    The pointer now appears as a fist holding the name of your database field, as shown in Figure 13-8.

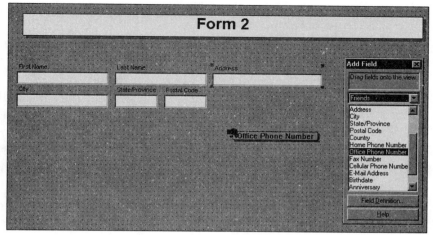

Figure 13-8:
Dragging a
database
field from
the Add
Field dialog
box to a
form.

5. **Release the mouse button after you've positioned the database field where you want that field to appear on the form and then click the Close (X) button to close the Add Field dialog box.**

Now that's great if the field you want is one that already exists. But to add an entirely new database field to a form, follow these steps:

1. **Open the Add Field dialog box, as described in the preceding steps.**

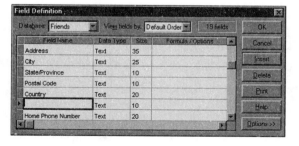

Figure 13-9:
The Field
Definition
dialog box.

2. **Click the Field Definition button in the Add Field dialog box.**

The Field Definition dialog box appears, as shown in Figure 13-9.

3. **Click the Insert button to create an empty row in the fields list at the center of the dialog box.**

4. **Type the name for your new field in the Field Name column and press Tab.**

   The cursor moves to the Data Type column, and the Data Type cell on this row becomes a drop-down list box.

5. **Click the Data Type drop-down list box, choose a data type (such as Text or Numeric), and then press Tab.**

6. **Type a size for your database field in the Size column and click OK.**

   The size of your database field is measured by the number of letters or numbers the field can hold. So a Size 4 field can hold a maximum of 4 letters.

7. **Click Close (X) to close the Field Definition dialog box.**

   The Add Field dialog box displays your newly created field.

8. **Follow Steps 3 through 5 of the preceding set of steps to place your newly created field on your form and close the Add Field dialog box.**

You may also want to delete a field from your form should you discover you no longer have a need for that field.

If you delete a database field from a form, Approach does *not* delete the actual data stored in your database. Deleting a database field simply keeps you from seeing certain data on your form, much like pulling a curtain over a window keeps you from seeing the parking lot outside but does not physically destroy the parking lot.

To delete a database field from a form, follow these steps:

1. **Click the Design button in the Action bar.**

   Approach displays your form on a grid.

2. **Click the database field that you want to delete.**

   Black handles appear around the database field.

3. **Press Delete.**

If you discover that you made a mistake and deleted the wrong field, choose Edit⇨Undo to save the day (and your database field). But you must choose the Undo command immediately — *before* you do something else — for the command to undo the delete.

Using the Tools Palette

As a shortcut to using menus all the time, Approach displays a Tools palette that you can move around the screen, as shown in Figure 13-10. The Tools palette enables you to quickly choose commands to perform the following tasks:

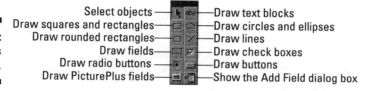

Select objects —— Draw text blocks
Draw squares and rectangles —— Draw circles and ellipses
Figure 13-10: Draw rounded rectangles —— Draw lines
The Tools Draw fields —— Draw check boxes
palette. Draw radio buttons —— Draw buttons
Draw PicturePlus fields —— Show the Add Field dialog box

✔ Draw text boxes and type text in those boxes.

✔ Draw squares and rectangles.

✔ Draw circles and ellipses.

✔ Draw rectangles with rounded corners.

✔ Draw lines.

✔ Draw a field.

✔ Draw a check box.

✔ Draw a radio button.

✔ Draw a macro button (which runs a series of recorded commands).

✔ Draw a PicturePlus field to hold a picture or OLE object. (*OLE objects* typically contain text or graphics created by another program and stored in another file.

✔ Display the Add Field dialog box.

To remove the Tools palette from sight, choose <u>V</u>iew⇨Show Tools <u>P</u>alette or press Ctrl+L.

To move the Tools palette around, move the mouse pointer over the Tools palette title bar, press and hold the mouse button, and move the mouse. Then release the mouse button after you've positioned the Tools palette where you want the palette on-screen.

Typing text and drawing circles, lines, and squares

For purely decorative purposes, Approach enables you to create text boxes and draw geometric shapes such as lines, circles, and squares on a form. Text that you type on a form and geometric shapes that you draw on a form have no effect on your actual data. To draw a text box on a form, follow these steps:

1. **Click the Draw text blocks button in the Tools palette.**

   The pointer turns into a crosshair accompanied by the letters *abc*.

2. **Move the pointer to where you want to create a text box, press and hold the mouse button, and drag to draw a rectangular text box.**

3. **Release the mouse button.**

   Approach draws a text box on the form. A flashing text-editing cursor appears in the upper-left corner of the text box.

4. **Type any text that you want, such as instructions explaining what the form does, decorative labels, or nasty words to your boss.**

5. **Click outside your text box.**

To draw a geometric shape on a form, follow these steps:

1. **Click the Draw squares and rectangles, Draw circles and ellipses, Draw rounded rectangles, or Draw lines button on the Tools palette.**

   The pointer turns into a crosshair.

2. **Move the pointer onto the form (where you want the shape), press and hold the mouse button, and drag to draw your geometric shape.**

3. **Release the mouse button.**

Adding radio buttons and check boxes

Radio buttons and check boxes can display your data in more visually appealing ways than can an ordinary database field. A database field may be called Marital Status, for example, and may contain Single, Married, or Divorced as its data. Rather than display a dull database field labeled Marital Status, however, you could use a radio button or check box to make the marital status data easier to see. A check box or radio button also has the advantage of restricting the user's input to predefined choices. And that avoids the problem of what to do with inappropriate responses such as "winner" in a Race field.

To draw radio buttons (or check boxes) on your form, follow these steps:

1. **Click the Draw radio buttons (or Draw check boxes) button in the Tools palette.**

   The pointer turns into a crosshair.

2. **Press and hold the mouse button and drag the mouse to draw a box in the location where you want your radio buttons (or check boxes) to appear.**

   A Define Radio Buttons dialog box appears, as shown in Figure 13-11. (A similar Define Check Box dialog box appears if you're creating a check box instead of a radio button. By the way, don't worry right now about the exact size of your radio buttons or check boxes; Approach automatically resizes them in Step 5.)

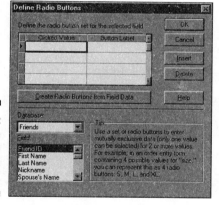

Figure 13-11:
The Define
Radio
Buttons
dialog box.

3. **Click in the Field list and select the name of the database field you want to display as a set of radio buttons (or check boxes).**

4. **Click the Create Radio Buttons from Field Data button (or its counterpart, the Create Check Box from Field Data button, if you're doing check boxes).**

   Approach automatically fills in values for the Clicked Value and Button Label columns based on information in that field in your database. (If you haven't stored any data in the database field you selected in Step 3, nothing happens at this step and you must manually enter something appropriate in the Clicked Value and Button Label columns.)

5. **Click OK.**

   Approach creates the radio buttons (or check boxes) you defined on your form.

Adding a field from the Tools palette

Although you can add database fields to your form by using menu commands, this task can be accomplished much more easily by using the Tools palette instead. The Tools palette provides two buttons for adding database fields to your form: the Draw Fields button or the Show the Add Field dialog box button (to display the Add Field dialog box).

To add a field by using the Draw Fields button, follow these steps:

1. **Click the Draw fields button in the Tools palette.**

   The pointer turns into a crosshair.

2. **Move the mouse to the form, press and hold the mouse button, drag the mouse down and to the right until the field is just the size that you want, and then release the mouse button.**

   The Field Properties InfoBox appears.

3. **Click the Basics tab and then click the database field that you want to add in the Field drop-down list box.**

4. **Click the Close (X) button to close the InfoBox.**

To add a field by using the Show the Add Field dialog box button, just click the button to open the Add Field dialog box and follow the steps listed in the section "Adding and Removing Fields," earlier in this chapter.

Saving Your Forms

While changing the appearance of your forms, make sure that you save your work periodically by choosing File⇨Save Approach File or pressing Ctrl+S.

Note: Approach automatically saves any data you type into your database fields. But Approach does not automatically save any changes you make to your forms. To prevent a power blackout from destroying all your hard work in creating a form, save your form frequently. Doing so may seem inconvenient at first but is a lot more convenient than trying to re-create an entire lost form from scratch. Really. Trust us.

Chapter 14

Finding Needles in Database Haystacks

· ·

· ·

*S*toring information in a database and viewing that information in different ways may be all well and good, but information is useless if you can never find it. If you have a database listing potential customers for a new product, you can use a database to help you filter out those people most likely to buy your product at full retail price.

You may, for example, demand of your database: "Hey, give me the name of everyone who works in Washington, D.C., makes more than $2,500,000 a year, and owns more than one home." Then your database may list those people most likely to buy carbonated beverages for their dogs, donate money to the "Save the Dandelion" foundation, and visit ski resorts located in the Himalayas.

By selectively displaying certain information stored in a database, Approach helps you uncover hidden information you may not otherwise discover. For those single people out there, this procedure is how computer dating services match people up. ("Find me all the single people interested in scuba diving, tennis, and iguana raising.")

Creating a Find

In the technical, confusing, and totally unnecessary jargon of computers, searching and finding information in a database is usually called a query. In an Approach database, however, the same process is called a *Find*.

Until you create a Find, however, Approach hasn't the slightest clue what information you want found. So, like the dumb brute of a program that it is, Approach displays a blank copy of your database form or worksheet on-screen and says, "Okay, fill in the blanks with all the data you want me to find, and then I'll go find that data for you."

To create a Find, follow these steps:

1. Choose Browse⇨Find⇨Find Using Form.

If you're currently in the Worksheet view, choose Worksheet⇨Find⇨Find Using Worksheet. Or better yet, press Ctrl+F or click the Find button on the Action bar (the row of buttons that usually appears between the SmartIcon palette and the view tabs).

Approach displays a blank form (or worksheet), along with five buttons in the Action bar: OK, Cancel, New Condition, Clear All, and Find Assistant, as shown in Figure 14-1.

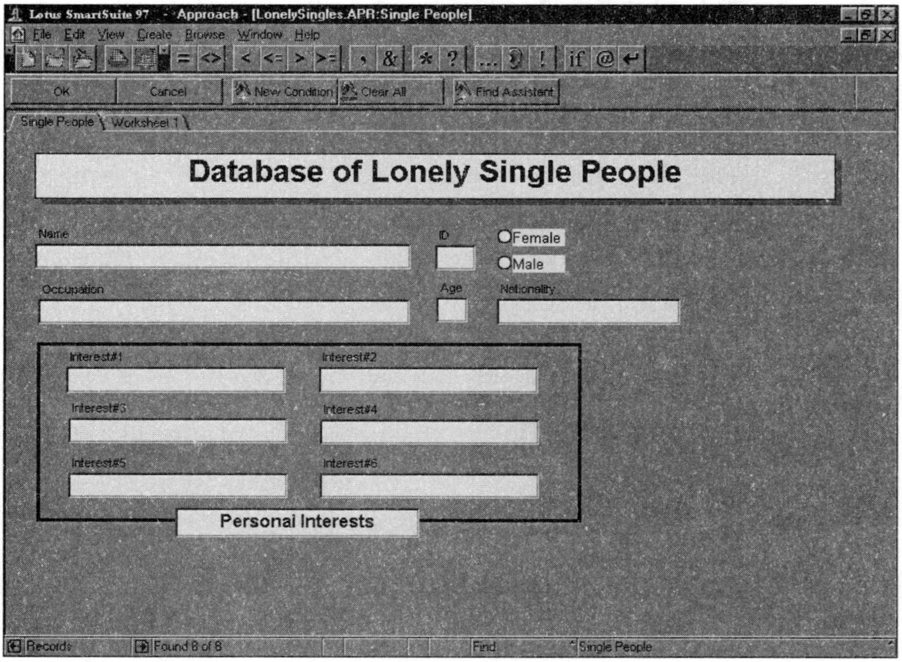

Figure 14-1: A typical blank form for a Find.

2. Click a database field and type the information that you want to find.

If, for example, you want to find all people of French nationality in the database of lonely single people, click the Nationality database field and type **French** (Finds aren't case sensitive, so you could type **french**, or even **fRENch**). If Approach can't find any record matching your Find, the program displays an error message.

3. Click OK.

Approach displays the first record containing the information that matches your Find. (If you are in Worksheet view, all matched records appear.) Approach also displays the total number of records found at the bottom of the screen in the status bar, as shown in Figure 14-2.

4. Click the Go to Next Record or Go to Previous Record button in the status bar to view the next or previous record that matches your Find.

If another match isn't found, nothing happens.

After you find the information you seek, guess what? Approach refuses to show you the rest of your database until you specifically tell the program, "Okay, I'm done with my Find. (What a stupid term!) Now show me the contents of my entire database again."

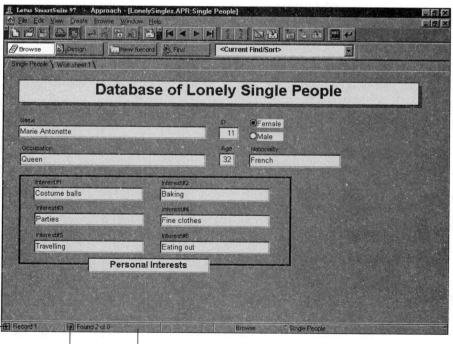

Figure 14-2:
A typical
Find result.

Go to Next Record button └─Approach displays the total number of records found here

└Go to Previous Record button

5. Choose Browse⇨Find⇨Find All; press Ctrl+A; or select All Records from the drop-down list in the Action bar.

To prove that it is now displaying all the records in your database, Approach displays a message listing the total number of records in your database at the bottom of the screen, such as `Found 8 of 8`.

Finding Records That Match a Single Criterion

Approach enables you to search for anything stored in a database, such as text, numbers, data displayed as a radio button or check box, or even empty database fields. Not only does Approach give you plenty of freedom in searching a database, but the program also provides employment for authors to write explanations for using all these confusing possibilities.

Finding text

Approach enables you to search for text in a database the following three ways:

- ✔ You can search for a *text string* (whether as part of a longer text string or not). Text strings are simply words or phrases such as *German*, *Napoleon Bonaparte*, and *Going Camping*. Text strings can even be parts of words, such as *Ger*.
- ✔ You can search for the *exact* text string.
- ✔ You can search for *part* of a text string.

Normally, if you ask Approach to find text, you just need to type the text into the database field that requires that Find information. If you want to search for *Sam* in a database, for example, you can just type **Sam** into the First Name database field. Not only does Approach then find all records containing *Sam*, but the program also finds all records containing *Sam*antha, *Sam*uel, or Hus*sam*. If this sort of return is what you want, fine. Just go ahead and type **Sam** in the First Name database field. (See if we care.)

If you want Approach to find only an exact text string (*Sam* instead of *Sam*antha), on the other hand, you must type an *equal sign* (=) in front of the text string, as follows: **=Sam**.

If you want to find all records that do *not* contain a specific text string, use the *not equal sign* (<>) in front of a text string. To find all records that do not have *George* in the First Name field, for example, you type: **<>George**.

Sometimes you may know part of a word that you want to find, but you don't know the exact word. Rather than throw your arms up in despair, you can use wildcards. _Wildcards_ enable you to tell Approach, "Okay, I know part of what I want to find, so I'll just type that part and let you find the rest."

Approach provides two different wildcards: the _asterisk_ (*) and the _question mark_ (?). The asterisk represents multiple characters, and the question mark represents a single character.

Suppose, for example, that you type the following into a City database field: **De***.

Approach finds all records beginning with _De_, such as _De_troit, _De_s Moines, or _De_Paul. (Actually, if you type **De** without the asterisk, Approach finds the same records because the program finds partial matches to Find entries by default. But this example gives you the idea of how the wildcard thing works.)

Here's where the asterisk earns its keep. Suppose that you type the following into a Last Name database field: ***ck**.

Approach finds all records that end with the letters _ck_, no matter how long the word, such as Bla_ck_, Lu_ck_, or Ale_ck_.

Now, say that you type the following into a First Name database field: **B???**.

Approach finds all records that are four characters long and begin with _B_, such as _B_lue, _B_orr, or _B_uck — and only those records. The program doesn't match longer words, such as _B_aker.

You can combine both the asterisk and question mark wildcards. Suppose, for example, that you type the following: **L?t***.

Approach finds all matching records, such as _Lotus_, _Latherton_, or _Litton_.

Finding numbers

Approach also enables you to find the following types of numbers:

- Exact numbers ("Show me all the people who make $35,000 a year.")
- Numbers that are greater than or less than a certain value ("Show me all the people who make less than $35,000 a year.")
- Numbers that fall within a specified range ("Show me all the people who make more than $35,000 a year but less than $50,000 a year.")

To find an exact number, just type the number you want to find in a database field. If you want to find all records containing a value of 35,000 in a Salary database field, type **35000** in the Salary database field. Don't bother typing commas or dollar signs ($) because Approach gets confused and doesn't recognize a dollar sign or a comma as part of a number.

To find a number greater than or less than a certain value, type one of the following in the Salary database field:

> **> 35000** (finds all records containing values greater than 35,000)

> **>= 35000** (finds all records containing values greater than or equal to 35,000)

> **< 35000** (finds all records containing values less than 35,000)

> **<= 35000** (finds all records containing values less than or equal to 35000)

Note: Whether or not you put a space between the symbol (=, >, <, >=, <=, and so on) and the Find string (either words or numbers) doesn't really matter. The program works equally well with or without the space.

To find all records that do *not* contain a certain value, use the not equal sign (<>): **<> 35000** (finds all records that do *not* contain 35,000).

To find a value that falls within a certain range, use the ellipsis (. . .): **35000 . . . 50000** (finds all records containing values that are equal to or greater than 35,000 but less than or equal to 50,000).

Finding data in radio buttons and check boxes

If a form displays data as a radio button or check box, just click the radio button or check box containing the value you want to find. For example, a form may display a person's sex as radio buttons labeled Male and Female. To search for all males, just click the Male radio button.

Finding blank (or nonblank) fields

How good data is depends on how accurately it was typed in. Just think of the last time you made a hotel reservation, but the hotel had no record of your reservation. All your information may have been typed into the computer database correctly, but someone may have forgotten to type your last name into the Last Name database field. So when the hotel clerk tries to find your reservation by typing your last name, the database never finds your last name because the name was never typed in its field. As far as the computer is concerned, your hotel reservation doesn't exist, and you must sleep in the lobby instead.

To help you find blank fields in your database, just type an equal sign (=) all by itself in a database field. If you want to find nonblank fields in your database, just type a not equal sign (<>) all by itself in a database field.

Finding Records That Match Multiple Criteria

Searching a database by using only one field can be too general, much like searching a database of single people and finding only names belonging to people of the opposite sex. Just as you can use a dating database to find specific names, you can use Approach to search a database by using multiple criteria. You can, for example, ask Approach: "Look in my high school database and show me all the people who live on this street and earn less than $50,000 a year." Then Approach may display the names of your high school prom queen, class president, and the guy voted Most Likely to Succeed. (But not *your* name, of course.)

By using multiple criteria to search through a database, Approach enables you to narrow your search so that you find exactly what you're looking for. To use multiple criteria to search a database, just type the information you want to find in two or more database fields. To find all males in a database who are younger than 30 years old, for example, you may enter the information shown in Figure 14-3.

If you search for data in two or more database fields, you're telling Approach: "Find me all records containing information A *and* information B."

Sometimes you may want to search for all records containing information A *or* information B. You may, for example, want to find all people in a database whose nationality is American or British. In this case, you type the following in the Nationality database field:

American, British

The comma tells Approach: "Find all records that contain either 'American' or 'British' in the Nationality database field."

Age database field   Male and Female radio buttons

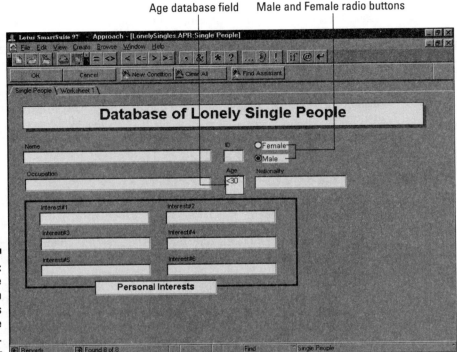

Figure 14-3:
An example
of a search
that uses
multiple
criteria.

"Hooked on Phonics" — Finding Sound-Alike Data

In spite of the insistence of our public school systems, not everyone knows how to spell correctly. Of course, in conversation, that doesn't really matter as long as you know what you're trying to say. If you search a database, however, you find that Approach is usually pretty picky about the commands it accepts.

If you tell Approach to find all names beginning with *C*, Approach may find names such as *C*aryn, *C*rystal, or *C*arol. But what if you don't have the slightest idea how something is spelled but remember how it sounds? If this were high school, you'd get a failing grade (or maybe not, considering the quality of too many of today's schools). Fortunately, Approach accommodates such problems by enabling you to search database fields phonetically (or, to use phonics, *fonetikalee*).

To tell Approach to search the database phonetically instead of just searching a database for, say, all names beginning with *C*, type the name the way it sounds and put a tilde symbol (~) in front of it. To search for *Carol Johnson*, for example, you could type the following in the Name database field:

~Karol Jonson

Approach does its best to figure out what you're trying to spell and digs up the names that most closely match what you write phonetically.

If you spell something phonetically but Approach says that it can't find anything, that could mean that no data matches your phonetic Find — or that Approach simply can't understand what you tried to phonetically write out. Try again with a different spelling.

Sending the Find Assistant on a Search

If entering all those symbols (=, <, ~, *, <>, . . .) into the database form seems confusing, you may want to try Approach's other way of defining Finds — the *Find Assistant*. Basically, the Find Assistant does the same things we've been describing on these last few pages. You just define the Find in a dialog box instead of a database form or worksheet. The difference is that you can choose the *operator* (equals, does not equal, and so on) from a list of descriptive words instead of typing arcane symbols.

To create a Find with the Find Assistant, follow these steps:

1. **Choose Browse⇨Find⇨Find Assistant from the menu bar; click the Find button and then the Find Assistant button on the Action bar; or press Ctrl+I.**

   (*Note:* The Find Assistant button appears on the Action bar after you enter the Find Definition mode by clicking the Find button.)

   Approach displays the Find/Sort Assistant dialog box, as shown in Figure 14-4.

2. **On the Find Type tab, click the Create a new find radio button and then select Basic Find from the Type of find list.**

   The Type of find list also gives you the option of some partially pre-defined Finds. For example, you can find duplicate records or the top ten records in some category.

3. **Click the Next button to access the Condition 1 tab, as shown in Figure 14-5.**

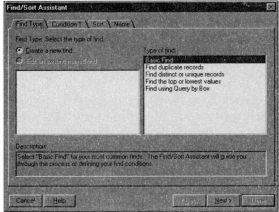

Figure 14-4:
The Find/
Sort
Assistant
dialog box
offers some
predefined
Finds as
well as the
capability to
define your
own Finds.

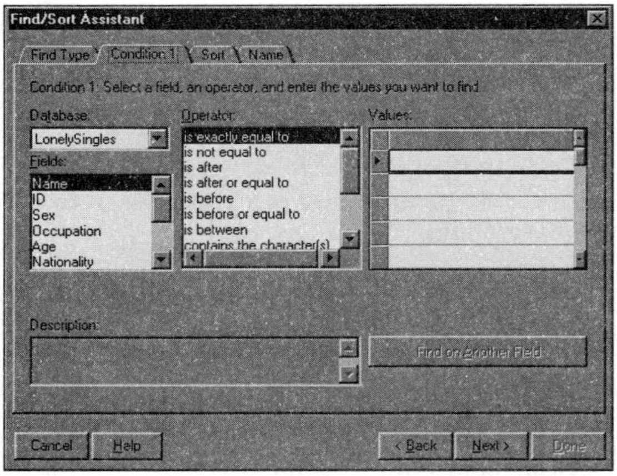

Figure 14-5:
Using the
Condition 1
tab of the
Find/Sort
Assistant
dialog box to
further
define a
Find.

4. **Select a database field from the Fields list box.**

5. **Select the kind of match you want from the Operator list box.**

   This list is where you can choose search criteria such as `is exactly equal to` or `contains the characters` (instead of those confusing symbols) to control the kind of match between the database records and the value you seek.

6. **Enter the text or number you want to find in the Values box.**

   Approach assembles a description of your Find in the Description text box at the bottom of the dialog box. Surprise! The description reads like a semi-intelligible sentence. After a Find criteria is defined, the Done button becomes available. You can define additional Find criteria or tell Approach to start searching for matching records now.

7. **Click the Done button to start the Find.**

   Approach displays the matching records just as the program does after you find records from a form or worksheet.

Saving a Find

Creating a Find can be simple or complicated — such as asking Approach: "Hey, find me all the names of people who live in Oregon, Washington, or Idaho, make more than $30,000 a year, own their own home, and subscribe to *Soldier of Fortune* magazine."

If you create a complicated Find that you may need to use again in the future, you can tell Approach to save that Find. Then, the next time you need to search your database for the same information, you just tell Approach: "Remember the last time I asked you to find everyone who lives in Oregon, Washington, or Idaho, makes more than $30,000 a year, owns their own home, and subscribes to *Soldier of Fortune* magazine? Well, find that information for me again."

Saving your Finds enables you to store often-used searches so that you don't need to specify the search criteria all over again. *Note:* Saving the find saves the criteria, not the results of the find. When you reuse the find, Approach performs a new search of the database using the saved criteria and displays the results — including all the latest updates to the database that match the find criteria. To save a Find, follow these steps:

1. **Create a Find by using your favorite of the techniques described in the preceding sections of this chapter and then have Approach display the matching records.**

   Note: This step isn't absolutely necessary, because you can define a new Find before you save that Find. You often must fine-tune the Find criteria, however, to obtain the results you want; saving a Find that you have already tested, therefore, usually works better than starting from scratch, because you know the existing Find works and produces the desired results.

2. **To save a named Find, choose Create⇨Named Find/Sort.**

   Approach displays the Named Find/Sort dialog box (see Figure 14-6).

3. **Type a name for your Find in the Edit name text box and press Enter.**

   Your new name replaces `<Current Find/Sort>` in the list box.

4. **Click Done.**

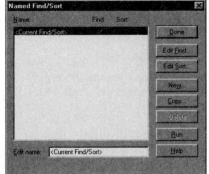

Approach saves the Find under the name you specified and closes the dialog box. Now you can reuse the Find any time you need it without redefining the Find each time.

To run a stored Find, follow these steps:

1. **Choose Create➪Named Find/Sort.**

   The Named Find/Sort dialog box appears, listing the available Finds in the Name list box.

2. **Click in the list the name of the Find that you want to run.**

3. **Click the Run button.**

   Approach finds the matching records for you according to the instructions in the saved Find.

You can also apply named Finds by selecting the name from the drop-down list box in the Action bar of your form. Approach applies the Find immediately. Now *that's* slick!

Chapter 15

Don't Be Out of Sorts Sorting Your Database

. . . .

. . . .

*A*ny database can store massive amounts of information, but what good are massive amounts of information if none of that information is organized? Imagine how frustrated you'd feel if you walked into a library in which someone had thrown all the books on the floor and you had to wade through the mess to find the three books that you really wanted to read.

To avoid this helter-skelter method of storing data, Approach enables you to sort your databases. By sorting your database, you can organize your data so that you can easily view the information you want. You may, for example, have a database listing names and phone numbers of potential customers. Approach can sort this data alphabetically by sales region or numerically by area code. By reorganizing your databases, Approach helps you make sense out of the information you keep in your databases.

Sorting Explained

Each time you type data into an Approach database, Approach cheerfully stacks the data in exactly the order you type that information. Because most people enter data in a way that's personally convenient — without concern for how the data's organized — most data isn't organized in a way that's useful.

Fortunately, you can tell Approach: "Hey, stupid, sort all my information." Approach then asks: "Okay, boss, but how do you want to sort your information?" After smacking Approach up side the head, you can tell the pesky program: "Sort the information alphabetically by last name." In the blink of an eye, Approach obeys your commands and sorts your data alphabetically.

Whenever you want to sort a database, you must tell Approach these two things:

✔ Which database field to use for sorting

✔ How to sort the data (the only choices being in *ascending* or *descending* order)

To sort a database alphabetically by last name, tell Approach to sort by using the Last Name database field. To sort by state, tell Approach to sort by using the State database field. And to sort by age, tell Approach to sort by using (what else?) the Age database field. Then, after you decide which database field to use for sorting, you must tell Approach whether you want to sort in ascending or descending order.

Ascending order sorts data from lowest to highest, such as from A to Z or 0 to 9. *Descending order* (surprise!) sorts data from highest to lowest, such as from Z to A or 9 to 0.

Changing the Sort Order by Using One Field

The easiest way to sort a database is to use one database field, such as the Last Name field or the Zip Code field. You can sort your database while in Worksheet view or Form view. For more on Worksheet view and Form view, see Chapter 12.

Because Worksheet view shows multiple records of your database at the same time, you can see your data more easily if the data is sorted in Worksheet view rather than in Form view.

If you used a Find to display a portion of your database records, press Ctrl+A before sorting your database. Otherwise, Approach sorts only the limited number of records that your Find displays. The remaining records remain in the order in which they were originally entered.

To sort a database in Worksheet view, follow these steps:

1. **Choose View⇨Browse & Data Entry; click the Browse button on the Action bar; or press Ctrl+B.**

2. **Click the Worksheet tab to view your data in the worksheet grid.**

3. **Click the database field (the column) that you want to use for sorting.**

   To sort by last name, for example, click the Last Name database field. Approach highlights the entire column (see Figure 15-1).

4. **Choose Worksheet⇨Sort to display a cascading menu of sorting options.**

5. **Choose either Ascending or Descending from this menu.**

   Approach magically sorts your database.

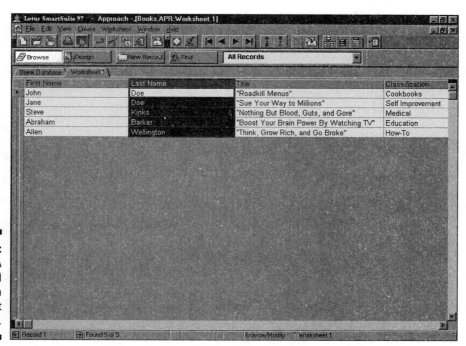

Figure 15-1:
A highlighted column in Worksheet view.

To sort a database in Form view, follow these steps:

1. **Choose View⇨Browse & Data Entry; click the Browse button on the Action bar; or press Ctrl+B.**

2. **Click the Form tab to view your data in Form view.**

   Note: Until you change the name of the form (as described in Chapter 13), Approach uses the generic name Blank Database on Form tabs, as shown back in Figure 15-1.

3. **Click the database field you want to use for sorting.**

   To sort by last name, for example, click the Last Name database field.

4. **Choose Browse⇨Sort to open the Sort cascading menu.**

5. **Choose either Ascending or Descending from this menu.**

   Approach sorts your database, although in Form view you can't easily tell that the program really does any sorting.

As a shortcut to sorting, just click the database field that you want to sort by and then click either the Ascending or Descending Sort SmartIcon (see Figure 15-2).

Ascending Sort SmartIcon ⎤ ⎡ Descending Sort SmartIcon

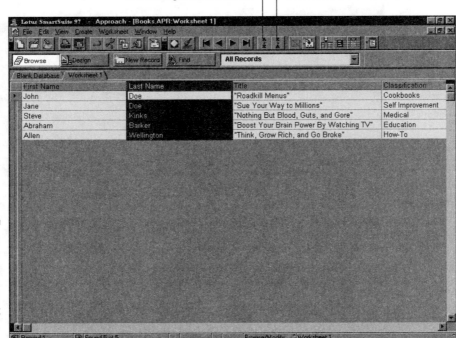

Figure 15-2:
The
Ascending
and
Descending
Sort
SmartIcons.

Multifield Sorting

Sorting by a single database field is nice, but for more power, Approach enables you to sort by using two or more database fields simultaneously. If using multiple database fields for sorting, you must tell Approach the order in which to sort your data. If you sort a database alphabetically by last name, for example, what happens if you have two Smiths or three Johnsons in your database? To avoid this dilemma, tell Approach: "Okay, sort my data by last name. And if you have any duplicate last names, sort the duplicates alphabetically by first name."

In this case, the Last Name field first tells Approach how to sort data. If any duplicates exist, the next database field tells Approach how to sort the duplicates, and so on.

To sort a database by using multiple fields in Worksheet view, follow these steps:

1. **Choose View⇨Browse & Data Entry; click the Browse button on the Action bar; or press Ctrl+B.**

2. **Click the Worksheet tab to view your data in the worksheet grid or click the Form tab to view your data in Form view.**

3. **Choose Worksheet⇨Sort⇨Define or press Ctrl+T in the Worksheet view (or choose Browse⇨Sort⇨Define in the Form view).**

   The Sort dialog box appears (see Figure 15-3).

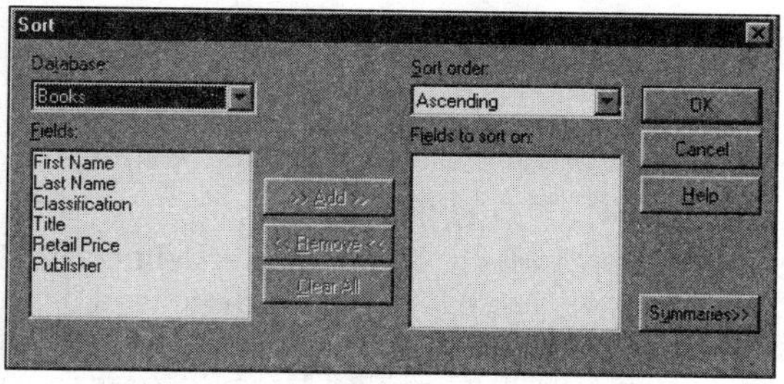

Figure 15-3:
The Sort
dialog box.

4. **In the Fields list box, click the first database field you want Approach to use for sorting.**

5. **Click the Add button.**

6. **Click the database field in the Fields to sort on list and then select either Ascending or Descending from the Sort order drop-down list.**

7. **Click the next database field in the Fields list box that you want Approach to use for sorting and click Add again.**

Repeat Steps 6 and 7 for each database field that you want to use for sorting.

8. **Click OK.**

Approach sorts your database in the order that you added fields. (Isn't it nice to boss your computer around for a change?)

Saving a Sort

Multifield Sorts are very useful, and you may find yourself setting up the same Sorts over and over again. If that happens, you can save time and effort by saving your Sort specifications so that you can reuse those Sorts in the future without redefining the Sort each time.

You do that by using Approach's Find/Sort Assistant dialog box. You discover one strange thing about saving a search this way — you must define a Find as well as a Sort. But that requirement is not really as strange as the idea may seem, because you often want to combine a Find and a Sort anyway. And if you really need to save only the Sort, just define a Find that finds all the records in the database.

To save a Sort definition, follow these steps:

1. **Choose Browse⇨Find⇨Find Assistant (or Worksheet⇨Find⇨ Find Assistant) or press Ctrl+I.**

This action opens the Find/Sort Assistant dialog box.

2. **Define a Find.**

If you need a refresher on defining a Find, see the "Sending the Find Assistant on a Search" section in Chapter 14.

If you want to sort all the records in the database, define a Find that finds all the records. For example, you can choose a Basic Find on the Find Type tab and then, on the Condition 1 tab, select any field and choose Is Not Blank from the Operator list. Click the Find More Records (or) radio button. Select the same field again and choose Is Blank from the Operator list. This procedure absolutely selects the entire database.

3. **Click the Sort tab to display the options shown in Figure 15-4.**

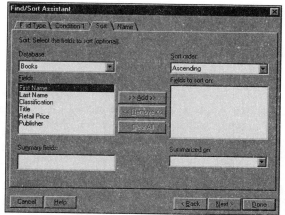

Figure 15-4:
The Sort tab of the Find/ Sort Assistant dialog box.

4. **In the Fields list box, click the first database field you want Approach to use for sorting.**

5. **Click the Add button.**

6. **Click the database field in the Fields to sort on list and then select either Ascending or Descending from the Sort order drop-down list.**

7. **Click the next database field that you want Approach to use for sorting and click Add.**

   Repeat Steps 6 and 7 for each database field that you want to use for sorting.

8. **Click the Name tab to display the options shown in Figure 15-5.**

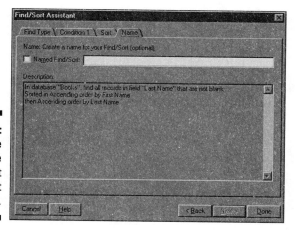

Figure 15-5:
The Name tab of the Find/Sort Assistant dialog box.

9. **Click the Named Find/Sort check box and type a name in the text box.**

10. **Click Done.**

    Approach applies the Find and Sort specifications to your database and also saves them for future use.

To use a saved Find/Sort, simply select the name of the Sort from the drop-down list on the Action bar. Approach finds the matching records and then sorts them according to the saved Find/Sort definition. The process is fast and easy! You don't even need to return the database to its original, unsorted, all-records-showing condition before applying a named Find/Sort.

Get Back — Returning the Database to Its Original Sort Order

After sorting, rearranging, and reshuffling your data in a myriad of multiple combinations, you may want to return your database to its original Sort order. To return a database to its original order, Approach gives you the following two choices:

✔ If you're in Form view, choose Browse⇨Find⇨Find All. (If you're in Worksheet view, choose Worksheet⇨Find⇨Find All.)

✔ Press Ctrl+A.

Your original Sort order? It's baaaaaack!

Chapter 16

Putting Your Database on Report

• •

In This Chapter

▶ Choosing a report type

▶ Toting up the results — Adding totals and calculations

▶ Making your reports look great

▶ Summing up and printing reports

• •

*F*orm view is great for displaying one record at a time and giving you the capability to customize its appearance. Worksheet view is great for displaying multiple records at once, but you're stuck viewing your data through a boring grid.

If a form or worksheet isn't sufficient, you can use a *report*. As do forms, reports enable you to customize their appearance. As with worksheets, reports enable you to view multiple records at once. But the main difference that makes reports so valuable is that they can also display calculations based on your data. If your database contains all the names of your salespeople, for example, a report may show you which salesperson is making the most sales and which salesperson has the highest expenses (and needs to be fired).

Standard versus Columnar — Choosing a Report Type

Approach offers the following two basic report types:

✔ *Columnar* reports

✔ *Standard* reports

A *Columnar report* displays your data in columns and rows, much like the Worksheet view. Columnar reports are best for cramming as much information as possible on a single sheet of paper. A *Standard report*, on the other hand, displays your data as a complete record, much like Form view does. Standard reports take more space to display but make studying individual records stored in your database easier. To see the difference, look at Figure 16-1.

Figure 16-1:
Comparison
between a
Columnar
(left) and a
Standard
(right) report
in the Report
Assistant
dialog box.

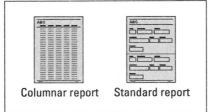

Columnar report   Standard report

To create a Columnar or Standard report, follow these steps:

1. Choose Create⇨Report.

The Step 1: Layout tab of the Report Assistant dialog box appears (see Figure 16-2).

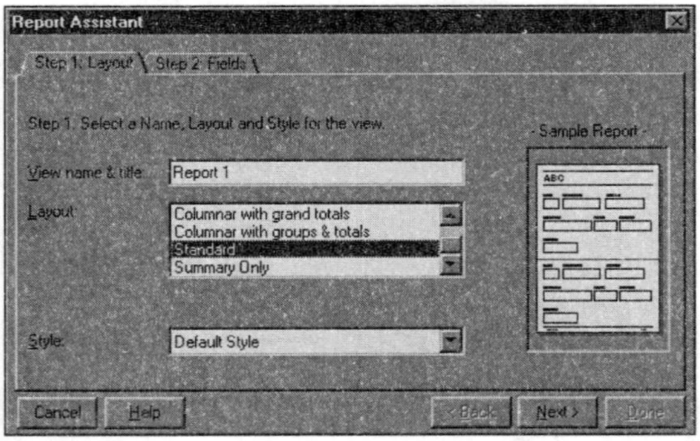

Figure 16-2:
The Report
Assistant
dialog box
displays
the Step 1:
Layout tab.

2. Type a name for your report in the View name & title text box.

3. Click either Columnar or Standard in the Layout list.

4. Click the Style drop-down list box and choose a style that appeals to you from the list.

Approach displays a preview of your report layout and style in the Sample Report box.

5. Click the Next button.

The Step 2: Fields tab of the Report Assistant dialog box appears (see Figure 16-3).

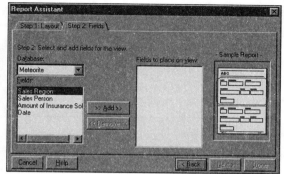

Figure 16-3:
The Report
Assistant
dialog box
displays
the Step 2:
Fields tab.

6. In the Fields list, click each database field you want to appear on your report and click the Add button.

Each database field you choose appears in the Fields to place on view list box.

7. Click Done.

Approach displays your report. Initially, the report appears in Design view. Click the Browse button on the Action bar to see the report without the distracting design grid. Then your report should appear much like the one shown in Figure 16-4, depending on the style and layout you choose.

Adding Totals

Standard and Columnar reports simply display your data in a neat format. To help you better understand your data, however, reports can display three different types of summaries (groups and totals), as shown in Figure 16-5. These report layouts offer the following options:

✔ Columnar with Grand Totals adds calculated totals to each column of a columnar report.

✔ Columnar with Groups and Totals enables you to group your information and calculate subtotals for each grouping in addition to the grand totals for the report.

✔ Summary Only enables you to dispense with all the details and look at the calculated totals only.

Lotus SmartSuite 97 - Approach - [Meteorite.APR:List of con artists]

File Edit View Create Browse Window Help

Browse | Design | New Record | Find | All Records

Blank Database \ Worksheet 1 \ List of con artists \

Meteorite Insurance: List of con artists

Sales Region	Salesperson	Amount of Insurance Sold	Date
East	Bill Banks	25000	1/24/96
East	Mary Doe	4400	2/4/76
East	Mary Doe	89000	2/20/76
East	Bill Banks	5900	3/3/96
North	Joe Smith	12500	2/6/96
North	Karen Cheat	90000	2/11/96
North	Karen Cheat	5600	3/1/96
North	Joe Smith	4700	2/3/96
North	Joe Smith	86000	3/5/06
South	Lisa Nordic	5100	2/5/06
South	Nancy Brown	8200	2/18/96

Wednesday, August 21, 1996   Page 1

Record 1 | Found 13 of 13 | Browse | List of con artists

Figure 16-4:
A typical
Standard
report.

Summaries serve two purposes: to group database fields together and to calculate a total result. Figure 16-6, for example, shows a typical report using the Columnar with Groups and Totals layout. A summary can group data together according to Sales Region or Sales-person. By reorganizing your data according to sales region, you can more easily see which salespeople are working in which sales region. By reorganizing your data according to salesperson, you can see which salesperson is selling a lot and which salesperson is doing practically nothing.

Figure 16-5:
The three
types of
summary
reports.

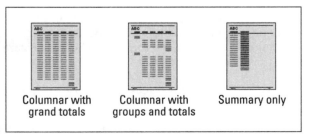

Columnar with   Columnar with   Summary only
grand totals   groups and totals

Summaries can also calculate a total result. You may, for example, want to know the total sales for each sales region. Instead of calculating this value yourself, have Approach do the job for you automatically. The following steps show how to group data and calculate a total result in a report:

1. **Choose Create⇨Report to access the Step 1: Layout tab of the Report Assistant dialog box (refer to Figure 16-2).**

2. **Type a name for your report in the View name & title text box.**

3. **Click the Style drop-down list box and choose your favorite style.**

4. **In the Layout list, click Columnar with Groups and Totals.**

   Note: At this point, you could choose any of the report layouts that offer summaries: Columnar with Grand Totals, Columnar with Groups and Totals, or Summary Only. After you choose a layout, Approach adjusts the tabs (Steps) in the dialog box to present the options and settings pertaining to that layout. We're going through the steps here for creating a report by using the Columnar with Groups and Totals layout because this type of layout demonstrates all the available options. The following list describes how the other layouts differ from the one used in this example:

   • *Columnar with Groups and Totals* includes tabs for Layout, Fields, Groups, and Totals.

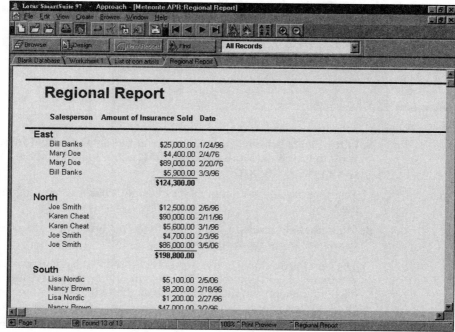

Figure 16-6:
An example
of a
summary
grouping
data
according to
Sales
region.

- *Columnar with Grand Totals* includes tabs for Layout, Fields, and Grand Totals (which includes the same options as on the Totals tab of the preceding layout type), but omits the Groups tab because those settings don't apply to this layout type.

- *Summary Only* includes tabs for Layout, Groups, and Summary (which is the same as Totals) but skips the Fields tab.

5. **Click the Next button to access the Step 2: Fields tab of the Report Assistant dialog box (refer to Figure 16-3).**

6. **Click each database field you want to appear on your report and click the Add button.**

   Each database field you choose appears in the Fields to place on view list box.

7. **Click the Next button.**

   The Step 3: Groups tab of the Report Assistant dialog box appears (see Figure 16-7).

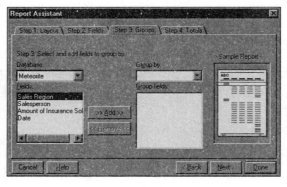

Figure 16-7:
Step 3 of the
Report
Assistant
dialog box:
the Groups
tab.

8. **In the Fields list box, click the name of the database field by which you want to group data and click the Add button to add that field to the Group Fields list box.**

   To group data by sales region, for example, click the Sales Region database field.

9. **Click the field name in the Group fields list box and make a selection from the Group By drop-down list.**

   The options available in the Group By drop-down list vary depending on what kind of field you select. The Default option always creates a group for each unique entry in the field (Smith and Smyth are separate groups). Other grouping options include grouping by the first letter of a text field (Smith and Smyth are grouped together with the other entries starting with S); grouping dates by month or year; or grouping numbers into groups of 10s or 10,000s.

10. Click the <u>N</u>ext button to move to the Step 4: Totals tab of the Report Assistant dialog box, as shown in Figure 16-8.

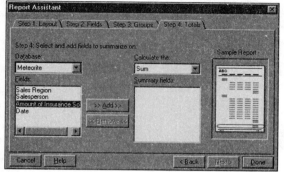

Figure 16-8:
Step 4 of
the Report
Assistant
dialog box:
the Totals
tab.

11. To have Approach calculate the sum of the data in a certain field, click the field name in the <u>F</u>ields list box and click <u>A</u>dd.

12. Select the field in the <u>S</u>ummary fields list and select a calculation from the <u>C</u>alculate the drop-down list.

   In addition to the obvious selection that Sums a column of numbers, Approach can calculate the average, the maximum, the minimum, the count (that is, the number of entries), and several other useful values. Repeat Steps 11-12 for each column that you want calculated.

13. Click <u>D</u>one.

   Approach displays your report in Design view (see Figure 16-9).

14. Choose <u>F</u>ile⇨<u>P</u>rint Preview.

   Approach now displays your report as it would look if you printed out the report.

Making Your Reports Look Great

Approach automatically creates reports for you, but you may still want to modify the appearance of your reports for the sheer joy of it (which probably means that you have waaay too much time on your hands). Approach enables you to add or modify the following parts of your report:

- ✔ A title page
- ✔ Headers and footers
- ✔ Line and color settings of database fields
- ✔ Position and size of database fields

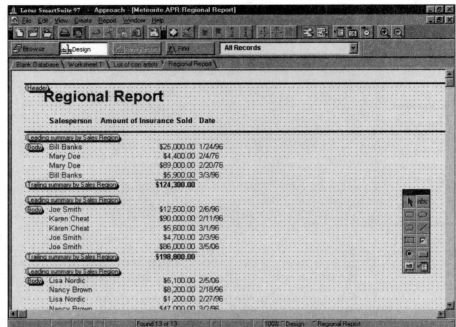

Before you can modify your reports, you must first display your reports in Design view. Choose View⇔Design, click the Design button on the Action bar, or press Ctrl+D.

Adding and modifying a title page

Title pages serve no functional purpose (much like your immediate supervisor). But (unlike a supervisor) title pages *can* be useful for decorative purposes. To add or modify a title page, follow these steps:

1. **Choose Report⇔Add Title Page.**

   Approach displays the Title Page Header at the top of your report.

2. **Add any text, lines, or other geometric shapes to the Title Page Header by using the Tools palette.**

   For more details on the Tools palette, see Chapter 13.

To hide your title page from view, choose Report⇔Add Title Page.

Adding and modifying headers and footers

Headers appear on the top of every page and can be useful for listing the database field as column headings. *Footers* appear at the bottom of every page and are more useful for listing mundane information such as page numbers, the date that the report was created, and the person to blame in case the report data is wrong.

To add or modify a header or footer, follow these steps:

1. **Choose Report⇨Add Header (or Add Footer).**

   Approach displays the header (or footer) on your report.

2. **Add any text, lines, or other geometric shapes to the header or footer by using the Tools palette, as described in Chapter 13.**

   Often you find that having Approach insert certain values, such as a page number, into your report for you is useful — especially in headers and footers. To insert a value, choose Report⇨Insert to open a cascading menu and then choose Today's Date, Current Time, Page Number, or Field Value from this menu.

To hide your header or footer from view, choose Report⇨Add Header (or Add Footer).

Changing line settings and colors of database fields

To make your database fields look pretty, Approach enables you to draw frames around the fields and change the background color. Of course, if you get carried away, your database fields can appear in eye-popping fluorescent green against a brilliant orange background. (Psychedelic, man!) Unless you're an artist, keeping frames and colors to a minimum is a good idea.

Using multiple colors can make your reports easier to read, but your reports still print out in black and white — unless, of course, you have a color printer.

To add frames or background colors to your fields, follow these steps:

1. **Click the database field on your report that you want to modify.**

   Approach highlights the entire column of database fields (see Figure 16-10).

2. **Choose Column⇨Column Properties, press Alt+Enter, or click the Show Info SmartIcon to open the Column Properties InfoBox (see Figure 16-11).**

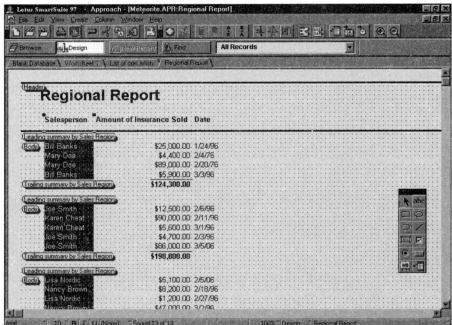

Figure 16-10: A report with a column of database fields highlighted.

Font, Attribute, and Color tab

Color, Border, and Line Style tab

Number Format tab

Basics tab

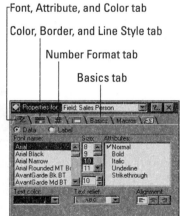

Figure 16-11: The Column Properties InfoBox for changing lines and colors of a database field.

3. **Click the Font, Attribute, and Color; Color, Border, and Line Style; Number Format; or Basics tab to change the settings of the highlighted database fields.**

4. **Make any changes you want in the different tabs of the InfoBox to modify the appearance of your database fields.**

Chapters 1 and 13 give you some additional guidelines on working with InfoBoxes.

5. **Click the Close (X) button after you're done making changes in the InfoBox.**

Moving and resizing database fields

As Approach creates a report, the program tries to cram in as many database fields as possible to fit on a single page. Most of the time this approach works, but sometimes Approach squeezes your database fields so narrowly that the data inside is partially hidden. Other times, Approach may display two separate database fields so close together that determining where one field ends and the next one begins is difficult. To touch up a report and make the thing readable, Approach enables you to move database fields around and resize them.

To move a database field, follow these steps:

1. **Click the database field that you want to move on your report.**

    Approach highlights your selected database field and turns the pointer into a hand.

2. **Press and hold the mouse button and drag the mouse.**

    Approach displays a box to show you the new position of your database fields (see Figure 16-12).

3. **Release the mouse button.**

    Approach moves your database field, along with its corresponding header, to the new location.

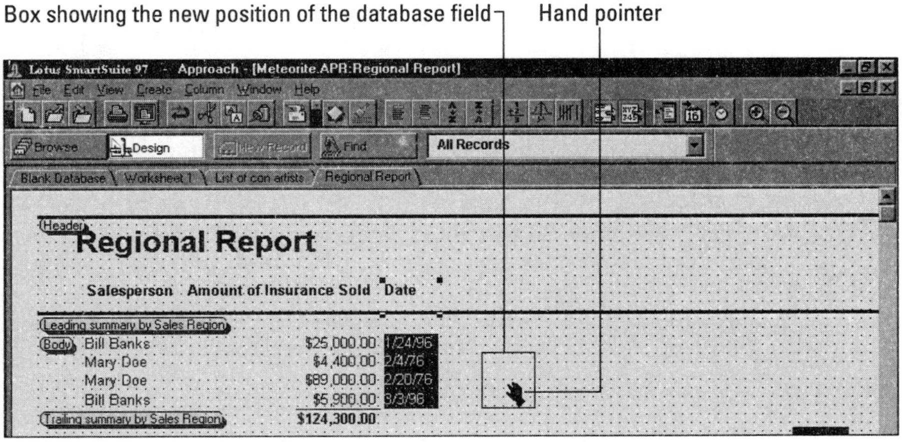

Box showing the new position of the database field ⌐   Hand pointer

Figure 16-12:
Moving a
database
field.

To resize a database field, follow these steps:

1. **Click the database field that you want to resize on your report.**

   Approach highlights your selected database field.

2. **Move the pointer to the edge of the highlighted database field.**

   Approach turns the pointer into a double arrow.

3. **Press and hold the mouse button and drag the mouse.**

   Approach shows the new size of your database field as a box, as shown in Figure 16-13.

4. **Release the mouse button after the database field is the size you want.**

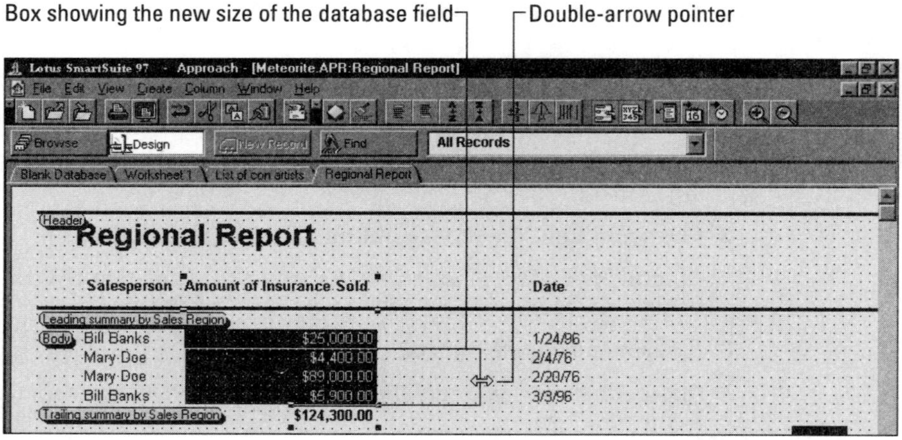

Box showing the new size of the database field ─┐   ┌─ Double-arrow pointer

Figure 16-13: Resizing a database field.

Finishing up — Adding Summaries and Printing Reports

Normally the best time to create a report with a summary is as you're creating the report in the first place. That way, Approach does most of the hard work in creating the summaries for you. Those of us who don't have the patience to plan ahead, however, can always add summaries to an existing Columnar or Standard report at a later time.

Make sure that you switch to Design view by choosing View⇔Design, clicking the Design button on the Action bar, or pressing Ctrl+D.

To display grouped data records on an existing Columnar or Standard report, follow these steps:

1. **Click the database field of the report that you want to use to group records together.**

   For example, click the Sales Region database field to group records according to sales region. Approach highlights your database field (see Figure 16-14).

2. **Click the Leading Summary or Trailing Summary SmartIcon.**

   Approach groups your records according to the database field you selected.

To add calculations to a report, follow these steps:

1. **Click a database field containing numbers that you want Approach to use to calculate a total result.**

   If you want Approach to calculate the total sales of insurance sold, for example, click the Amount of insurance sold database field. Approach highlights your database field.

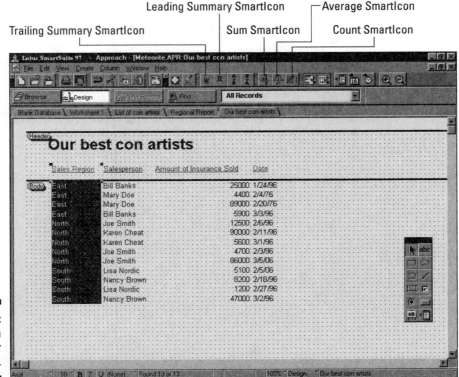

Figure 16-14:
Modifying a Columnar report.

2. Click the Sum icon.

Approach displays the total you requested.

You can also click the Average icon to calculate average sales or the Count icon ... well, you get the idea.

Printing Reports

After spending countless hours (or minutes) making your reports look pretty, printing the reports so that you can share your masterpieces with others only makes sense. Before wasting paper (and contributing to global deforestation), however, view your report on-screen first. That way, if something is totally out of whack, you can fix the problem before wasting time and printing out a report you may have to throw away after all. To preview your report on-screen, follow these steps:

1. **Choose File⇨Print Preview or click the Print Preview SmartIcon.**

2. **Click the left mouse button to see your report in finer detail (or the right mouse button for lesser detail), or choose View⇨Zoom In (or Zoom Out) from the menu bar.**

3. **Choose View⇨Zoom To⇨100% or press Ctrl+1 to return your report to its actual size.**

4. **Choose File⇨Print Preview or click the Print Preview SmartIcon again to stop viewing your report on-screen in Preview mode.**

When you're ready to print your report, choose File⇨Print, click the Print SmartIcon, or press Ctrl+P to open the Print dialog box (and then click the Print button in the dialog box). Now just stand back and watch that sucker print!

Chapter 17

Playing Matchmaker — Joining Databases

- -

- -

*I*f people shiver in fear of computers, they're usually afraid of databases. One database may store our names, addresses, and phone numbers. Another database may store our names, credit history, and driving record. Still another database could store our police record, the types of library books we checked out last month, and the magazines we subscribe to. (Scary.)

By themselves, such databases are fairly innocent. A computer, however, can examine each separate database and pick out your name from all of these databases. Then, by examining each database containing your name and joining this information together, a computer can piece together a fairly accurate personality profile of you.

This threat of computer databases watching over our lives has many people frightened to death. Theoretically, governments can join information from separate databases and use computers to monitor our lives. Realistically, however, most governments can barely deliver mail without going broke. On the other hand, joining separate databases together can produce a powerful tool for uncovering hidden information, and that's what this chapter is all about.

What's the Deal with Joining?

If you run a business, you may keep two separate databases, one containing your customers' names and addresses and another your suppliers' names and addresses. What if one of your customers also happens to be one of your suppliers? Typing this same information into two separate databases increases the chance of an error in one of the databases. Even worse, if this customer/supplier later changes addresses, you need to correct the address in both databases.

To avoid the problem of typing duplicate information into separate databases, the computer industry created something called *joining*. Joining enables two or more databases to share stored information. In this way, you can type information into one database, and the second database can access that same information. Joining serves two main purposes: eliminating the need to store duplicate information in separate databases and flexibility in displaying data stored in separate databases.

Joining establishes a relationship between two (or more) databases. Database programs that can do this kind of stuff are called *relational* databases and such programs are much more powerful than so-called *flat file* databases that must store all their information in one database. If you hear someone talking about relational databases and see dialog boxes labeled Relational Options, you needn't become confused; using such terms is just another way of saying joining.

To join separate databases, each database must have a common database field that acts as a link. One database, for example, may list employees, while another database may list the sales staff and the products each salesperson sells. The employee database could contain the names and addresses of janitors, executives, and secretaries as well as salespeople. The salesperson database, however, lists only the names of the salespeople, along with the information about the products each one sells. To join these two databases, you could use a common database field, such as a Name database field (see Figure 17-1). After you join the databases, you can look up a product in the sales database and discover the name and the address of the salesperson handling that product. Approach can get the salesperson's address from the employee database by cross-referencing the salesperson's name.

A database listing all products and the people who make them

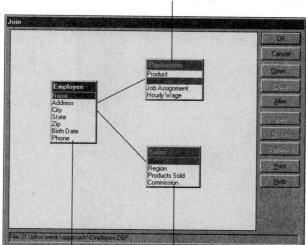

Figure 17-1:
An example
of a
common
database
field joining
separate
databases.

A database listing all employees

A database listing all salespeople and the products they sell

Getting Ready to Join

Before you can join two or more databases together, you must first create all
the databases you want to join and then make sure that each database has a
common field to share.

Approach can join databases stored in different file formats, such as joining a
dBASE IV file to a Paradox file or a Paradox file to an Access file. As long as
Approach can use a particular database file format, the program can join that
file to another database file.

How to join databases

After you decode that you want to join two or more database files, follow these
steps:

1. **Open one of the database files that you want to join.**

2. **Choose Create⇨Join from the menu bar.**

   The Join dialog box appears, displaying your current database and its
   fields (see Figure 17-2).

Fields   Database name

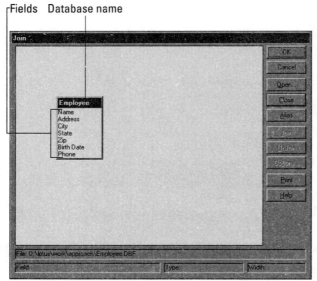

Figure 17-2:
A database
and its
fields.

3. **Click the Open button to open the Open dialog box. (Honest!)**

4. **In the Open dialog box, click the name of the database file you want to join to your current database and then click Open.**

   Approach displays your second database in the Join dialog box.

5. **Click the common database field that you want to use to join your databases and press and hold the mouse button.**

   Approach highlights your chosen database field.

6. **Drag the mouse to the common database field stored in the other database that you want to join.**

   Approach displays a line, showing that your two databases are now joined by a common database field (see Figure 17-3).

7. **Repeat Steps 3 through 6 for each database file you want to join.**

8. **Click OK.**

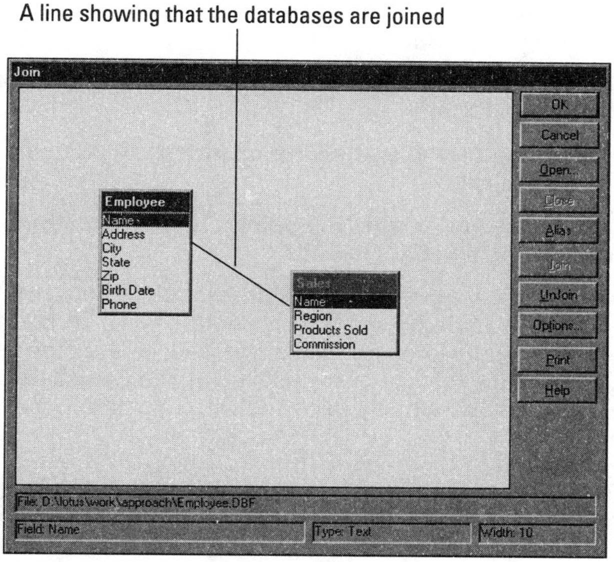

A line showing that the databases are joined

Figure 17-3:
The Join
dialog box,
displaying
two joined
databases.

Using joined databases in forms and worksheets

After you join two databases together, guess what? You can display all the fields stored in one database on the forms or worksheets of the other database. As far as Approach is concerned, joined databases are just like one big database with lots of database fields from which to choose.

To use joined databases in forms and worksheets, follow these steps:

1. **Choose View⇨Design, click the Design button on the Action bar, or press Ctrl+D.**

   This action switches Approach into Design view.

2. **Click the Form or Worksheet tab to display a form or worksheet.**

3. **Choose Form⇨Add Field in Form view; in Worksheet view, choose Worksheet⇨Add Field.**

   The Add Field dialog box appears, listing all the database fields stored in the joined databases. The drop-down list above the field names list enables you to select the database from which to display fields.

4. **Click the field that you want to add to your form or worksheet and press and hold the mouse button.**

   Just to see how this step works, select a field from the joined database to add to this database form.

5. **Drag the mouse pointer onto the form or worksheet, taking the database field along for the ride.**

6. **Release the mouse button after the pointer is at the location where you want to display the database field.**

   You just added a field from another database to the form in the current database. After you switch back to Browse view, you can enter and edit data in that field, search for data in the field, and use the field to sort your database. In short, you can do all the things with the field from the joined database that you can do with a field from the current database.

As is true of the Add Field dialog box, many Approach dialog boxes that enable you to select fields include a Database drop-down list so that you can select from which of the joined databases you want to select a field. This allows you to use fields from joined databases in Finds, Sorts, and Reports as well as in Form and Worksheet views. Pretty cool, huh?

Setting your options for joining

Joined databases create special problems for Approach. Because data is shared among separate databases, Approach has no idea what to do if you add or delete a record from one of the joined databases. Adding or deleting a record to one database means that you must also update any databases joined to the first database so that all those databases also reflect your changes.

To avoid these problems, you can tell Approach what to do if you add or delete records from joined databases. If you add a new record to a database joined to another database, Approach can automatically insert a new record into all joined databases. By default, Approach adds a new record to all joined databases to make sure that all your databases remain current. Likewise, if you delete a record in a database joined to another database, Approach can automatically delete all related records in all joined databases. If Approach didn't perform this updating, you would need to open each database file individually and update them yourself.

(Situations do come up, of course, in which too much automation can be a problem. If you add a record to the department roster, for example, you also want to add a corresponding record to the master employee database. You don't, however, want Approach to automatically duplicate every record you add to the master employee database and place that record in each of several department databases joined to the master database. Similarly, just because you delete a record from a department roster doesn't mean that you want to delete that record from the master employee database. In such cases, you need to update your databases manually.)

To set or change options for your joined databases, follow these steps:

1. **Choose Create⇨Join from the menu bar.**

   The Join dialog box appears (refer to Figure 17-3).

2. **Click the Options button (you may need to click the line joining two database fields before clicking the Options button).**

   The Relational Options dialog box appears (see Figure 17-4). By default, Approach assumes that you want to insert a new record into your joined database.

Figure 17-4:
The
Relational
Options
dialog box.

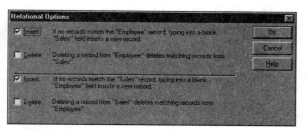

3. **Select the check boxes for the options that you want to use and then click OK.**

   The Join dialog box reappears.

4. **Click OK.**

Unless you specify otherwise, Approach assumes that if you delete a record in one database, you don't want to delete related records in joined databases. This default prevents you from accidentally erasing globs of data stored across several joined databases.

Unjoining Database Files

If you *unjoin* a database, Approach deletes any forms, worksheets, and reports that rely on database fields spread across your joined databases. Before unjoining databases, make sure that you don't need any previously created forms, worksheets, or reports as well. If you don't check first, you'll be sorrrrry.

To unjoin a pair of database files, follow these steps:

1. **Choose Create⇨Join from the menu bar.**

   The Join dialog box appears (refer to Figure 17-2 if you need to).

2. **Click the line joining separate databases.**

   Approach highlights the selected line by displaying the line in bold.

3. **Click the UnJoin button.**

4. **Click Close.**

   If you have any forms, worksheets, or reports that rely on database fields stored in joined databases, Approach displays a warning dialog box to clue you in on the consequences of your impending action.

5. **Click Yes if you're sure you want to delete all these forms, worksheets, or reports that rely on fields stored in joined databases.**

   If you click No, Approach does not unjoin your databases. If you choose to continue unjoining your databases, the Join dialog box removes your unjoined database from view.

6. **Click OK.**

Chapter 18

Final (Approach) Touches and Shortcuts

● ●

In This Chapter

▶ Producing charts from database numbers

▶ Entering data automatically

▶ Using Approach to verify data

● ●

*A*pproach provides everything you need to use, create, and modify databases. Approach goes one step farther, however, and provides additional tools for making your databases more useful.

To make sure that you type data correctly, Approach can automatically type certain data for you. To help you make sense out of your data, Approach can turn your data into charts and graphs. Although these features aren't necessary to use Approach, they can make Approach much easier (and fun) to use.

Turning Database Numbers into Charts

If you store numbers such as sales results or commissions into a database, you may find that determining exactly what the numbers mean can often be difficult. Just glance at the stock market listing of any newspaper, and you see a database loaded with numbers that don't tell you a thing. To help you understand what your stored numbers may mean, Approach can turn your numbers into *charts*. Through charts, you can spot trends or patterns in your data that you may not have noticed by staring at a massive listing of numbers. Approach can create the four types of charts shown in Figure 18-1.

Although Freelance Graphics and even 1-2-3 have fancier charting capabilities, the charting capabilities of Approach are nice for creating charts quickly and easily, without needing to transfer data between separate programs.

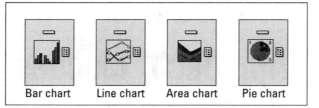

Figure 18-1:
The four
types of
Approach
charts.

Bar chart   Line chart   Area chart   Pie chart

Creating bar, line, or area charts

Bar, line, and *area charts* plot data over an *X-axis* (horizontal) and a *Y-axis* (vertical). For example, you can plot values (Y-axis) over time (X-axis). To create a bar, line, or area chart, you must specify the fields to use for the X- and the Y-axes. Bar charts are especially useful for making comparisons between items, such as sales results of different people or sales regions. Line and area charts are useful for seeing values change over time, such as with stock prices.

After opening a database, follow these steps to create a chart:

1. **Choose Create⇨Chart from the menu bar.**

   The Step 1: Layout tab of the Chart Assistant dialog box appears (see Figure 18-2).

Figure 18-2:
Step 1 of the
Chart
Assistant
dialog box:
the Layout
tab.

2. **Type a name for your chart in the View name & title text box.**

3. **Click Bar chart, Line chart, or Area chart in the Layout list box.**

4. **Choose the type of chart you want to create (2D Charts or 3D Charts) from the Style drop-down list box.**

   3D charts look neat, but 2D charts are sometimes easier to understand.

5. **Click the Next button.**

   The Step 2: X-Axis tab of the Chart Assistant dialog box appears (see Figure 18-3).

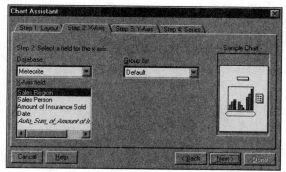

Figure 18-3:
Step 2 of the Chart Assistant dialog box: the X-Axis tab.

6. **From the X-Axis field list box, select the name of the field that you want to represent the X-axis of your chart and then click Next.**

   The Step 3: Y-Axis tab of the Chart Assistant dialog box appears (see Figure 18-4).

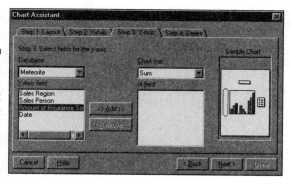

Figure 18-4:
Step 3 of the Chart Assistant dialog box: the Y-Axis tab.

7. **Click the name of the field in the Y-Axis field list box that you want to represent the Y-axis of your chart, make a selection from the Chart the: drop-down list, and click Add; repeat this step for any additional fields you want to chart and then click Done.**

   Approach displays your chart (see Figure 18-5).

X-axis

Y-axis

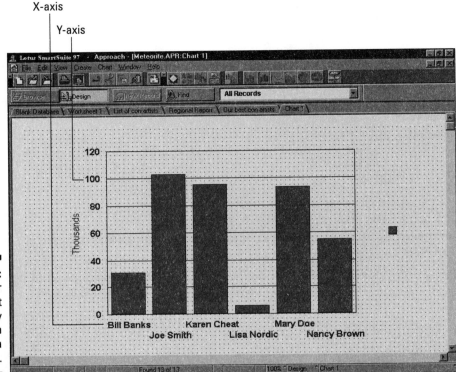

Figure 18-5:
A typical bar
chart
created by
Approach
from a
database.

You can create stacked bar charts, line charts, area charts, and more with only
slight variations of this same technique. The process of creating any chart with
an X-axis and a Y-axis is essentially the same. Of the commonly used chart
types, only pie charts are significantly different.

Creating pie charts

Pie charts display the parts of data that make up a whole, such as plotting each
salesperson's sales results in relationship to overall sales results. To create a
pie chart, you must specify what each wedge of your pie chart represents. Pie
charts are best for showing how separate parts add up to the whole — for
example, seeing the amount each sales region contributes to a company's total
profits (or losses).

After opening up a database, follow these steps to create a chart:

1. **Choose Create⇨Chart from the menu bar.**

   The Step 1: Layout tab of the Chart Assistant dialog box appears (refer back to Figure 18-2).

2. **Type a name for your chart in the View name & title text box.**

3. **Click Pie chart in the Layout list box.**

4. **Choose the type of chart you want to create (2D Charts or 3D Charts) from the Style drop-down list box.**

5. **Click the Next button.**

   The Step 2: Pie Fields tab of the Chart Assistant dialog box appears (see Figure 18-6).

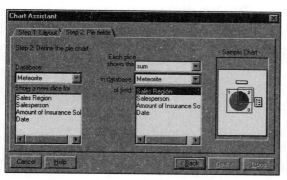

Figure 18-6: Step 2 of the Chart Assistant dialog box for creating pie charts: the Pie Fields tab.

6. **Click the database field you want to represent each wedge of your pie chart in the Show a new slice for box.**

   If you want each wedge to represent the sales results of different salespeople, for example, click the database field containing the salespersons' names. This database field must contain text, which Approach uses to label each wedge in a pie chart. Approach creates a separate pie slice for each unique entry in the selected field — in this case, a separate pie slice for each salesperson.

7. **Next, tell Approach what data to use to calculate the sizes of the pie slices in your chart by making selections from the three list boxes on the right side of the dialog box page.**

Don't let this confusing dialog box befuddle you. Basically, you make selections from the list boxes to fill in the blanks in a sentence. The sentence reads: Each slice shows the (*calculation*) in database (*database name*) of field (*field name*). Your answers tell Approach how to calculate the value that determines the size of each pie slice.

For example, suppose you want the pie slices to represent the amount of insurance sold by the different agents. You select the Salesperson field in Step 6. In the top list box, choose Sum to calculate the total value of insurance sold, as opposed to the other options such as counting the number of sales or calculating the average sale amount. Accept the default database name (unless you need to select a field from a joined database), and then select the field that holds the data on the amount of insurance sold. This database field must contain numbers, which Approach uses to create the size of each wedge in a pie chart.

8. **Click Done.**

Approach displays your pie chart (see Figure 18-7).

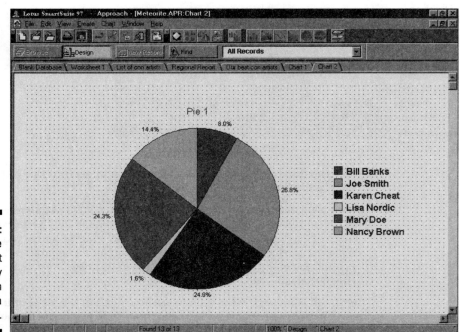

Figure 18-7:
A typical pie chart created by Approach from a database.

Automating Data Entry

To save time and make sure that your database stores accurate information, Approach can type data into your database fields automatically. Approach can type the following information into each new record that you create:

- ✔ The date or time that the record was created or modified
- ✔ The data stored in the last record you added
- ✔ A serial number that increases or decreases with each record
- ✔ A calculation based on data you type into another field
- ✔ Data that you specify

To make Approach type data automatically in each new record you create, you must tell Approach in which database field to store this information. To do so, follow these steps:

1. **Choose Create➪Field Definition from the menu bar.**

   The Field Definition dialog box appears.

2. **If the bottom half of the Field Definition dialog box isn't visible, click Options and the dialog box changes to display its bottom half, as shown in Figure 18-8.**

3. **Click the database Field Name to which you want data automatically added.**

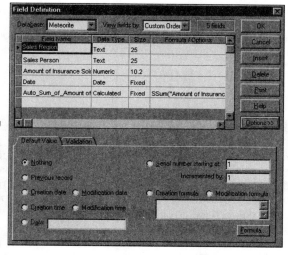

Figure 18-8:
The Field Definition dialog box with its bottom half displayed.

4. **Click one of the automatic data entry option buttons in the Default Value tab area.**

   - To enter the same data stored in the last record you added, click the Previous Record radio button.

   - To enter a date, click the Creation Date or Modification Date radio button.

   - To enter a time, click the Creation Time or Modification Time radio button.

   - To enter repetitive data, click the Data radio button and type the data you want to enter in the Data text box.

   - To enter a number that increases or decreases with each new record, click the Serial Number Starting At radio button and type in the text box the number at which you want Approach to start counting. In the Incremented By box, type a positive or negative number by which to increment or decrement the value.

   - To enter a formula that will perform a calculation and enter the result in a field, click Creation formula (if you want to calculate the result of the formula only when you create the record) or Modification formula radio button (if you want to calculate the result of the formula every time the record is modified) and then type the formula into the text box. You can click the Formula button to open the Formula dialog box, where you can build the formula by making selections from lists instead of having to type the formula yourself.

   - If you don't want to define an automatic entry for this field, click the Nothing radio button.

5. **Click OK.**

Now, when you create a new record in your database, Approach automatically fills in default values for the fields according to your instructions. It's a great time-saver.

Verifying Data

Data is only as good as its accuracy. If some jerk types his name in the Address field and his address in the Zip Code field, your database is worthless. To ensure that your database actually contains useful information, Approach can validate data as someone types the information. If a user types incorrect information, Approach displays an error dialog box and forces the user to type the correct information.

You don't need to verify data for fields to which Approach adds data automatically.

To have Approach verify data, follow these steps:

1. **Choose Create⇨Field Definition from the menu bar.**

   The Field Definition dialog box appears.

2. **If the bottom half of the Field Definition isn't visible, click Options.**

3. **Click the database Field Name that you want Approach to verify.**

4. **Click the Validation tab in the bottom half of the Field Definition dialog box.**

   The Validation options appear in the bottom half of the Field Definition dialog box (see Figure 18-9).

Figure 18-9:
The
Validation
options of
the Field
Definition
dialog box.

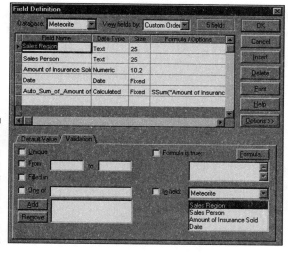

5. **Click one or more data validation options.**

   - If you don't want a database field to contain duplicate data stored in another record, click the Unique check box.

   - If you want a value to fall within a specified range, click the From check box and type a minimum and maximum value in the From and To text boxes.

   - If you want to make sure that the user types something into a field, click the Filled In check box.

   - If you want a field to have certain values, click the One Of check box, type an acceptable value in the text box, and then click the Add button.

- If you want to make sure the field contains an entry that will cause the formula to test true, click the Formula i̲s true check box and enter the formula in the text box. One use of this feature might be to accept only numbers above your minimum order quantity.

- If a field must have a value that's also stored in another field, click the I̲n Field check box and select a joined database and a field from the list boxes.

6. Click OK.

Now, when you enter data into new records in your database, Approach compares your entries to the validation standards you've defined and rejects any entries that don't meet the specifications.

This concludes the part of this book on Approach. To find out more about the many powerful options and applications of Approach, pick up a copy of *Approach 97 For Windows For Dummies*, by Eric and Deborah Ray (IDG Books Worldwide, Inc.).

Part V

Freelance's Presentation Power

The 5th Wave   By Rich Tennant

©RICHTENNANT

"Frankly, I'm not sure this is the way to enhance the colors on the Kodak CD photo."

In this part . . .

Don't fret and sweat over your upcoming presentation at the shareholders' meeting. Freelance Graphics gives you the tools you need to get prepared and organized. This part shows you how to put together all the materials you may need for a professional presentation. If you don't need to worry about your presentation materials and organization, maybe you can actually get some sleep the night before so that you really look like you know what you're doing. (You do, don't you . . .?)

Chapter 19

Boot Camp for Freelance Graphics

- -

In This Chapter

▶ Introducing Freelance Graphics

▶ Picking a look

▶ Picking a layout

▶ Adding text

▶ Adding clip art

▶ Inserting a new page

▶ Saving your presentation

- -

*J*ust the thought of public speaking causes many a mere mortal to break into a cold sweat. Worrying yourself sick about a presentation you must make probably doesn't make your talk go any smoother. But fear not — Freelance Graphics can! Freelance makes putting together all the materials you need for a truly stunning presentation easy — well, relatively easy. With the presentation materials under control, you can safely concentrate on the more important issues — such as remembering to show up on time so that the show can go on.

Presenting Freelance Graphics

If you ever must present information to an audience — or create snappy presentation materials for someone else to use — you should be pleased to know that using Freelance Graphics makes the entire experience practically painless. By using the power of Freelance Graphics (henceforth referred to just as *Freelance* to emphasize its user-friendly nature), you can delight and amaze audiences — and persuade them to your point of view every time. If you're wondering exactly what a presentation graphics program such as Freelance can do for you, check out some of the following nifty features:

- ✔ Creating presentations with a uniform look is a piece of cake with more than a hundred professionally designed SmartMaster sets.

- ✔ Create title pages, bulleted lists, charts, tables — you name it — by using Freelance's preformatted page layouts.

✔ Create speaker notes to help you get through your presentation without freezing.

✔ Create astonishing on-screen slide presentations with big-time special effects and transitions but with small-time effort.

Getting the Show on the Road

You start Freelance the same way you start any of the other SmartSuite 97 programs; just follow these steps:

1. **If SuiteStart is running, click the Lotus Freelance Graphics icon in the taskbar's system tray; otherwise, click the Start button in the taskbar, point to Programs, point to Lotus SmartSuite, and then choose Lotus Freelance Graphics 97.**

   The Welcome to Lotus Freelance Graphics dialog box appears, as shown in Figure 19-1.

Figure 19-1: The Welcome to Lotus Freelance Graphics dialog box enables you to start from scratch or edit an existing presentation.

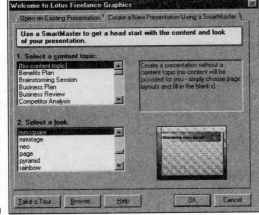

2. **Make sure that you have the Create a New Presentation Using a SmartMaster tab selected.**

To work on an existing presentation instead of creating a new one, select the Open an Existing Presentation tab and select a presentation file you worked on recently from the list of presentations. If you don't see the presentation listed, click the Browse button to open a dialog box that enables you to locate the file on your system. Click Open to open the presentation.

3. **Choose the SmartMaster design you want to use as the basis of your presentation.**

   Note: To choose a design, first you choose a content topic (which includes a set of preformatted presentation pages you can use) and then you choose a look (color scheme and background graphics) for your presentation.

4. **After you make your choices from the lists in this dialog box, click OK to open the New Page dialog box.**

5. **Choose a page layout from the list on the Page Layout tab of this dialog box and click OK.**

6. **Enter your text in the page layout template that appears.**

   Congratulations, you've created the first page of your presentation.

That's the overall procedure of creating a presentation, offered in a bare-bones nutshell (mixing of metaphors intended). But, of course, each of the preceding steps involves much more effort than described in this section's overview, and the following sections go into the gory details.

You've got the look

The first step on the road to creating a stunning Freelance presentation is to pick a *look* from the more than one hundred professionally designed SmartMaster sets that come with the program. You pick a look for your presentation from the lists in the New Presentation dialog box as part of the process of creating a new presentation file. Because these SmartMaster looks are designed by professionals, you don't need to worry about things such as artistic balance, color, fonts, type size, and so on. Of course, you *can* make all these decisions yourself, but why bother if the work's been done for you?

Don't feel pressured to make a final choice for your presentation's look right now. You can change your mind at any time during the process of creating your presentation. After you create some presentation pages, you can choose Presentation➪Choose a Different SmartMaster Look to open the Choose a Look for Your Presentation dialog box. Then you can select a different look from the list and click OK to apply that look to all the pages in your presentation.

Okay, but how do you decide which SmartMaster look to use? Freelance thoughtfully provides you with a preview of any SmartMaster look you highlight in the lists in the New Presentation or Choose a Look for Your Presentation dialog boxes. An easy way to browse through the list of SmartMaster sets is to use the scroll bar or the down-arrow key. As you scroll down the Select a look list, a thumbnail-sized preview of each highlighted SmartMaster appears on the right side of the dialog box. If you're a do-it-yourself kind of guy or gal, choose `No look   blank background` in the lists of looks in either the New Presentation or Choose a Look for Your Presentation dialog boxes to make all the creative decisions yourself. Unless, however, you possess no small measure of graphic design talent, don't try this one at home.

Getting a head start with a Content Topic

Freelance SmartMasters can affect more than the look of your presentation. SmartMasters can provide templates for the content as well. A SmartMaster content topic serves as the skeleton for your presentation with an assortment of predesigned pages, arranged in a suggested order, complete with text placeholders. You just fill in the blanks with your own text and data to produce a professional-quality presentation in a hurry.

Picking a layout

After you choose the look you want for your presentation, you need to pick the kind of page layout you want to create. Whichever SmartMaster set you choose, Freelance provides thirteen page layouts with the appropriate elements included. As soon as you choose your SmartMaster set, in fact, the New Page dialog box appears, as shown in Figure 19-2. Just as when you choose a SmartMaster set, you see a preview of the various page layouts in the right side of the New Page dialog box. You can click a layout name or use the up- or down-arrow keys to highlight a layout in the list in the dialog box.

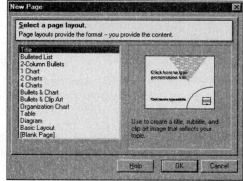

Figure 19-2:
The New Page dialog box lists the page layouts at your disposal.

If you choose to use a content topic, the New Page dialog box has two tabs. The Page Layouts tab offers the same choices as the standard New Page dialog box. The Content Pages tab offers a selection of predesigned pages, as shown in Figure 19-3. Again, you highlight a topic in the list to see a preview of the page in the right side of the dialog box.

Figure 19-3:
The Content
Pages tab
enables you
to choose
one of the
predesigned
pages that
are part of
the Content
Topic you
chose for
this
presentation.

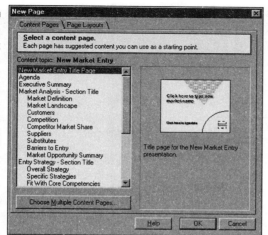

To choose the page layout you want, click an item name in the list on either the Page Layouts or Content Pages tabs of the New Page dialog box and then click OK. A page layout template appears — complete with dummy elements ready for you to replace with whatever you want on the page — as shown in Figure 19-4. If you chose a content page, some of the text may already be filled in for you.

In choosing a page layout, keep the following points in mind:

✔ You don't need to choose a layout that *exactly* matches what you have in mind for the page. You can add, rearrange, or even delete elements in any of the layouts. Picking a layout that is at least *close* to what you want, however, is a good idea.

✔ If you're creating a title page — something almost every presentation has — choosing the title layout usually makes a great deal of sense.

✔ If none of the layouts come close to what you want, choose the Basic Layout, which gives you only the graphic elements of the SmartMaster set and a title for the page. If even the Basic Layout has more stuff than you want, choose [Blank Page] to get just the background color with no graphic or text elements at all.

✔ If you realize that you chose the wrong page layout, don't panic. Just choose Page⇨Switch Page Layout and select a different layout from the Switch Page Layout dialog box.

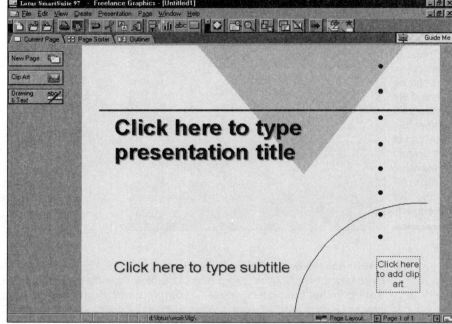

Figure 19-4:
A page
layout
template
with the
elements for
a title page,
usually the
first page
you create
for a
presentation.

Add text (and stir)

With your chosen page layout on-screen, replacing text elements with your own text is as simple as clicking and typing. As you can see from the example in Figure 19-4, each element in the Title page layout tells you to click the element to add your own data or graphics. To type the text for the presentation title on the presentation's title page, for example, follow these steps:

1. **Click the page layout element that reads** Click here to type presentation title.

   A text box appears in place of the instructions for you to type your title.

2. **Type the text you want for the presentation title.**

3. **Click the OK button or just click anywhere on the page outside the title element's frame to accept the title.**

   The text box window and its buttons disappear, leaving the text you typed.

All the elements in all the page layouts work the same way. Click the element and add the data. Some data require additional or different steps. Adding a chart or symbol, for example, requires more than just typing, but all the instructions are right there for you. If, for example, you click a title page where the text reads `Click here to add clip art`, Freelance takes you right into a dialog box where you can choose clip art to add. If you want more details on a lot of this stuff, check out *Freelance Graphics 96 For Windows 95 For Dummies,* by William Harrel and Roger C. Parker (published by IDG Books Worldwide, Inc.) for the full scope. In the meantime, keep the following in mind as you add elements to your page layout:

✔ You can't get too lost adding elements in a page layout. Notice the Tips button in the title text box. Every element of every page layout has a Tips button or a Help button. Click the Tips or Help button to access a dialog box explaining how to create the particular element you're working with.

As you enter text, you can use the Bold, Italic, and Underline SmartIcons. You can also change fonts and sizes by using the Font and Size buttons on the status bar, just as you can in the other SmartSuite 97 programs. (You may not want to change the font and size, however, because that affects the consistency provided by the SmartMaster.)

✔ You can edit text as you create it by using the Backspace and Delete keys. If you need to edit text after accepting a text entry, double-click the text element to select that text and reopen the text box with the insertion point so that you can make your changes.

Adding clip art

Because adding clip art is part of creating a normal title page, this section is a good place to sneak in a bit about this nifty feature.

Clip art in Freelance is just a little graphic — a picture — stored in a Freelance symbol library. Freelance includes zillions of clip art images for every occasion. Assuming that you select the Title layout, as described in the preceding steps, you can add clip art by following these steps:

1. **Click the page layout element that says** `Click here to add clip art.`

   The Add Clip Art or Diagram to Page dialog box appears, as shown in Figure 19-5.

2. **Choose Clip Art in the View area in the lower-right corner of the dialog box.**

3. **Select a category from the Category drop-down list.**

   After you click a category name, the first six clip art images appear at the bottom of the dialog box. (Some categories have fewer than six images.)

4. **Choose a clip art image by scrolling through the images in the chosen category and double-clicking the one you want to insert. Click outside the clip art image to accept the image.**

   The clip art image appears on the page.

Figure 19-5:
The Add Clip
Art or
Diagram to
Page dialog
box,
displaying
six Arrows
category
symbols.

Inserting a New Page

After you know how to create a title page, you already know just about everything you need to know to add new pages. To add a new page, simply choose Create➪Page to display the New Page dialog box. Surprise, this dialog box is the same one you use to create the first page of your presentation. So you already know how to use the thing. (Check out the section "Picking a layout," earlier in this chapter, if you need a refresher on using the New Page dialog box.)

Here are a couple of points to remember as you add pages to your presentation:

✔ Clicking the New Page button is an even quicker way to open the New Page dialog box. (You find the New Page button located in the upper-left corner of the Freelance window in Current Page view.)

✔ After you click OK, Freelance inserts the new page in your presentation following the page you were on when you opened the New Page dialog box. The new page appears in the Current Page view editing window, and the creation process goes on. Don't worry too much about keeping the pages in your presentation in order as you create them. Freelance's Page Sorter view enables you to rearrange the pages easily after you create them. See Chapter 21 for details on moving among the presentation's pages, rearranging presentation pages, and changing views.

Saving Your Presentation

Saving a Freelance presentation is just the same as saving a document in any other SmartSuite 97 program. Choose File➪Save, enter a name in the File Name text box of the Save As dialog box, and then click Save. Freelance saves all your presentation pages in one file.

Chapter 20

Presenting (Ta Daaah!) Tables and Charts

● ●

In This Chapter

▶ Adding tables

▶ Adding charts

● ●

*I*f you really want your presentation to persuade your audience that you know what you're talking about, you probably need to throw in more than just some fancy titles. Good news. Freelance enables you to add just about any element of persuasion, including tables and charts. And, just like text and symbols in title pages, charts and tables are just a click away.

Adding Tables

One good presentation device is putting data in a table — rows and columns — to give your data an air of organization and authority. Okay, of course your data *is* authoritative, but you must persuade your audience of that fact.

Although you can create a table on any of the page layouts, typically you create a table by inserting a new page using the Table layout. To insert a new page containing a table, follow these steps:

1. **Choose Create⇨Page or click the New Page button (located just below the Current Page tab) to display the New Page dialog box.**

2. **Select the Page Layouts tab (if you're using content topics) and double-click Table in the list of available layouts.**

   The new page, with the elements for the Table layout, appears, as shown in Figure 20-1. The two standard elements on a Table page layout are a page title and, of course, a table.

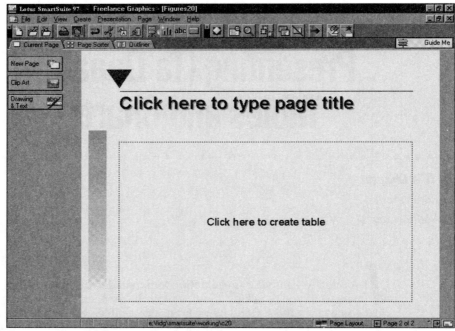

Figure 20-1:
A new page created by using the Table page layout.

3. **Click the text that reads** `Click here to type page title` **to open the text box for the title.**

4. **Type the title of the page and click OK in the text box.**

5. **Click inside the box containing the text** `Click here to create table.`

   The Table Gallery dialog box appears, as shown in Figure 20-2, giving you four available styles.

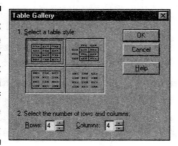

Figure 20-2:
The Table Gallery dialog box provides a choice of basic table styles.

6. **Click the box displaying the table style you want to use.**

7. **Click the up- or down-arrow buttons next to the Rows or Columns box to change the number of rows or columns in your table.**

   The default is four rows and four columns, but you can specify the numbers you need to present your data. If you are unsure of the number of rows or columns needed, you can add or delete rows and columns at any time.

8. **Click OK.**

   The empty table with the specified attributes appears on the page. Figure 20-3 shows the table after entering some text by using the default settings.

As the empty table first appears on the page, selection handles surround the table. These handles enable you to size or move the table. You can size a table by positioning the mouse pointer over one of the selection handles so that the pointer turns into a double-headed arrow; then just press and hold the left mouse button and drag the handle until the table is the size you want in that direction. You can move a table by positioning the mouse pointer inside the selected table, pressing and holding the left mouse button, and dragging the table to a new location.

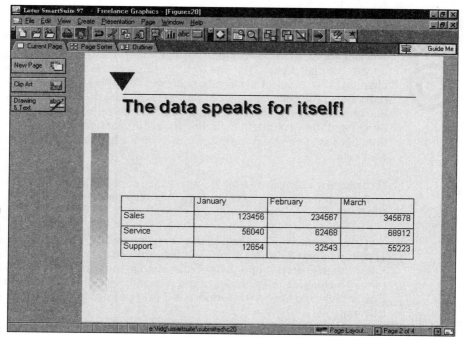

Figure 20-3:
This table
uses the
default four
rows and
four
columns.

Entering table text

To access the Edit mode so that you can enter text in a selected table, click the *cell* (one of the rectangles in the table) in which you want to enter text. A thick gray border appears around the table, and a text insertion point appears in the cell you clicked. (If you haven't selected the table yet, click the table once to select it and then pause and click again in the cell.) Type the text you want to enter and then click the next cell in which you want to enter text — or press the Tab key to move to the next cell or Shift+Tab to move to the previous cell. You can also use the up- and down-arrow keys to move within the table.

If you enter more text in a cell than can fit, the words automatically wrap to the next line, just as in Word Pro tables, and the row height expands to accommodate the extra lines. (See the section "Tabular, Dude!," in Chapter 6, for more on working with Word Pro tables.)

After you enter all the text, click outside the table to accept the entries.

Editing table attributes

These tables are not created in stone. Any attributes you want to change — table style, number of columns and rows, drop shadows, fonts, and so on — you can change during the creation process.

You can apply certain attributes, such as text formatting, colors, and borders, only to the current cell (the one the insertion point is in as you make the change) or to all selected cells. For changes to apply to more than one cell, you must select the cells you want to change by pressing and holding the left mouse button and dragging the insertion point over the cells you want to modify. You don't need to worry about including the entire contents of a cell in the selection, because you select the entire cell as you drag the insertion point to the next cell.

To make any changes to a table's attributes, choose Table➪Table Properties while the table (or any cell in the table) is selected. The Table Properties InfoBox appears, as shown in Figure 20-4.

You can choose which aspect of the table you want to change by clicking the appropriate tab in the InfoBox. If, for example, you click the Font, Attribute, and Color tab (the default option), you can change the text attributes for the entire table. To change the attributes of the selected cell instead of the entire table, choose Selected Cell in the Properties for drop-down list box in the InfoBox's title bar.

Font, Attribute, and Color tab
Alignment tab
Color, Pattern, and Line Style tab
Columns and Rows tab
Table Layout tab

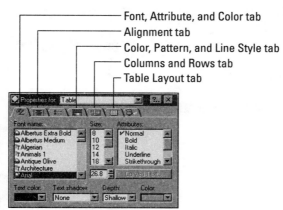

Figure 20-4:
The Table
Properties
InfoBox.

You can also open the InfoBox by right-clicking the table and choosing either Cell Properties or Table Properties from the pop-up menu.

You can modify the following attributes in the InfoBox:

✔ You can change the fonts, size, alignment, and so on of the table's text. In fact, you can make just about all the changes to your table's text that you can in Word Pro or any of the other SmartSuite 97 programs. Just choose the attributes you want to change from the appropriate drop-down lists, check boxes, and buttons.

B _I_ U   You can also change selected table text to bold, italic, or underlined by selecting the text and clicking the SmartIcons for those attributes or the corresponding buttons on the status bar.

✔ You can use the Color, Pattern, and Line Style tab in the InfoBox to assign borders, drop shadows, and background colors to table cells.

✔ The Table Properties InfoBox also enables you to change the size of a column or row and change the table style from one of the four table styles to another.

If you make a change that you didn't mean to, remember that you can almost always undo that change by choosing Edit⇨Undo Set Attributes (or by pressing Ctrl+Z).

Figure 20-5 shows our table after making a few minor modifications.

To add or remove columns or rows, use the Table⇨Insert or Table⇨Delete commands. For example, you can select a cell in the row where you want to add another row and then choose Table⇨Insert⇨Row. Freelance adds a new row to your table below the row where the cursor is located.

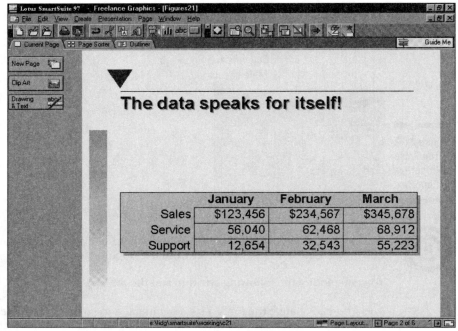

Figure 20-5:
A table
with new
fonts, text
alignment,
and style.

Adding Charts

What would a presentation be without charts? If we learned nothing else from the 1992 presidential race — at least on *Larry King Live* — charts are required accoutrements for effective presentations. Wait a minute — that guy with all the charts *lost!* Oh well, charts are still important. (And he probably wasn't using *Freelance* charts anyway.)

You usually add charts, as you do tables, by inserting a new page, using one of the page layout options that include one or more charts. Of course, you can add a chart to any page layout.

Note: The concepts for creating charts in Freelance are the same as for creating charts in 1-2-3. If this information all seems like foreign territory to you, take a look at Chapter 10 of this book before diving in — or at least before you get confused and frustrated.

To create a page containing a single chart, follow these steps:

1. **Choose Create⇨Page or click the New Page button (located just below the Current Page tab) to open the New Page dialog box.**

2. Click 1 chart **in the list on the Page Layouts tab of the New Page dialog box, and then click OK.**

A new page with a page-title element and a chart element appears. Initially, this page looks very similar to the blank table page shown back in Figure 20-3.

3. Click the text that reads Click here to type page title **and then type a title for the page.**

4. Click inside the box containing the text Click here to create chart.

The Create Chart dialog box appears, as shown in Figure 20-6.

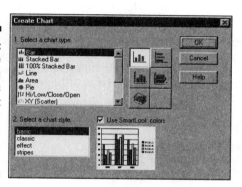

Figure 20-6:
The Create Chart dialog box features more chart types than you can shake a pointer at.

5. Click the chart type you want to use in the Select a chart type list at the left side of the dialog box.

6. Click one of the buttons in the middle of the dialog box to select a variation of the basic chart type.

The buttons change to reflect the available variations for the chart type you chose in Step 5.

7. Select the style you want in the Select a chart style area.

The style selection controls chart formatting details such as color scheme and the appearance of grid lines and such. The box just to the right of the Select a chart style area shows a preview of the chart you are about to create, including chart type, variation, and style.

8. Click OK to display the Edit Data dialog box, opened to the Data tab.

If this dialog box looks somewhat familiar to you, it should (provided, of course, you have already read Part III of this book). Its grid of numbered rows and lettered columns looks much like a 1-2-3 worksheet. You enter text for Legend and Labels and numbers to chart in the cells, just as you do in a 1-2-3 worksheet. The options and grid in the Edit Data dialog box vary depending on the chart type you choose. If you choose a pie chart, for example, only one column for a data series is available, because a pie chart can have only one data series.

9. **Enter the labels for each data series in the Labels column, the labels for the legend in the Legend rows, and the numbers for the data series in the appropriate cells.**

The *Labels* identify the different divisions in a chart. If your chart shows the earnings for each quarter, for example, you may have axis labels for 1st quarter, 2nd quarter, 3rd quarter, and 4th quarter. You can also add an axis title that labels the entire set of entries. In this case, the axis title may be "Quarters." We tell you how to add axis titles in just a bit.

You may need to experiment a little to discover how to enter the data so that it produces the chart you expect. But the procedure is not too difficult to figure out — and viewing your data charted in different ways may generate some insights and pleasant surprises. Don't be afraid to experiment!

Figure 20-7 shows a filled-in Edit Data dialog box for a bar chart.

Figure 20-7:
The Edit
Data dialog
box
displaying
filled-in data
for a bar
chart with
three data
series.

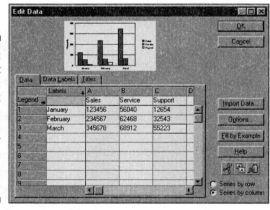

Notice that, if you select the chart, the menu choices in the menu bar change. To explore all the options for creating and modifying Freelance charts, take a look at what's available under the Chart menu.

10. **After you have the chart data filled in, click OK to see the chart on the new page, as shown in Figure 20-8.**

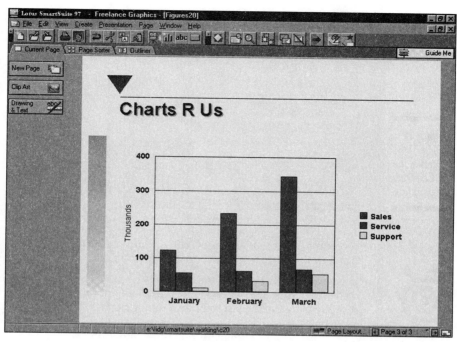

Figure 20-8:
A simple bar
chart — but
one that
sure adds
pizzazz
to the
presentation.

As you're creating and modifying charts in Freelance, keep the following points in mind:

✔ You can see a preview of what the chart looks like in the Edit Data dialog box. But remember: This representation *is* just a preview — not an exact representation of what the chart looks like on your page — but this preview is helpful nonetheless.

✔ Just as you can for 1-2-3 charts, you can add headings, notes, and axis titles to your freelance charts. You can add them while you're creating the chart by clicking the Titles tab in the Edit Data dialog box. The tab displays a group of text boxes, as shown in Figure 20-9.

✔ You can choose a different chart type by double-clicking the chart to open the Chart Properties InfoBox, selecting the Type tab, and then choosing a different chart type. (If the Plot Properties InfoBox appears, just click the chart *outside* the plotting area.)

✔ Another quick way to change chart types is to simply select the chart and then click the SmartIcon for the chart type you want to use.

✔ Don't forget to save your work (by clicking the Save the Current File SmartIcon) before making too many changes to your chart. That way, you can retrieve the original if you mess up too badly.

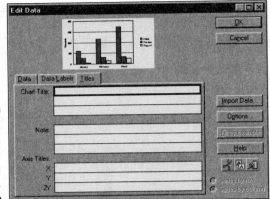

Figure 20-9:
The Titles
tab of the
Edit Data
dialog box.

✔ To edit a chart you already created, right-click the chart and choose Edit Data from the pop-up menu to display the Edit Data dialog box.

✔ Just as in 1-2-3 charts, you can modify each element of a Freelance chart independently. The legend is a chart element, for example, so you can double-click the legend to open a dialog box for editing the chart legend.

Note: Because 1-2-3 is a full-featured spreadsheet program, 1-2-3 enables you to do a lot more with numbers and charts than Freelance does. If you already have a perfectly good chart created in 1-2-3 — or even just the data for a perfectly good chart entered in some other program — you needn't re-enter all the data into Freelance. You can copy charts from 1-2-3 or import data from 1-2-3 and a variety of other programs.

Chapter 21
Final Touches and Shortcuts
à la Freelance

In This Chapter
▶ Changing views
▶ Freelance drawing
▶ Creating a screen show

*O*kay, so you've created a bunch of spiffy pages for your presentation — an eye-catching title page, an informative table, a compelling chart or two, and maybe some pages with other elements, such as bulleted lists and organizational charts — now what? Time to add some final flourishes and get this presentation put together.

Changing Views

Freelance gives you several ways to look at your presentation's pages on-screen: *Current Page* view, *Page Sorter* view, and *Outliner* view. So far, you've seen pages only in the Current Page view, which is the view you're in as you create a new page. Current Page view is also the view you use to edit pages. You can change views by choosing the view you want from the View menu, but the easiest way to change views is by clicking one of the view tabs just below the menu bar and SmartIcon palette.

Sorting presentation pages

To change to the Page Sorter view, click the Page Sorter tab. Page Sorter view displays all the pages in your presentation as thumbnails (small versions) so that you can see a bunch of them on a single screen. You can use the scroll bar to see any of the thumbnails that don't fit on one screen.

Figure 21-1 shows a presentation in Page Sorter view.

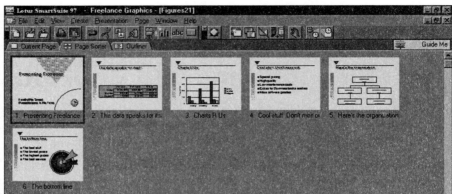

Figure 21-1:
Page Sorter
view gives
you a bird's-
eye view
of your
presentation.

In Page Sorter view, you can remove, duplicate, add, and sort pages, as follows:

✔ To remove a page from your presentation while in Page Sorter view, click the page you want to zap and then press Delete.

✔ If you change your mind after pressing Delete, you can bring the zapped page back by choosing Edit➪Undo Delete Page(s).

✔ To duplicate a page, click the page you want to copy and then choose Page➪Duplicate (or press Alt+F7). Freelance places an exact copy of the page right after the original.

Note: You rarely want an *exact* duplicate of a page. Usually, you need to modify the new page in some way, which you must do in Current Page view. You can change to Current Page view to edit your copy by double-clicking the page or by selecting the page and clicking the Current Page tab.

✔ To add a new page, click the page that is just before the location where you want to insert your new page and then choose Page➪New Page. The New Page dialog box appears so that you can choose the layout to use for the new page. Unless you make another choice in the dialog box, the new page uses the same layout as the page you're on when you add the new one. Click the layout you want in the dialog box and then click the OK button to insert the new page.

Note: Just as when you duplicate a page, you must edit a new page in the Current Page view. Double-click the new page to see that page in Current Page view.

✔ To change the order of the pages in the presentation, just click the page you want to move in Page Sorter view and then press and hold the mouse button as you drag the page to its new location. A gray vertical bar and an outline of the page show you where the moved page is going to land, as shown in Figure 21-2.

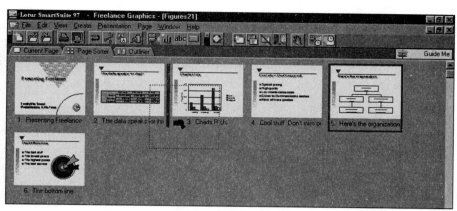

Figure 21-2:
Page 5
of this
presentation
is about to
be dropped
between
pages 2
and 3.

> ✔ **Note:** If you change the position of a page in the Page Sorter view, the page
> number that appears below the page changes to reflect its new location.

Outliner view

Although graphic elements often seem to be the most important parts of your
presentation, the words also need to be right — or the whole thing can fall
apart. In Current Page view, you can see only the text on the current page. In
Page Sorter view — unless you have a large, expensive, high-resolution computer screen — any text, other than large titles, is difficult to see. The *Outliner
view* enables you to view just the text in all the pages of your presentation,
including titles, subtitles, and bulleted lists.

To switch to Outliner view, click the Outliner tab. Your presentation appears in
Outliner view, as shown in Figure 21-3. Notice the row of buttons across the top
of the page just below the view tabs. These buttons come in handy for manipulating your presentation pages and text.

Outliner view enables you to work with your text in the following ways:

> ✔ The thumbnail representations of your presentation pages on the left side
>   of the outline give you some clues about what graphical elements are in
>   the page. These thumbnails are small but are adequate for distinguishing
>   bar charts from organization charts from title pages.

> ✔ You can hide the thumbnails by clicking the Hide/Display Thumbnails
>   button (at the far left of the row of buttons, just below the Current Page
>   view tab).

> ✔ You can *promote* (change to a higher outline level) or *demote* (change to a
>   lower outline level) the headings in titles or bulleted lists by clicking the
>   line containing the title you want to change and then clicking the Promote

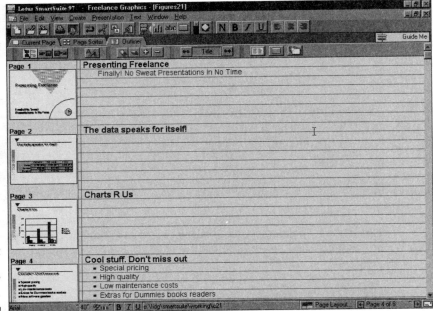

Figure 21-3:
Outliner
view
displays
your
presentation
as if the text
were written
on a yellow
notepad.

button (the one displaying a left arrow, located in the row of buttons just below the view tabs) or the Demote button (the one displaying a right arrow, on the same line). You can also demote an item by pressing Tab or promote an item by pressing Shift+Tab. While you're working in Outliner view, Freelance indents the different levels of headings in traditional outline form. You need to remember, however, that the indents don't carry over to your finished presentation pages.

If you promote a Level-1 heading, that head becomes the page title for a new page. If you find that you've inadvertently done so, you need to choose Edit⇨Undo Change Level.

✔ To enable you to more easily see the important stuff — and conceal unnecessary details — you can *collapse* (that is, *hide*) all the text of any level below that of the page title, either for the entire presentation or just for selected pages. To collapse all the text except the title for a particular page, click any of the text on the page and then click the minus sign (–) button in the row of buttons below the view tabs. To collapse the text for the entire presentation, as shown in Figure 21-4, click the Collapse All button (the one with stacked minus signs).

Note: Any pages with hidden text levels display a plus sign next to the page number at the left of the screen.

✔ To expand the collapsed text for one page in Outliner view, click any of the text on that page and then click the plus sign (+) button in the row of buttons below the view tabs. To expand the text for the entire presentation, click the Expand All button (the stacked plus signs).

✔ While in Outliner view, you can double-click one of the thumbnails to switch to Current Page view with that page displayed.

✔ You can also add or edit text while in Outliner view, which can be very handy.

Figure 21-4:
A
presentation
in Outliner
view,
collapsed to
show just
the titles.

+Page 1	Presenting Freelance
Page 2	The data speaks for itself!
Page 3	Charts R Us
+Page 4	Cool stuff. Don't miss out
Page 5	Here's the organization
+Page 6	The bottom line

Freelance Drawing

Just as in the other SmartSuite 97 programs, you can spruce up your Freelance pages by using a variety of drawing elements. The drawing tools are available in a Toolbox that appears on the left side of the Current Page view window after you click the Drawing & Text button. The Toolbox (as shown in Figure 21-5) includes tools for creating polygons, rectangles, lines, arrows, open curves, polylines, circles, arcs, text boxes, and freehand drawing.

Figure 21-5:
The Drawing
& Text
toolbox.

In addition to these drawing tools, you can create various shapes with text inside. The Toolbox even enables you to draw special connectors between shapes. The Shapes with text and Connectors tools, however, are mostly used for drawing diagrams from scratch. If you're the adventurous type who enjoys creating complex drawings, see *Freelance Graphics 96 For Windows 95 For Dummies,* by William Harrel and Roger C. Parker (IDG Books Worldwide, Inc.) for more information.

To use one of the drawing tools, click that tool in the Toolbox and then move the mouse pointer to the part of the page on which you want to place the element. Then simply press and hold the mouse button and drag the mouse to create the drawing. Chapter 11 gives you a bit more detailed instruction on using the more common drawing tools (as used in 1-2-3).

Note: You must do all your drawing on a presentation page while in Current Page view.

To help you place drawing objects more precisely, you can display the *drawing ruler* along the top and left sides of the window. You display the drawing ruler by choosing <u>V</u>iew⇨Show <u>R</u>uler. With the drawing ruler displayed, *guide markers* appear in the ruler as you move the mouse pointer (now shaped like a crosshair) so that you know exactly where you are drawing your shapes. A finished object is shown in Figure 21-6.

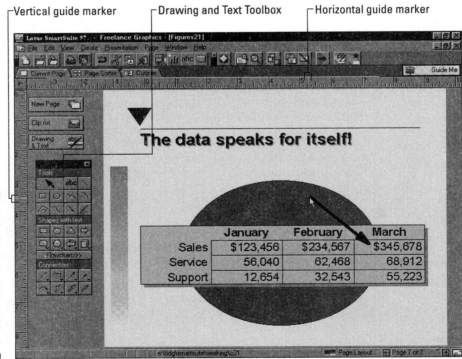

Figure 21-6:
Notice the light-shaded guide markers on the horizontal ruler and the vertical ruler.

Roll Camera: Creating a Screen Show

Ways to actually give your presentations abound. You can, of course, simply print your presentation pages to use as handouts or as overhead transparencies. You can save your presentation files so that they can be transformed into 35mm slides. You can even publish your presentation on the Web.

To create slides, you must save your Freelance file in a special format that requires a special software installation. Most likely, you must also send the file to an imaging center for processing. Information on these procedures can be found by choosing Help⇨Help Topics and then clicking the Index tab and typing **slides** in the text box at the top of the tab. Choose Slides from the list and click the Display button.

In addition to all those presentation methods, you can create your own on-screen presentation — called a *screen show.* You can even choose your effects for the transitions from one page to the next.

You can set up screen show effects in any view, but you can more easily work with the flow from page to page in Page Sorter view.

To create a screen show, follow these steps:

1. **Select a page and choose Page⇨Screen Show Effects.**

   The Page Properties InfoBox appears.

   Note*:* You don't need to select a page in Current Page view. The screen show effects affect the current page. (Gee, I bet you'd never have guessed that.)

2. **Click the Screen Show tab (the one displaying a picture of a movie camera) to see the options shown in Figure 21-7.**

Figure 21-7:
The Screen
Show tab of
the Page
Properties
InfoBox.

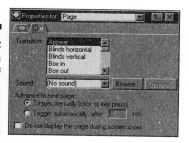

3. **Scroll through the Transition list box and choose the effect you want.**

   Determining exactly what the effects do just from their names isn't always easy, so you need to experiment to see which ones provide the desired effect.

4. **(Optional) If you want a sound to play after the page appears in the screen show, choose a sound from the Sound drop-down list box or click the Browse button to locate a sound file elsewhere on your system.**

5. **If you want the screen show to run automatically, you can choose the Trigger Automatically, After *X* Seconds option and type in the text box the number of seconds you want the page to remain on-screen before the next page appears.**

   The default display time is three seconds.

   You can omit a page from a screen show without deleting that page from your presentation file by clicking the Do Not Display This Page During Screen Show option.

6. **Repeat Steps 3 through 5 for the remaining pages in the presentation.**

   The InfoBox stays open until you click the Close (X) button, so you can select another page and set its screen show properties. In Outliner or Page Sorter views, you can select another page by clicking the page. In Current Page view, you can use the arrow buttons in the status bar (or any of the standard Freelance navigation techniques) to go to another page.

7. **Choose Presentation➪Run Screen Show➪From Beginning or press Alt+F10 to start the presentation.**

   Again, you can create and run a Freelance screen show starting from any view.

Before you begin your presentation, you may want to consider the following points:

- By default, the screen show runs manually, which means that you must click the mouse (either button) or press any key to move to the next page.

- If you want the screen show to run automatically, you must set the timing for each page, as described in Step 5 of the preceding steps, or set all the pages to advance after a fixed time delay. To do that, start in Current Page or Page Sorter view, choose Presentation➪Set Up Screen Show to open the Set Up Screen Show dialog box, click the Page Effects tab, choose After *X* Seconds, enter in the text box the number of seconds you want each page to remain on-screen, and click OK.

- If you want the screen show to run continuously — for example, at a trade show for your products — open the Set Up Screen Show dialog box (by choosing Presentation➪Set Up Screen Show), click the Options tab, choose Run Screen Show in a Continuous Loop, and click OK.

- Freelance saves the screen show settings with the presentation file.

Part VI
Organize Your Life

The 5th Wave   By Rich Tennant

"OH SURE, IT'LL FLOAT ALRIGHT, BUT INTEGRATION'S GONNA BE A KILLER."

In this part . . .

*I*f you find you constantly have trouble keeping up with all those little scraps of paper on which you scribble important notes, you need some organization in your life. This part shows you how to use Organizer — SmartSuite 97's answer to the pocket day planner — to keep track of every aspect of your day-to-day activities. After reading this section, you may actually have fun getting organized. (Yeah, right!)

Chapter 22

Organizer Boot Camp
(And Beyond . . .)

. . . .

In This Chapter
▶ Investigating Organizer
▶ Exploring Calendar
▶ Making appointments
▶ Creating To Do lists

. . . .

*H*ave you ever wished you could take your appointment book and shove the thing into your (now, now, keep it clean!) . . . er, computer? Have you ever considered stuffing your entire desk, drawers and all, into your briefcase? Wouldn't you love, just once, to find your appointment book right where you left it instead of hunting for it under mounds of paperwork? Anyone who has missed an important appointment, searched in vain for their appointment book, or left vital information behind on a business trip can relate, right?

Well, good news, soldier! Now you can organize your entire life (well, most of it) and have it all at your fingertips. All your fingers need to do is enter the information from your elusive appointment book into Lotus Organizer. Then just sit back and have Organizer keep track of your appointments. Heck, the program can even remind you a few minutes (or hours or days) before your appointment is scheduled.

Organizer: The Big Picture

We don't want to overwhelm you with euphoria, but Organizer can also track your incoming and outgoing calls, dial up other computers and fax machines for you, remind you of important dates, enable you to schedule events, keep a notepad, and do much more. After you enter the stuff you want Organizer to remind you about, the program can do its reminding thing even if you're working in another program! Is that awesome or what!?

Organizer at a glance

You own a day planner, right? (If not, bear with us anyway.) Does the planner manage your time, jump into your briefcase or purse, beep you at the time for an appointment, remind you when a birthday or holiday comes up, and warn you if you book conflicting appointments? No?!? Then check out the following feats that Organizer can do:

- The *Calendar* feature enables you to keep track of your appointments and calls. You can set alarms to remind you of stuff, and you can set up repeating appointments (such as that lunch with Mom every Thursday) simply by clicking the mouse button a couple of times.

- The *To Do* section enables you to keep a list of things you need to do and when they need to be done. To Do lists can be sorted by priority, status, or date.

- The *Address* section is like a Rolodex on speed. Oh, and you can also use the feature to dial phone numbers for you.

- The *Notepad* is a wonderful tool for jotting down notes, reminders, lists, memos — anything that you could put on a piece of paper and then promptly misplace.

- The *Calls* section helps you keep track of incoming and outgoing calls, duration of phone conversations, status of the calls — and this feature even has a place for taking notes.

- The *Planner* is great for scheduling meetings, projects, and stuff such as that. If you're on a network, you can use the Planner to track Calendar entries for a bunch of people.

- The *Anniversary* section enables you to store all those important dates.

- If you work on a network, you can also schedule meetings and invite co-workers, accept or decline a meeting invitation, and share work with a group of people. You can dial and receive telephone calls as well as send and receive messages.

Come on in, the water's fine!

The first thing you see after you start Organizer is a cute little notebook with charming icons around it. Don't let the scene fool you. Organizer is no powder puff, so dive right in and get acquainted.

If you have SuiteStart running, a row of small icons appears in the System Tray at the right end of the taskbar. You can start Organizer by clicking the icon that looks like a notebook. To start Organizer from SmartCenter, open the SmartSuite drawer, click the Lotus Applications folder, and then double-click the Lotus Organizer icon. If you don't have SuiteStart or SmartCenter running, you can access Organizer from the Windows 95 Start menu. Click the Start button, point to Programs, point to Lotus SmartSuite, and then choose Lotus Organizer 97.

After you start Organizer, an open notebook appears on-screen, with a bunch of icons, called the Toolbox, to the left. The Toolbox icons are incredible one-step time-savers. For example, you can drag an entry to the Clipboard icon in the Toolbox and copy the entry to other sections as many times as you like. You can open any of the entry dialog boxes by clicking a Toolbox icon, schedule group meetings, send and receive mail, make or log phone calls, and more. Pretty slick, huh?

Organizer's set up just like those day planner binders, complete with section tabs. To move to a different section, all you need to do is click its tab.

If you don't know what a SmartIcon does, move the mouse pointer to that icon and wait for Bubble Help to appear. (That's the yellow balloon with the message on it — remember?) Bubble Help also works with the Toolbox icons.

The Calendar — Up Close and Personal

After you first start Organizer, you see an appointment book open to the current week, as shown in Figure 22-1. To the left are the Toolbox icons. Directly beneath the Toolbox are four other icons — the View icons. In Calendar, these icons give you a choice on how you want to view your appointments. You can choose from among the following view options:

- ✔ One day per page
- ✔ One week on two pages (the default view)
- ✔ One week per page
- ✔ One month on two pages

Setting appointments

Setting an appointment in Organizer is easy and fun. A Create Appointment dialog box helps you select the criteria for your appointment, including what tune plays if you set an alarm as a reminder!

To set an appointment, you need to open the Create Appointment dialog box, set the date and the time and length of the appointment, enter a description for the appointment, and then exit the dialog box. You can also perform some

One day per page

Clipboard   Entry icon

Drag within the same page   One month on two pages

Move to another page   Backtrack SmartIcon   Current date icon

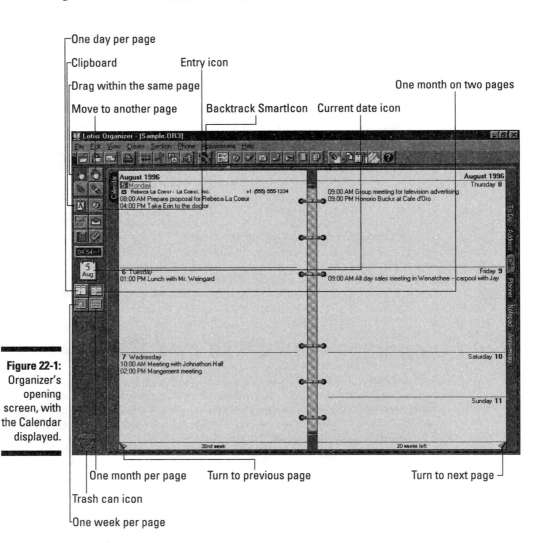

Figure 22-1:
Organizer's
opening
screen, with
the Calendar
displayed.

One month per page   Turn to previous page   Turn to next page

Trash can icon

One week per page

optional steps within the Create Appointment dialog box, such as setting a
repeating appointment, setting an alarm, choosing a category, and selecting
cost codes.

To set an appointment, follow these steps:

1. **Double-click the day for which you want to enter the appointment or
   click the Entry icon on the Toolbox (the icon with the little clock on it).**

   The Create Appointment dialog box appears, as shown in Figure 22-2.

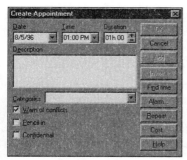

Figure 22-2:
The Create
Appointment
dialog box.

2. **Click the Date drop-down arrow and then choose a date for the appointment from the monthly calendar page.**

   Use the left and right triangles on either side of the month name to move forward or backward a month at a time.

3. **Click the Time drop-down arrow to set the time and length of the appointment.**

   The TimeTracker opens as part of the Time drop-down list, as shown in Figure 22-3. The clock thingy on the TimeTracker provides you with three important pieces of information: The clock and bar at the top in the TimeTracker show the appointment's starting time; the Duration bar in the middle shows the appointment's length; and the clock and bar at the bottom show the ending time. Along the left edge of the TimeTracker, any existing appointments appear as a blue bar, and the current appointment appears as a green bar. If the current appointment conflicts with an existing appointment, the bar appears in red.

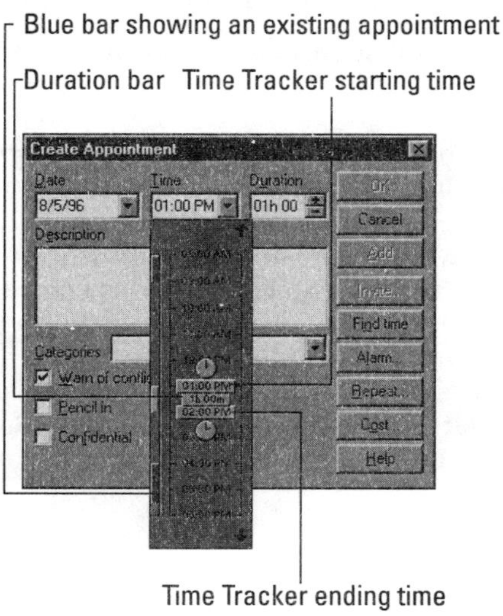

Blue bar showing an existing appointment

Duration bar   Time Tracker starting time

Figure 22-3:
The Time
drop-down
list with the
TimeTracker
displayed.

Time Tracker ending time

4. **Click the top clock button in the TimeTracker, press and hold the mouse button, and drag the clock up or down the Time list to set the appointment starting time.**

   Release the button as you reach the desired appointment time.

   You can't drag the starting clock down past the ending clock (or the ending clock up past the starting clock, for that matter). If you want the appointment to start later than the current ending time or end earlier than the current starting time, just point to the new time to which you want to move the appointment and click. This action moves the entire clock thingy to the new starting time.

5. **Click the bottom clock and drag it to set the ending time.**

   The time in the Duration bar changes to reflect your starting and ending times. You can move the entire appointment to a different time by clicking the duration bar and dragging the clock thingy to the new time; the starting and ending times adjust automatically.

   Note: You can also change the duration time by clicking the plus (+) or minus (-) sign next to the Duration text box in the Create Appointment dialog box. This method closes the Time drop-down list and TimeTracker, so if you use this approach, skip the next step.

6. **Click the Time drop-down arrow again to close the Time list and TimeTracker.**

   Click the Find Time button if your day is nearly booked. Each time you click the Find Time button, the next available time appears in the Time text box.

7. **Click the Description text box and type a description for your appointment, as you want the description to appear on your Calendar.**

   You could, for example, type **Lunch with David at Lenny's Restaurant**.

8. **Click the Add button to create more appointments or click OK to exit the dialog box.**

You can also choose some of the other options before closing the dialog box. Those options are explained in following sections.

To save your new file, click the Save Current File SmartIcon or choose File⇨Save from the menu bar. If you are on a network, you may want to use an abbreviated version of your name as the filename so that others can access your planner. (Make sure that you select a filename that conforms to the file-naming rules of your network.) To open your file after you start Organizer, click the Open File SmartIcon or choose File⇨Open from the menu bar. Check with your network guru on how to open and save on the network, as well as how to handle group scheduling.

Ladies and gentlemen, choose a category

One convenient Organizer feature is the capability to assign any Organizer entry to a *category*. Then you can use the categories to pull together information on related entries scattered across several Organizer sections and view the entries by category.

Categories are very helpful for tracking projects and different kinds of activities. (Maybe you don't really want to know how much time you spend in meetings. But if you do, Organizer can tell you.) Organizer comes with an assortment of predefined categories — mostly for kinds of activities, such as calls, meetings, and travel — and you can create new categories to fill your needs. A single Organizer entry can belong to several different categories. So you can assign a meeting to consult on the Smith project, for example, to the Meeting, Smith Project, and Consulting categories.

To assign a category to an appointment, you must be in the Create Appointments dialog box, which you access by clicking the Entry icon in the Toolbox, or the Edit Appointments dialog box, which you access by double-clicking an existing appointment. Click the drop-down arrow for the Categories text box and select the category you want from the drop-down list. You can choose more than one category by clicking all that apply. If none of the categories suits your needs, type your own category in the Categories text box. After you're done, simply click outside the Categories text box and drop-down list.

Could you repeat that, please?

Appointments that repeat are fairly common. With a regular desktop planner or calendar you must write every meeting or appointment in by hand, right? This task can become very tedious — and maybe even dangerous. (What if you forget to enter one?) Organizer can set all your repeating appointments or meetings for you, whether they repeat every week, month, quarter, or whenever — and you only need to enter the appointment once!

To set a repeating appointment click the Repeat button in the Create Appointment dialog box to open the Repeat dialog box (see Figure 22-4).

Note: If you are currently in the Calendar and not the Create Appointment dialog box, double-click the existing appointment to open the Edit Appointment dialog box, which is identical to the Create Appointment dialog box. Then click the Repeat button in this dialog box.

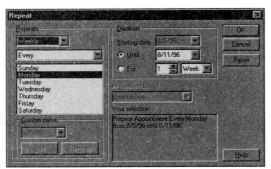

Figure 22-4:
The Repeat
dialog box.

After the Repeat dialog box appears, click the drop-down arrow next to the first text box in the Repeats area to view your choices for how often to repeat the appointment. (The default choice in the drop-down list is Weekly.) Select the one that works best for you. Suppose, for example, that you attend quarterly financial planning meetings. These meetings always occur on the first day of the month, so you select the Monthly [Dates] choice from this drop-down list.

Then you move down to the second text box. (In Figure 22-4, Every appears in this text box.) Click the drop-down arrow to open the list of choices. Staying with the quarterly example, you choose the Every third month on the selection.

You next select the days or dates from the list box right below the two drop-down list boxes. (In Figure 22-4, this box lists the days of the week. Had you chosen Monthly [Dates], as in our example, you'd instead see days of the month listed here, such as 1st, 2nd, 3rd, and so on.) In our example, you choose 1st from this list. You can use the scroll button for more choices than the list currently shows.

The Starting Date for the recurring appointment is already set in the Duration area of the dialog box, so all you need to do is add an ending date. Click the Until radio button and choose a date from the drop-down list. If you want the appointment to repeat for a period of time, however, click the For radio button and select the appropriate length of time from the accompanying text boxes. Say, for example, that you want a monthly appointment that starts in January to continue through September. You click the For radio button and then select 8 in the first text box and Months in the second (to specify 8 additional monthly repetitions of the original appointment). Notice that Organizer sets the Until date for you if you go this route.

Now click the drop-down arrow next to the At Weekends text box, and choose how to handle dates that fall on a weekend. In our example, you might select Move to Nearest Weekday.

You can also enter specific dates in the Repeat dialog box. To do so, first select Custom in the top list box in the Repeats area. Next, go to the Custom Dates area, just below the Repeats area. Click the Custom Dates drop-down arrow and select from the list all the dates you want to include, clicking the Add button each time. Your chosen dates appear in the list box above the Custom Dates area.

After you finish creating your repeat appointments, click OK to return to the Create Appointment dialog box. Then, after you click OK to close the Create Appointment dialog box, Organizer copies your appointment in your Calendar to the recurring dates just as you specified in the dialog box.

What's the secret code?

The capability to assign *customer* and *cost codes* is a valuable tool in Organizer, especially if you already use cost or customer codes in your business or in other software. *Customer codes* assign a number or alphanumeric code to each customer or company you deal with. These codes help you track that customer throughout the computer or network and provide a cross-referencing ability. *Cost codes* work in a similar manner, except that this type of code can help you track how and where you're spending money. Tracking costs is ideal for a project that's on a budget. Customer codes and cost codes work much like categories. You can use them to select and display appointments and other Organizer items so that you can view only the items pertaining to a specific customer or cost center.

To use cost or customer codes, click the Cost button in the Create Appointment dialog box. (If you've already returned to the Calendar, double-click the existing appointment to open the Edit Appointment box and click Cost there.) The Cost dialog box appears.

Enter a Customer Code and a Cost Code in the appropriate text boxes. If you have previously entered codes, you can click the drop-down arrows next to these text boxes to reveal your existing code choices. Click OK to return to the Create Appointment dialog box after you have your codes set.

An alarming situation!

One of our favorite options in Organizer is the Alarm option. You can have a message flash on-screen and choose a little ditty or other sound to remind you of your appointment. As long as Organizer is running in the background, the alarm and message work no matter what Windows program you're running. You can also set the alarm to go off a day or more in advance or several hours in advance of your appointment — the choice is yours!

To set an alarm, follow these steps:

1. **In either the Create or Edit Appointment dialog box, click the Alarm button.**

   You can access the Create Appointment dialog box by clicking the Entry icon on the Toolbox. Double-clicking an existing appointment opens up the Edit Appointment dialog box.

   After you click the Alarm button, the Alarm dialog box appears (see Figure 22-5). Notice that the Alarm dialog box is preset to the date and time of the appointment. If that's the day you want the alarm to go off, skip to Step 3. If not, continue on to Step 2.

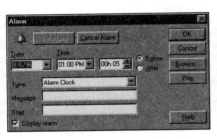

Figure 22-5:
The Alarm
dialog box.

2. **Click the Date text box's drop-down arrow and select a date from the monthly calendar page that appears if you want the alarm to sound on a day other than the date of the appointment.**

   Use the left and right triangles on either side of the month heading to move forward or backward a month at a time.

3. **If you want the alarm to sound at a time other than the time of the appointment, click the Time text box's drop-down arrow.**

   The TimeTracker opens. The clock shows the time of the alarm (which is the starting time of the appointment initially). You can simply drag the clock up the TimeTracker to the time you want the alarm to go off. (*Note:* Moving this clock has no effect on the starting time of the appointment.)

4. **Click the Before or After radio button to tell Organizer to run the alarm either before or after the time you select.**

   You can use the Before or After setting in combination with the Time setting to control the exact time the alarm sounds. For example, you may want to leave the Time set for the start of the appointment and set the alarm to sound 10 minutes before that time. Or you can set the Time and leave the Before/After setting at zero to sound the alarm exactly at the time you set. You can even combine the two settings if you want. The tools are there. You get your choice of how to use them.

5. **Click the plus (+) or minus (-) buttons next to the accompanying text box (to the right of the T̲ime text box and to the left of the radio buttons) to increase or decrease the number of minutes before or after the time that appears in the T̲ime text box that you want the alarm to sound.**

Preferences, shmeferences — just play me a tune

Organizer enables you to choose from myriad alarm sounds to delight your ears and amaze your co-workers. With the Create Appointment dialog box or the Edit Appointment dialog box open, click the drop-down arrow next to the Alarm dialog box's T̲une text box, and a list of alarm tunes appears.

1. **Scroll through the T̲une list and click a selection to choose a tune.**

2. **To listen to the tune, click the Pla̲y button.**

   Note: Some computers can't play all the tunes. If one doesn't play, try another.

3. **Click the Me̲ssage text box to type in a reminder.**

   As the alarm goes off, Organizer not only plays your musical selection, but also displays your reminder text in a different version of the Alarm dialog box, as shown in Figure 22-6.

4. **Click OK to return to the Create Appointment or Edit Appointment dialog box.**

Figure 22-6:
This version
of the Alarm
dialog box
appears to
remind you
of an
appointment.

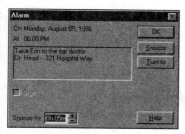

In this version of the Alarm dialog box there is a T̲urn To button. If you are in another part of Organizer or in another program, you can click T̲urn To, and Organizer takes you to the page where the alarm originated. Suppose, for example, that you are working in Word Pro as the alarm goes off. You can't remember some specifics about the entry, so you click T̲urn To, and Organizer takes you to the page in the notebook where the entry is.

Launch time!

If you need to start another program at a specific time, you can set an alarm for a reminder and use the Start option on the Alarm dialog box to start that program automatically (refer to Figure 22-5).

You're probably wondering: "Why would I need to take this action if I can start a new program simply by using the Start menu?" Well, you are absolutely right. You *can* start a program that way. But suppose you have an appointment at 3 p.m. and you need to run a report to take with you. You know that whenever you work in 1-2-3 you lose all track of time. So you set an alarm by using the Start option, which not only reminds you in time to run the report, but also takes you directly into the new program without any searching through the cascading Start menus. Neat!

While in the full Alarm dialog box, click the Start text box and type the full path name of the program you want to start or the file you want to open after the alarm goes off. (If you're like us and can't remember a full path name, you can click inside the Start text box and then click the Browse button. Select the program you want to launch by double-clicking the program folder to open the program and then scrolling through its files. After you find the file you want, double-click the file or click the file once and click Open. The entire path is now visible in the Start text box.) Click OK.

After the alarm goes off, a message box appears to tell you that the program is launching. As soon as you click OK, the new program launches — even if you have the alarm set to go off a few minutes early as a warning. If you need time to finish up what you're currently working on, just click the Snooze button after the Alarm dialog box appears. You know that the amount of time set in the Snooze For text box is enough to finish what you're doing before the new program starts.

Editing in the Calendar section

You can edit the description of an entry in the Calendar section two ways. You can double-click the appointment you want to edit, which opens the Edit Appointment dialog box, or you can edit directly on the page.

If all you need to do is change the appointment day, just drag the entry to a new day on the calendar. If you need to move your appointment to a day or month that's not displayed on the screen, click the grabbing hand icon in the Toolbox, click the appointment, and then find the appropriate date (either by using the Turn to next page area at the lower-right corner of the Organizer page or by clicking the Calendar tab and clicking the appropriate date on the yearly calendar that appears).

To edit on the page, follow these steps:

1. **Click the entry in the Calendar to highlight that entry.**

   A highlight box appears around the appointment. The mouse pointer now changes from a hand into an I-beam while inside the box.

2. **Click again at the place you want to edit within the highlight box.**

   A flashing cursor appears inside the highlight box, and the TimeTracker also appears. You can now edit the description of the entry and change the time, too. (***Note:*** If the cursor isn't exactly where you want it inside the box, move the I-beam to the correct spot and click again.)

3. **After you finish editing the appointment, close the highlight box by clicking anywhere on the Calendar page outside the box and the TimeTracker.**

After you click the appointment area of the page to close the highlight box, all the times for that day appear. To avoid having these times appear on-screen, you can click the date to close the highlight box without displaying the times. If the times are already visible and really bug you being there, turn the page and then turn back again to get rid of them.

Moving around in the Calendar

After you start Organizer, the notebook is always open to the current week. You can move around in the calendar in the following two ways:

- ✔ To move a page at a time, click the turned-up corners at the bottom of the notebook pages. The mouse pointer turns into a pointing hand and the pages turn one at a time. (If you have a sound card, the action is accompanied by the sound of turning pages.)

- ✔ To move to another month, click the tab labeled Calendar at the top left-hand side of the notebook, and — lo and behold! — the notebook flips pages to display a calendar of the entire year. Double-click the desired date, and Organizer flips right to that week for you.

If you are ready to return to the current date's page, you can flip back to the yearly calendar and double-click the date again, or you can click the Backtrack SmartIcon (the one with the footprints traipsing across it). You may need to click the icon two or three times, depending on how many times you moved around. Better still, just click the current date icon below the Toolbox.

Here's a nifty shortcut for moving around the Calendar: Just press the letter on your keyboard that corresponds to the first letter of the month you want to turn to, and Organizer flips to that month. Suppose, for example, that you want to go to June. You press J and — wait a minute! Organizer switched to January, not June! In the case of months with the same starting letter, you need to press the first *three* letters. So, for June or July, you need to press J-U-N or J-U-L.

To move an appointment to another page or month, click the grabbing hand icon in the Toolbox (refer to Figure 22-1). Then click the appointment entry in the Calendar that you want to move. Turn the pages or flip to another month. Click the new day for the appointment, and the appointment drops right in place.

To simplify copying an entry, just click the entry and use the pointing hand icon to drag that entry to the Clipboard icon in the Toolbox (refer again to Figure 22-1). Now you can drag the entry from the Clipboard to as many places in the Calendar as you like. You can also copy the entry to a To Do or Notepad page.

Delete and undelete

Deleting in Organizer couldn't be easier. Just click the item you want to delete and drag that item to the Trash Can icon. The item even appears to burn up! Following are the basics on deleting and undeleting:

✔ To delete an appointment from the Calendar, click the appointment and drag the appointment to the Trash Can icon at the bottom left of the Calendar (refer — yes, *again* — to Figure 22-1). If deleting a repeating appointment, a Delete Repeating Appointment dialog box appears. Radio buttons on the dialog box enable you to indicate whether you want to delete just this one appointment, the entire series, or just selected portions of the series. Choose which repeating appointments to delete and click OK.

✔ If you delete an appointment and then realize that you trashed the wrong one, you can retrieve the appointment — as long as that appointment is the most recent deletion. Choose Edit➪Undo Appointment Delete from the menu bar.

The Undo command can't undo the deletion of repeating appointments.

Tie a String Around Your Finger — or Create a To Do List

To do or not to do? That is the question. Well, maybe yes and maybe no — because a To Do list is a very effective way to help you manage your time. You can devote an entire page (or pages) to a single project, create lists, track any number of tasks for which you are responsible, and more. You can track your tasks by their status, start date, and priority.

Create a To Do list by clicking the To Do tab in your Organizer notebook. The notebook flips to a section divided by Overdue, Current, Future, and Completed tabs (see Figure 22-7). Double-click the empty page to open the Create Task dialog box (see Figure 22-8).

Date view icon

Status view icon

Priority view icon   Entry icon   Catagory view icon

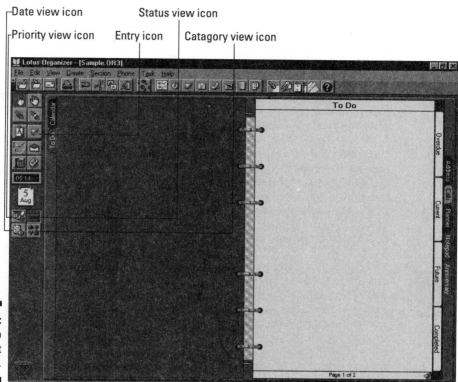

Figure 22-7:
A To Do
page at first
glance.

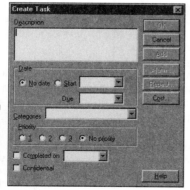

Figure 22-8:
The Create
Task dialog
box.

Notice in Figure 22-7 that the Entry icon in the Toolbox has changed from a clock to a checked box. Clicking this icon also opens the Create Task dialog box.

After the Create Task dialog box appears, the cursor is already in the Description box. Type a description of what you need to do. For example, you may write: **Follow up on new advertisers for restaurant promotion.**

Decide whether a date is necessary for this task. You can choose to have No Date, a Start date, a Due date, or both a Start and Due date. Click the drop-down arrow for Start, and the nifty monthly calendar appears. Select the desired start date, and the monthly calendar closes by itself. Next, select a due date the same way (optional) by clicking the Due drop-down arrow.

Click the drop-down arrow next to the Categories text box and choose a category, or type in your own category name in the text box. Click the appropriate radio button for the Priority of the task; in other words, how important is this task in reference to other current projects? The Completed On text box marks the project or task as being finished and the date the task was completed. And the Confidential text box is used in networking situations if you don't want others to read or write to your entry.

You can set an alarm and choose cost codes in the To Do section just as you can in the Calendar section. Just click the Alarm button in the Create Task dialog box and follow the instructions in the section "An alarming situation!" earlier in this chapter. As do the Create and Edit Appointment dialog boxes, the Create Task dialog box (and its companion Edit Task dialog box, discussed later in this chapter in "How To Do an edit — get it?") has a Repeat button. Refer to the section "Could you repeat that, please?" earlier in this chapter, for information on using this feature.

After you finish creating your task for the To Do list, click the Add button to continue creating tasks or click OK to return to the To Do list notebook.

View options

After you open the To Do section, you see four View icons, located below the Toolbox (refer to Figure 22-7). These guys are great for helping organize the To Do lists. They can sort and separate your entries. Each time you click one, the To Do section sorts all entries by that view choice.

- ✔ *Priority* entries are sorted by the priority number. After you select the Priority view icon, the page tabs enable you to view all at once your priority 3 tasks, priority 2 tasks, priority 1 tasks, or tasks with no designated priority.

- ✔ *Status* entries are sorted by their status and separated into the following files: *Current, Future, Overdue,* and *Completed.* Click the appropriate tab to view a file.

    If you want a future task located in the Future category, both the start date and the due date must fall sometime after the current date. Suppose, for example, that a proposal must be turned in one week after the task is assigned — say, on May 8. If you put the date you were assigned the proposal in the $\underline{S}$tart date text box of the Create Task dialog box and put the day the proposal's due in the D$\underline{u}$e date text box, Organizer files the proposal by its start date, which makes that task a Current project. By setting the $\underline{S}$tart date a couple of days before the D$\underline{u}$e date, however, you can have Organizer file the project or task in the Future category until the start date you specify. When the start date arrives, Organizer moves the task into the Current category.

✔ *Date* entries are sorted by their *start dates* only. The tabs along the right side of the page enable you to select a month and year. After you have the correct month, you can leaf through its pages by clicking the Turn to next page/Turn to previous page areas in the lower corners of the display.

✔ *Category* sorts entries by category. If you have an entry with more than one category, that entry appears on each category's page. Click the tab for the first letter of the category you wish to view.

You may notice that the description of each task appears in color on the To Do list (if you use a color monitor, of course). The color of the text signifies the status of each entry, no matter which view you are using, as described in the following table.

Color	Status of entry
Red	Overdue
Green	Current
Blue	Future
Black	Completed

How To Do an edit — get it?

You can edit any task by double-clicking its entry in the To Do list, which opens the Edit Task dialog box. The Edit Task dialog box looks and works just as the Create Task dialog box does. Use the Edit Task dialog box to change a date; change or add a priority, an alarm, or a cost code; or create a repeating task.

You don't need to open the Edit Task dialog box to edit the description of an entry or mark the task as completed. You can make those changes directly in the To Do section, as described in the following steps:

1. Click the entry in the To Do list to highlight that entry.

A highlight box appears around the task, and the mouse pointer changes from a hand to an I-beam if the pointer is over the description text.

2. **Click again where you want to edit or insert text.**

   The text color changes to black on white and a flashing cursor appears inside the highlight box.

3. **Edit the description.**

4. **After you finish, click anywhere inside the highlight box (but outside the description text) to close Edit mode.**

After you finish a task, you don't need to open the Edit Task dialog box to mark the Completed On text box. Simply click the gray box, called the Completed button, that appears to the left of the task on the To Do page, and a check mark appears in the box. If you go into the Edit Task dialog box, you find the Completed On text box filled in with the same date on which you marked the task's gray box on the To Do list. Pretty slick, huh?

You cannot use the Clipboard to copy a task to another page. If you try, the task simply reappears as a duplicate entry on the original page. You cannot use the pointing hand or grabbing hand icons to move or copy tasks either. The To Do tasks are very specific. These tasks are separated by their dates, priority, and status.

Copying To Do tasks

Organizer is big on sharing information, enabling you to copy appointments without having to retype all the information. Guess what? You can also copy tasks in the To Do section of Organizer in any of the following three ways:

- ✔ *Select more than one category for the task in the Create Task dialog box or the Edit Task dialog box.* Organizer includes the task in each category you select.

- ✔ *Use the Clipboard icon in the Toolbox.* Here's how: Drag the task to the Clipboard icon, copy the task back onto the page, and then double-click the copied task to open the Edit Task dialog box and change its information in the dialog box.

  This method also enables you to drag tasks to the Calendar. Simply drag the task to the Clipboard icon, click the Calendar tab near the Toolbox, click the appropriate date on the yearly calendar that appears, and drag the task to the appropriate date. You can then double-click the task to open the Edit Task dialog box and change the information.

- ✔ *Create a repeating task.* Click the Repeat button in either the Create or Edit Task dialog boxes, select Custom in the first drop-down list box of the Repeat dialog box, and then choose dates in the Custom Dates drop-down list box.

And what do you do after you're done with a To Do entry? If you don't want to keep a completed entry for your records, simply drag the entry to the Trash Can to delete that entry.

Chapter 23

Putting All the Little Black Books in One Place

In This Chapter
- ▶ Using the address file
- ▶ Keeping a phone log
- ▶ Creating a planner

*R*olodex cards, phone books, day planners, calendars — where do they all end? Why, with Organizer, of course! Keep these aids all in one place and within easy reach. After all, when was the last time you misplaced your computer?

If you use the *Address section* of Organizer as your new little black book, you get an organized, versatile address file. But the fun doesn't stop there! You can access information from the address file to help you fill in similar data in the Address section, as well as in the Calls section. Organizer brings the info to you — all you need to do is click the name, company, and so on to select the info. The *Calls section* of Organizer enables you to monitor the phone calls you make. By using categories and cost and customer codes, you can assign your calls to a group or project for tracking expenses. Using the *Planner* is a great way to plan blocks of time. What's really neat is that you can have all your engagements in Planner show up in the Calendar, too, which keeps you from overbooking your appointments! What a deal!

Addressing the Issues

You can most readily compare the Address section with your old-fashioned Rolodex — but with a couple of twists (instead of spins). For one thing, you get two cards for each entry — a *Business card* and a *Home card*. The Home card is really neat. This card has a place for the spouse's and children's names and any personal info. The Business card includes extra fields, too.

To add new address information to the Address section, follow these steps:

1. **Click the Address tab on the right-hand side of Organizer's right page.**

   After you're in the Address section, the Toolbox's Entry icon changes into a cute little postcard. (Don't confuse this icon with the Toolbox button displaying an open envelope — that's your link to e-mail.)

2. **Click the Entry icon (or double-click the blank address page) to open the Create Address dialog box, as shown in Figure 23-1.**

   The dialog box opens with the Business card tab selected.

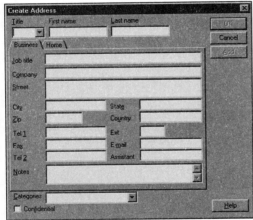

Figure 23-1:
The
Business
card tab of
the Create
Address
dialog box.

3. **Fill in the text boxes with the new address information.**

   Start with the Title, First Name, and Last Name boxes. Then click the Job Title box or one of the other text boxes in the Business tab. Click each text box or press Tab to move forward through the boxes; press Shift+Tab to move back to the previous box.

4. **Type any notes or reminders in the Notes text box.**

   For example, you could type **Mr. Hall prefers to be called between the hours of 1 and 5 p.m.**

5. **Click the Home tab.**

   After filling in the Business card, you can fill in a card with more personal information by clicking the Home tab.

6. **Click the Categories drop-down list box and choose a category (if you want to put the address record in a category, that is).**

Organizer provides several preset categories, such as Calls, Clients, Follow up, Personal, and so on. You could keep all your friends in one category, for example, and all your business associates in another. You may also select a category to keep track of projects, companies, or clients. If you don't find one you like, type a new one in the Categories dialog box.

7. Click the Add button or OK button to record the information.

Click Add if you want to enter another address record. If you don't want to enter any more records right now, click OK or press Enter to enter the current record and close the dialog box.

The address entry appears on the appropriate letter-tabbed page of Organizer's Address section.

Note: Because pressing Enter is just like clicking OK, pressing Enter closes the dialog box and takes you back to the Organizer page where you started. Don't worry if this happens — just double-click the address to open the identical Edit Address dialog box and finish entering your information.

If you have more than one contact within a company, you can have Organizer fill in the redundant data for you. After you fill in the company name, press Tab. A Similar Address Found dialog box appears, as shown in Figure 23-2. If the information listed in this dialog box is correct for the current record, click OK; Organizer adds the company information for you. Fill in any phone extension and any message in the Notes text box, and you're done.

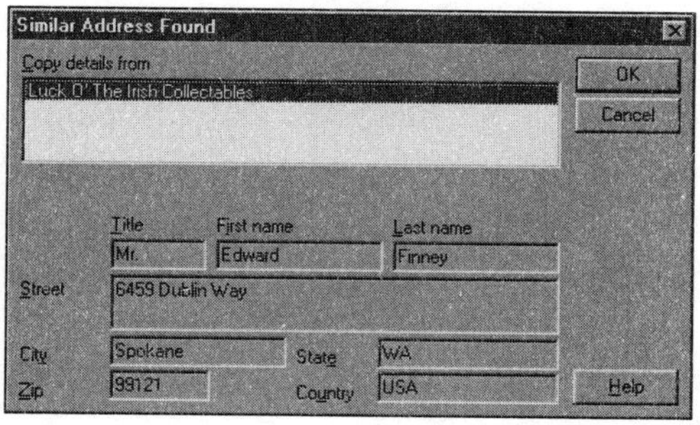

Figure 23-2:
The Similar
Address
Found
dialog box.

You can also use the Clipboard icon in the Toolbox to copy similar information. From the Address book, drag a similar address card to the Clipboard and then drag that address back to the Address book. Double-click either address card to open the Edit Address dialog box.

View — a la mode

After you open the Address section of Organizer, you see four new View icons below the Toolbox. These offer four different ways to view the address files in the notebook. You can view by Address, Contact, Phone, and View All. In View All mode, each Address card is on its own page (see Figure 23-3).

Searching for Mr. Goodboy

Searching for an address card is simple as long as you have any piece of information from the card. If you want to find a new contact, knowing the contact's first name is enough information to conduct a search.

To search for an address card, follow these steps:

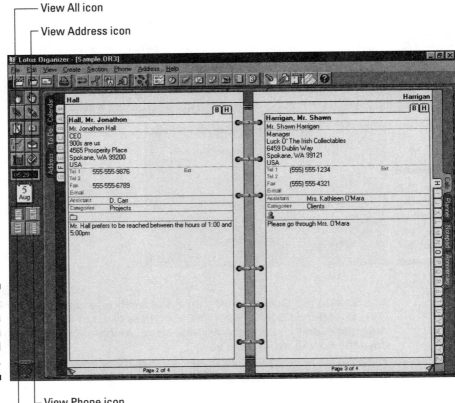

View All icon

View Address icon

Figure 23-3:
Address cards in View All mode.

View Phone icon

View Contact icon

1. **Click the Find Text SmartIcon (the one that looks like a flashlight), or choose Edit⇨Find.**

   The Find dialog box appears (see Figure 23-4).

Figure 23-4:
The Find
dialog box.

2. **Type what you want to search for in the Find text box.**

3. **Click the Case Sensitive check box if you want the search to find only exact case matches.**

   If you want to find *McDonald* but not *MCDonald,* checking Case Sensitive ensures that Organizer finds only the addresses that match *McDonald.*

4. **Click the Whole Word check box if you want the search to find only the specified word and not the same letters occurring within another word.**

   With Whole word checked, for example, you find instances of the word *the* but not the word *there.*

5. **Click the Section radio button and then the drop-down arrow for its text box, and select from the list what sections of Organizer to include in the search.**

   The Section list box deals with where you want your search to take place. Do you want to search only in one section of Organizer (the Address section, for example) or in all sections?

6. **Click Find Next or Find All.**

   The Occurrences box displays all the data that matches your search request. If you search for only one occurrence or want to view occurrences one by one, click the Find Next button. If you want to view a list of occurrences, click the Find All button.

Use the Clear List and Append to List radio buttons if performing more than one search in the same Find dialog box. Clear List clears the Occurrences box for each search, while Append to List maintains all matches from previous searches in the Occurrences box. After you exit the Find dialog box, the Occurrences box clears automatically.

After you finish the search, either close the dialog box or highlight one of the matches in the Occurrences box, click the Turn To button, and then click Close. You should be at the highlighted entry.

Feeling out of sorts

You can choose the order in which the address cards appear by using the Sort option. Changing the sort order is useful if you need to access certain information more frequently than others. Suppose that the normal view of the address cards is alphabetical by last name. You may deal with companies more than names; therefore, you may find that displaying the cards by company name is more logical for you.

To change the sort order of your address cards, make sure that you click the Address tab and then follow these steps:

1. **Choose View⇨Address Preferences from the menu bar.**

    The Address Preferences dialog box appears, as shown in Figure 23-5.

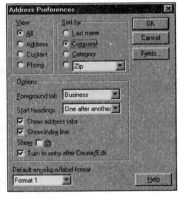

Figure 23-5:
Sorting
address
cards in the
Address
Preferences
dialog box.

2. **Click the radio button for the View that you want.**

    Actually, you can even leave these options alone. The View icons below the Toolbox govern these options; you can change views as often as you like by clicking those icons. You can, however, change the default View icon (the one that is in effect as you open the section) by choosing a new view here.

3. **In the Sort by area, click the radio button for the field by which you want to sort the addresses.**

If you want to view cards by company, for example, click Company (of course). This sort field is also the first field that appears on your address card. To select a field that is not offered, click the bottom radio button and select from the drop-down list a different kind of information by which to sort the cards (for example, Zip code).

4. **Click the Foreground Tab drop-down list box in the Options area and choose which tab you want your address cards to display: the Business tab (B) or the Home tab (H).**

   You can also choose Selected, which means that whichever tab you used last on each record is the one that appears. Choose Selected if you do not primarily use one tab over another.

5. **Click the Start Headings drop-down list box and choose how to display the pages.**

   Choose `One after another` in this list if you have blank pages. The other options keep the blank pages, while `One after another` displays only the filled-in pages.

6. **Click the Show Address Tabs check box if you want the address tabs to show.**

   The Show Address Tabs check box enables you to decide whether you want the Business (B) and Home (H) tabs to show. The box is selected by default, which means the tabs appear above the cards.

7. **Click Show Index Line if you want the index line to show.**

   The Show Index Line check box enables you to decide whether you want the title of your sort information to show. If you decide to use company names as your display and sort choice, the company name shows on the index line, above each card.

8. **(Optional) Click the Show check box with the lock beside it to show whether you marked any information as confidential.**

   This option is generally used in a networking situation in which other people can access your files.

9. **Click the Turn to entry after Create/Edit check box if you want Organizer to go to that entry after you close either the Create or Edit Address dialog boxes.**

   This entry is selected by default.

10. **Click OK after you finish.**

Your address list is now sorted by company name.

Number, Please

The *Calls section* of Organizer helps you keep a record of your phone calls —
incoming and outgoing. You can keep track of who you spoke with, how long
the call lasted, and the status of a follow-up call. You can assign a cost code to a
call and set an alarm to remind you of a scheduled future call. The calls and
address sections work well together because you can access address card
information from the Create Calls dialog box.

Before you can use all the features in the Calls section of Organizer, your
computer must have a modem linked to a phone line. You also need a telephone
handset plugged into the modem. (If you need to know more about modems,
contact your computer guru or read *Modems For Dummies*, by Tina Rathbone,
published by IDG Books Worldwide, Inc.) Without a modem and a telephone
handset, you can use the Calls features of Organizer only as a manual record of
your calls.

To keep track of your phone calls, follow these steps:

1. **Click the Calls tab to move to the Calls section.**

   The Entry icon in the Toolbox now displays a phone receiver.

2. **Click the Entry icon (or double-click any blank area on a Calls page) to open the Create Call dialog box, as shown in Figure 23-6.**

Figure 23-6:
The Create
Call dialog
box.

3. **Enter the contact information in the text boxes of the Contact tab.**

   Type the first name of the person you are calling (or plan to call) in the
   First Name text box. If the names you are entering are in your Address
   section, Organizer helps you fill in the rest of the information. You can type
   the person's last name in the Last Name box, or you can click the drop-down

arrow and select the name from the list. The box closes by itself and, like magic, Organizer automatically fills in the company name and phone number. If you type the last name yourself, Organizer doesn't fill in the company and phone fields for you.

If you want to enter a different phone number, select The phone number entered below in the Phone At drop-down list and fill in the information in the Phone Number area.

Confirm the settings in the Dialing From and Dial Using drop-down list boxes. Normally, you don't need to change these settings, which control what modem to use and the dialing format for outgoing calls. Organizer picks up the information from your Windows 95 telephony settings. The settings appear in this dialog box for convenience. The Dialing Properties and Configure buttons open the standard Windows 95 dialog boxes for setting dialing properties and configuring your modem. (For more information on using the Windows 95 telephony features, refer to *Windows 95 For Dummies*, by Andy Rathbone, published by IDG Books Worldwide, Inc.)

4. Click the Notes tab.

Organizer displays the options shown in Figure 23-7.

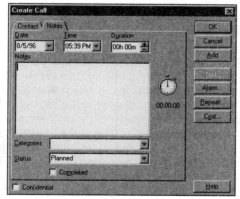

Figure 23-7:
The Notes
tab of the
Create Call
dialog box.

5. Select the appropriate information for the call in the Date, Time, and Duration list boxes.

What you enter here depends on what information you are filling in. Are you listing a call you already made or received? Are you scheduling a date to call someone or follow up on a call?

You can use the plus (+) and minus (-) signs next to the Duration text box to set or adjust the length of the call. You can also set the Duration of the call by using the TimeTracker, discussed in Chapter 22, or you can use the Stopwatch, which is explained in the following section of this chapter.

6. **Type any reminders for yourself in the Notes text box.**

   For example, you may type **Have new proposal and layouts ready when calling.**

7. **In the Status box, select the setting to reflect the status of this call.**

   The Status drop-down list box tells you the result of the call or tells you that the call is a future call. If you intend to make the call at a future time, the text in the box should read Planned. If you are going to place the call right away, do not change the information in this box — Organizer automatically updates the information after you go into the Dialing dialog box, which is described in the following section. If you are logging an incoming call, click the drop-down arrow for the Status list box and select a status from the list that appears.

8. **Click the Categories drop-down list box and choose your category(s).**

   You can use the same category you assigned for this person elsewhere and/or a category pertaining to the call only.

9. **Click the Completed check box if the call is finished and needs no follow-up.**

   The call remains in your Calls section even though you marked this call as completed.

10. **Set an alarm, assign cost codes, or configure repeating calls as needed.**

   As in setting appointments in the Calendar, you can set an alarm to remind you to make a call. Click the Alarm button in the Create Call dialog box, and choose in the Alarm dialog box the date and time for the alarm, along with a tune, if you like. For details on using the Alarm dialog box, see Chapter 22. As for appointments, you can use the Repeat button to set up calls that repeat. If you make a call regularly, click the Repeat button in the Create Call dialog box. Set up the repeating call in the Repeat dialog box, the same as you would an appointment. For more information, refer to Chapter 22. Use the Cost button in the Create Call dialog box to assign a cost and customer code to the call. The codes assign the costs to a group, project, or client. See Chapter 22 for more info.

11. **If you plan to complete the call at a later time, click the OK button to close the dialog box and record the call record in Organizer; otherwise, proceed to the following section and follow the steps there.**

When I'm calling you

Now you're ready to make a call. (If you're on a network, however, check first with your network guru.) Follow these steps to make a call in Organizer:

1. **Click the Dial button in the Create Call dialog box to open the Dialing dialog box, as shown in Figure 23-8.**

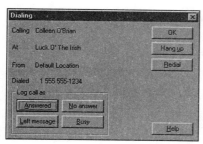

Figure 23-8:
The Dialing
dialog box.

Follow the steps in the preceding section to create a call if you haven't already done so.

If you have a modem installed and configured, Organizer uses the modem to dial the number immediately, and the Call Status dialog box appears over the Dialing dialog box. After the phone starts ringing, pick up the telephone handset and click Talk in the Call Status dialog box to continue your conversation and return to the Dialing dialog box. Click Hang Up in the Call Status dialog box to break the connection (and close both dialog boxes).

2. Click one of the buttons that describe how to log the call.

If you click the Answered button, the Stopwatch immediately begins to tick. Whichever button you click to log the call (Answered, Busy, No Answer, Left Message), the Status text box in the Create Call dialog box automatically updates with that information.

3. After the call is over, click the Stopwatch icon to stop the timer.

The elapsed time appears in the Duration text box for you.

The Hang Up and Redial buttons of the Dialing dialog box are for use with a modem. If you have a modem, the Calls section can perform a number of related options. Check with your network administrator or computer whiz for more help with these options.

Incoming calls and dialing shortcuts

If you receive a phone call you want to track, start or switch to Organizer and choose Phone⇨Incoming Call from the Organizer menu bar. The Create Call dialog box appears. Click the Notes tab and then click the Stopwatch icon to start the timer running. You can fill in the rest of the information at your leisure.

The Telephone icon in the Toolbox is present in every section of Organizer. Use this icon as a shortcut to dialing a number. Click the icon, and the Dial dialog box appears, as shown in Figure 23-9.

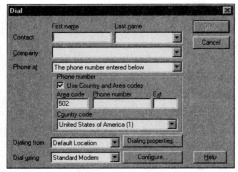

Figure 23-9:
Open the
Dial dialog
box by using
the
Toolbox's
Telephone
icon.

Fill in the information as you would in the Create Call dialog box and then click
Dial. The Dialing dialog box appears. As soon as you click your choice (<u>A</u>nswered,
<u>B</u>usy, <u>N</u>o Answer, <u>L</u>eft Message), the Create Call dialog box reappears, all filled
in. Again, if you choose <u>A</u>nswered, the Stopwatch starts running.

Editing calls

You can edit any call by double-clicking the call listing in your notebook, which
opens the Edit Call dialog box. This dialog box looks and works just like the
Create Call dialog box. Use the Edit Call dialog box to add notes, add or change
a category, or change the company or other name. The Edit Call dialog box also
has a Follo<u>w</u> Up button that you can click to create a follow-up call.

A follow-up call can be set for any date and time. The Create Follow Up Call
dialog box, which appears after you click Follo<u>w</u> Up, is identical to the Create
Call dialog box. After you exit the dialog boxes and return to the Calls page, you
see that the follow-up call is listed directly below the original call.

You can edit the description of an entry in the Calls section without using the
Edit Call dialog box by following these steps:

1. **Click the entry once to highlight that listing.**

   A highlight box appears around the call card. The mouse pointer turns into
   an I-beam whenever the pointer touches any text inside the edit box.

2. **Click the text you want to edit again.**

   A flashing cursor appears inside the highlight box. You can edit the
   company, notes, and status.

3. **Edit the text.**

4. **Click the name above the highlight box after you finish your edits.**

   This action closes the Edit mode.

A call with a view

The Calls section also has four View icons below the Toolbox. You can choose to view your Calls section by Name, Date, Company, and Category. The Name, Company, and Category views have their respective titles indexed above each card, with alphabetical index tabs along the side (see Figure 23-10). The Date view has the date indexed above the cards and monthly index tabs along the side. In the Category view, if you have a call with more than one category assigned to that call, duplicate cards appear.

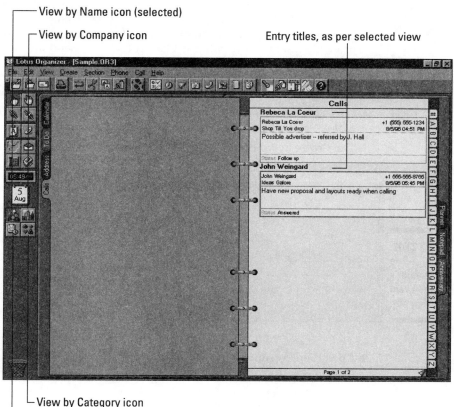

View by Name icon (selected)

View by Company icon

Entry titles, as per selected view

View by Category icon

View by Date icon

Figure 23-10:
The Calls
section in
the Name
view, with
the titles
reflecting
the name of
each entry.

Planning with a Purpose

The Planner is ideal for scheduling events that take one or more days, such as conferences, vacations, business trips, and so on. By marking events with color blocks or strips, the Planner makes seeing your scheduled events at a glance quite easy.

The following steps explain how to enter a Planner event:

1. **Move to the Planner section by clicking the Planner tab.**

   After the Planner opens, the page takes up both sides of the notebook. You can "fold" the Planner page by clicking the little Planner icon (with the little red horizontal arrow) in the top right-hand corner of the page. You probably want to work with the Planner folded out and then fold it down to single-page size so that you can access other section tabs on the left side of the Organizer notebook. As you move the mouse over the page, the dates appear in a text box below the page.

2. **Click the Toolbox Entry icon, which now resembles (amazingly enough) a Planner page.**

   The Create Event dialog box appears, as shown in Figure 23-11.

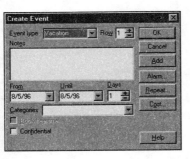

Figure 23-11:
The Planner's Create Event dialog box.

3. **Click the drop-down arrow by the Event Type text box and select the desired event from the list that appears.**

   If the option you want is not visible, the list has a scroll button that you can use to view more options. If you have a week's vacation coming up on June 1, you can select Vacation from the drop-down list.

4. **Choose the Row in which you would like your event to appear in the Planner.**

   Although you can't see it until you assign an event, the Planner divides each day into four rows, from top to bottom. You may want to choose rows according to the importance of the event. For example, you may have an all-day meeting in row one and a lunch date in row two. Simply click the + or – keys to make your selection.

5. **In the Notes text box, write any messages or reminders.**

   For example, you may need to remind yourself to give all files for the Luck O' the Irish to a co-worker before leaving for your vacation.

6. **Choose the dates for the event in the From and Until date boxes.**

   If your vacation starts on September 1 and ends on September 11, click September 1 from the drop-down calendar in the From list box and September 11 from the Until list box. Notice that Organizer then fills in the Days box for you. You can also select the beginning date in the From date box and then select the number of days in the Days box to have Organizer fill in the Until box for you.

7. **Click the Categories box and choose a category for this event from the drop-down list.**

   Remember that categories help you track people, events, and expenses.

The Book Free Time check box, if checked, books the events into your calendar for you. Use this option to keep from double-booking an appointment or event. Use this option in conjunction with the Show Through feature, explained later in this chapter.

The Repeat button enables you to schedule a recurring event or meeting in advance as many times as you like. See Chapter 22 for details. Likewise, the Cost button enables you to assign cost and customer codes to your planner events, just as you can assign codes to calendar appointments and other Organizer items. See Chapter 22 for more info.

Planning to alarm you

As you may remember from the earlier sections, the Alarm button enables you to set an alarm as a reminder. You can set the alarm from either the Create Event or the Edit Event dialog box. Setting an alarm in the Planner is the same as setting one for appointments. For details, see Chapter 22.

Entering events directly

Two View icons appear below the Toolbox in the Planner. One (the icon on the right) is for viewing the Planner by the year, and the other (the icon on the left) is for viewing the Planner by the quarter. Using the Quarterly view has an advantage. Remember that, in the Create Event dialog box, you can assign events to up to four rows for each day, rows that otherwise don't appear. The Quarterly view shows all four rows of the Planner clearly, while the Yearly view shows only two rows without overlapping. For the following example, click the icon that switches to the Quarterly view. Notice that the side tabs change from yearly to quarterly indexing.

The Planner displays colored key codes at the bottom of the page (see Figure 23-12). After you select one of these with the mouse, the mouse pointer turns into a highlighting marker. Now you can choose where to mark the Planner. Just above the key codes is a text box that shows you the date the mouse pointer is on or the dates covered by any box the mouse pointer is on. Move the mouse around the Planner, and you see how that box tracks your moves.

Click the key code you want and move to the Planner. Suppose, for example, that you have an all-day conference on May 5. You could click the Conference key and move the mouse pointer to May on the Planner. After the tracking box reads, just click the mouse. May 5 now shows a conference. Wait a minute! What if you want an alarm set here? No problem — touch the event on the Planner page with the mouse pointer. After the pointer changes to a hand, click the right mouse button and a pop-up menu appears displaying all the options available in the Create Event dialog box. See? You can do all your work right from the Planner page.

Mouse pointer   Date box

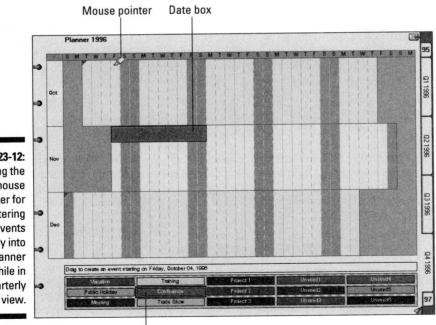

Figure 23-12:
Using the mouse pointer for entering events directly into the Planner while in Quarterly view.

Key codes

You can easily set aside several days for an event. Suppose that you want to attend a series of meetings in Seattle from October 14 through 18. You could set this event by clicking the Meeting key at the bottom of the Planner page. After you move the mouse to October 14 on the Planner page (so that the date appears in the tracking box), you click and hold the left mouse button and drag the Meeting color block that appears through October 18, as shown in Figure 22-13.

You can use the rows to set up more than one event on the same day. Suppose that you want to attend a training seminar in Seattle on October 15. Click the Training key, move the mouse up to October 15, and click right below the first event (not above the event block). Now you have two events for the same day.

The only significance to the rows is the significance you attach to them. You don't need to put a day's first event at the top — you can have your most important blocks at the bottom, if you so desire. And if you want to move blocks around, simply click the block you want to move and drag the block to the correct location. You can also change a selected block's length by moving the mouse to an end of the block (where the cursor changes into a two-headed arrow) and then clicking and dragging until the block is the desired length. To delete a block, simply click that block and press the Delete key. Poof — it's gone.

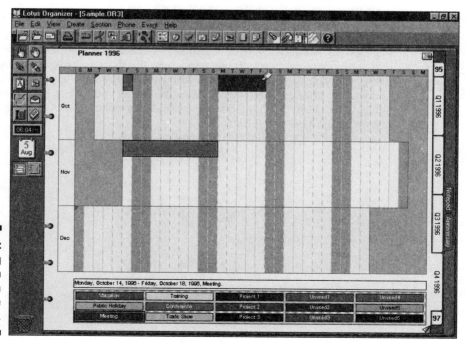

Figure 23-13:
Marking more than one day at a time on the Planner.

If you want all these bookings to show into the Calendar, choose Section⇨
Show Through or click the Show Through SmartIcon to open the Show Through
dialog box (see Figure 23-14). Select Calendar in the Show Into drop-down list
and then highlight Planner in the From list box to enable the events to show
through from the Planner to the Calendar; then click OK. After you return to the
Calendar section of Organizer, all the Planner's events appear in your Appointment book.

Figure 23-14:
The Show
Through
dialog box.

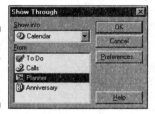

You may feel like looking at the Calendar section to make sure that the events
are there, but you may notice a problem — you can't find the Calendar tab. This
missing tab, however, is not really a problem. Click the Planner icon at the top-
right corner of the Planner page (with a page and a red arrow) and the page
folds up, revealing the rest of the notebook.

 If you want to assign your own key codes in the unused keys of the Planner
page, do so by choosing View⇨Planner Preferences. A Planner Preferences
dialog box appears in which you can adjust the Planner to suit your needs. Click
the Key button, and a master chart with the Planner keys appears. Click the key
you want to change, drag over the existing name, and type in your own key
name. Click OK to close the dialog boxes after you finish, and the new name(s)
appear in the keys at the bottom.

Chapter 24

Organizer — Final Touches and Shortcuts

*Y*ou've probably never been in the doghouse for forgetting an important date, right? You have? Then set up Organizer to remind you of those important times and never be in trouble again (you hope).

You Say It's Your Birthday

The Anniversary section of Organizer is a simple, painless way to remember important recurring dates, holidays, birthdays, and so on. You can use the Show Through feature to transfer any events from Anniversary to Calendar so that you remember the dates. (For more information on the Show Through features, check out the "Entering events directly" section in Chapter 23.)

Click the Anniversary tab, and Organizer turns to the Anniversary section with the page open to the current month. Four View icons appear below the Toolbox that enable you to view your Anniversary calendar by Month, Year, Zodiac signs, or Category. (Bear in mind, however, that viewing by category isn't very useful because, by default, Organizer puts all traditional holidays on a separate page labeled "Uncategorized.")

Remember that a category helps you track certain projects across all the Organizer sections. So, why would you want to assign a category to an anniversary? Well, an anniversary is more than just birthdays and such, although you may want to add the birthdays of co-workers or friends and family. You can also enter other long-term planning dates — such as project milestones and the due dates for quarterly tax payments — and select an appropriate category for each entry. You can find more information on categories in the section "Ladies and gentlemen, choose a category," in Chapter 22.

To use the Anniversary section to remember important dates, follow these steps:

1. **Double-click the month of your choice or click the Entry icon in the Toolbox (which now looks like a calendar page).**

   The Create Anniversary dialog box appears, as shown in Figure 24-1.

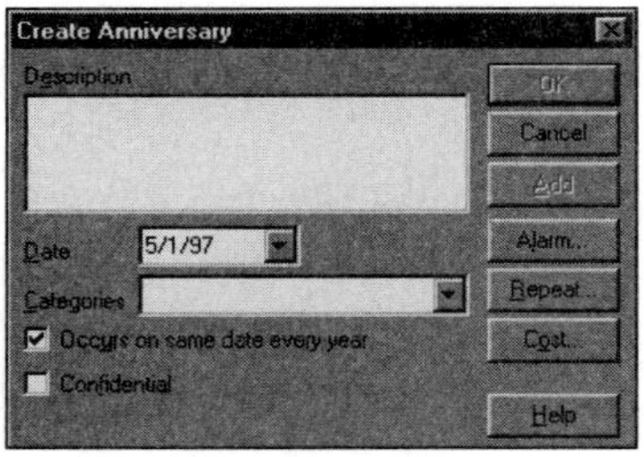

Figure 24-1:
The Create Anniversary dialog box.

2. **Type the name or description of the anniversary date in the Description text box.**

3. **Click the Date drop-down arrow and select the correct date from the list.**

   Suppose that you want to enter Mother's Day. This holiday always falls on the second Sunday in May, so for 1997 you select May 11.

4. **Click the Categories drop-down arrow and select a category, if desired.**

   The default holidays aren't assigned categories, but you can assign new entries to categories if you want. For instance, Mother's Day may be assigned to the Personal category. (You can go back and edit the existing anniversary entries and assign them to categories, if you want to go to the trouble of doing it.)

5. **Select the Occurs on same date every year check box, if appropriate.**

   The Occurs on same date every year option is selected by default. But in some cases, such as Mother's Day, the anniversary does not fall on the same date every year. If so, you must click the check box to deselect this option.

6. **If the anniversary doesn't occur on the same date each year, click the Repeat button to open the Repeat dialog box so that you can enter this anniversary for following years; schedule the dates for recurrences of this anniversary in the Repeat dialog box and then click OK to return to the Create Anniversary dialog box.**

   If the anniversary doesn't fall on the same date each year, Organizer needs some help scheduling recurrences of the anniversary for following years. For dates such as Mother's Day, you need to enter each date into the Repeats dialog box as a separate Custom date. (For more information on setting recurring dates, refer to Chapter 22.)

   For example, to set the dates for Mother's Day, select Custom from the top list box in the Repeats area of the Repeat dialog box. Next, in the Custom Dates area, click the drop-down arrow button to display the calendar, click the right-arrow to scroll to next May, and click the correct date (the second Sunday, remember?). Click Add to add this date to the list of dates in the Repeats area. Repeat this procedure for each year you want to schedule the anniversary. In the Duration area, click the For radio button; then click the plus (+) button a few times to specify an appropriate number of years and select Years from the drop-down list. After you finish scheduling recurrences of the anniversary, click OK to close the Repeat dialog box and return to the Create Anniversary dialog box.

7. **(Optional) Set an alarm as a reminder (refer to Chapter 22 for information).**

8. **(Optional) Set any cost codes needed (refer to Chapter 22 for information).**

9. **Click OK to return to the Anniversary section.**

If you want the dates you are setting to appear in the Calendar, click the Show Through SmartIcon to open the Show Through dialog box, as described in Chapter 23. Select Calendar in the Show Into drop-down list box and then select Anniversary in the From list box before you click OK. After you return to the Calendar tab, you see all your anniversaries displayed in your Appointment book.

Keeping Notes — Plus a Whole Lot More

Organizer's *Notepad* is one of the most valuable tools for the person who keeps a notepad on their desk and can't find the thing half the time. You can keep notes, certainly, but you can also import spreadsheets, text files, pictures, graphs, maps, and so on onto a Notepad page and then link that page to another page as a reference.

Click the Notepad tab, and Organizer turns to a Notepad Contents page. Every time you enter a Notepad page, Organizer automatically updates the Notepad Contents page with the new page numbers and titles.

Another nice feature of Notepad is that you can have as many pages as you like for any entry. Notepad enables you to create chapters, too, to keep pages together. To enter a Notepad page, follow these steps:

1. **Click the Entry icon in the Toolbox (which now looks like a notepad) to open the Create Page dialog box, as shown in Figure 24-2.**

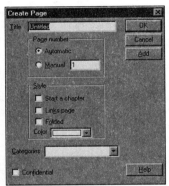

Figure 24-2:
The Create Page dialog box for Notepad.

2. **Each entry has its own page, so give your page a title in the Title text box.**

3. **Select the Automatic radio button in the Page number area if you want Organizer to add the new page to the end of your Notepad, or choose Manual if you want to assign the page number yourself.**

   You need to place the page manually if you want to insert your new page between existing pages — perhaps to group the new page with other pages related to the same project.

4. **(Optional) In the Style area you can check options to designate the page as the one to Start a chapter, as a Links page, or as a Folded page and even define its Color if you want.**

   The *Start a chapter* option makes your new page appear in bold on the Notepad Contents page. Having a page as a chapter heading can be handy if you're grouping Notepad pages on the same projects.

   The *Links page* option creates a page of links to other Organizer items. We find that using the Link icon in the Toolbox is a better choice for linking pages, however, because this option enables you to combine text and links on the same page. (See the section "Just a link in the chain," later in this chapter.)

The *Folded* option creates a double-width page to accommodate oversized items such as tables imported from a 1-2-3 worksheet.

The *Color* option enables you to select the color of the page. Just click the drop-down arrow button to display a color palette and then click the color of your choice in the palette.

5. Click the Categories drop-down list box and choose a category, if one applies.

A category can help you organize Notepad during a sort or if you're in the Category view and can help you track projects throughout Organizer.

6. Click OK to create the page, close the Create Page dialog box, and go to the newly created page, or click the Add button to add the page to your Notepad section and begin defining another page.

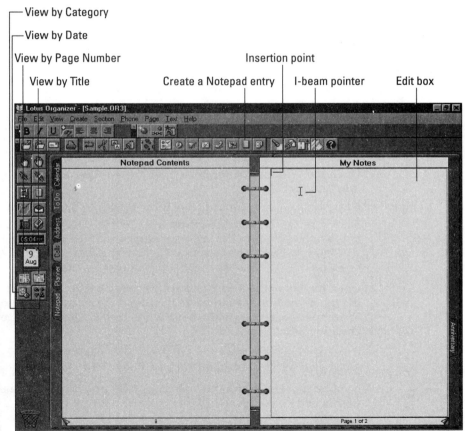

View by Category
View by Date
View by Page Number
View by Title
Insertion point
Create a Notepad entry
I-beam pointer
Edit box

Figure 24-3:
A blank
Notepad
page ready
for you to
start typing
your notes.

Organizer displays the newly created page in the Notepad section. Click once anywhere on the blank page area (between the title at the top and the page number footer at the bottom) to put an edit box around the page. Click again for an insertion point cursor to appear, as shown in Figure 24-3. Now, just start typing your notes. If you reach the bottom of the page, just keep going; you can make the page as long as you like. Organizer adds a scroll bar to the right side of the page to enable you to scroll the page if all your notes can't fit on one screen.

Adding a File from Another Application

Importing a file from another application may seem technical, but the task is actually quite easy and the results are astonishing. By importing a file, map, graph, or spreadsheet onto a Notepad page, Notepad becomes a powerful tool to help you organize information, remember information from other programs, and keep pertinent facts with your notes. You may, for example, find that importing a spreadsheet on a client helps you remember important facts in designing a new proposal for the client's firm.

To import a file from another application, just follow these steps:

1. **Save your Organizer file by clicking the Save File SmartIcon.**

   Always save your work before opening other applications — the safe thing to do.

2. **Open the Windows program containing the file you want to import into Notepad.**

   If you're opening another SmartSuite 97 program, you can click its SuiteStart icon or start the program by double-clicking its icon in the Lotus Applications folder in SmartCenter's SmartSuite drawer. For other Windows programs, such as WordPad, you probably need to select the program from the Start menu in the Windows taskbar.

3. **Open the file in the new Windows program, select the portion of that file (up to the entire contents of the file) that you want to see on the Notepad page, and copy the selection to the Windows Clipboard by choosing Edit⇨Copy.**

   If you need assistance with any of these procedures you can refer to *Windows 95 For Dummies,* by Andy Rathbone (IDG Books Worldwide, Inc.).

   If you're copying from another SmartSuite 97 program, you can use the Copy SmartIcon to copy the selected data to the Clipboard.

4. **Switch back to Organizer.**

You can click the Organizer icon in SuiteStart, double-click the Organizer icon in SmartCenter, or press and hold the Alt key and press Tab until the Organizer title and icon are highlighted in the dialog box that appears.

5. **Click the Notepad section tab and create a page by clicking the Entry icon.**

6. **Title the page and click OK.**

7. **Click the new page to put an edit box around that page and click again with the I-beam pointer to get the blinking text insertion point cursor on the page, then click the Paste SmartIcon (or choose Edit⇨Paste or right-click the page and choose Paste from the pop-up menu).**

Organizer pastes the information from the Clipboard onto the Notepad page. Figure 24-4, for example, shows a Lotus 1-2-3 spreadsheet that's been imported into Notepad. Notice that the columns at the top and bottom wrap to second lines because the page is not wide enough to hold all the information. Click the right mouse button and choose Page from the pop-up menu that appears (or choose Page⇨Page from the menu bar). Select the Folded check box in the Page dialog box that appears and then click OK. A Folded Page icon appears at the top of the Notepad page. Click the icon to view the entire spreadsheet across the page, as shown in Figure 24-5.

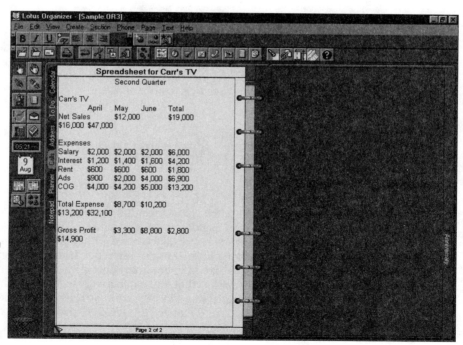

Figure 24-4:
Importing a spreadsheet into Notepad.

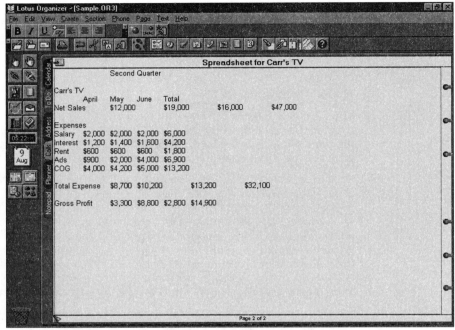

Figure 24-5:
The same
imported
spreadsheet
viewed
using a fold-
out feature.

If you want to add text to an existing Notepad page, such as adding names to a list, go to the page you want to edit, click the page once to select that page, and then click the page to place the insertion point where you want to edit. After you finish editing, click the page title to stop editing.

Almanac — a Desk Reference at Your Fingertips

You've seen them before — those almanacs that contain all kinds of useless information and a little bit of useful information as well. The chances are good that one is sitting on a shelf near you, all covered with dust. Well, that doesn't happen with the handy-dandy little *Almanac* reference feature in Organizer. First of all, this almanac can never go on your shelf. Second, the Organizer Almanac is filled with relevant information that you can actually use! (You can, for example, look up U.S. area codes and foreign country telephone codes, time zones, world air mileage, U.S. and metric conversions, birthstones, wedding anniversaries, and much more.)

This Almanac is simply a pre-configured Organizer file. To access the Almanac, you must first save your current Organizer file by choosing File⇨Save. Then choose File⇨Open to open Almanac just as you open any other Organizer file. (Almanac is easy to locate in the default folder for Organizer files.) After Almanac is open on-screen, click the Reference tab and check out all the cool things the feature offers, as shown in Figure 24-6. You can turn to any page by double-clicking that page number in the Contents page displayed in the figure. (Yes, this example is of a contents page in the Notepad section of Organizer. In the Almanac, the Notepad section is simply been renamed Reference.)

After you browse around in the Reference section of Almanac, you can click the Holidays tab and check out the international holidays. Just as the Reference section is a renamed Notepad section, the Holidays section of the Almanac is a renamed Anniversary section. The book opens to the current month. The View icons are the same as in the Anniversaries section of Organizer — Month, Year, Zodiac signs, and Category. You can copy a holiday to your Anniversaries section by clicking the Copy SmartIcon.

Note: Do not attempt to drag an item from Almanac to the Toolbox Clipboard — this procedure does not work well for copying repeating holidays.

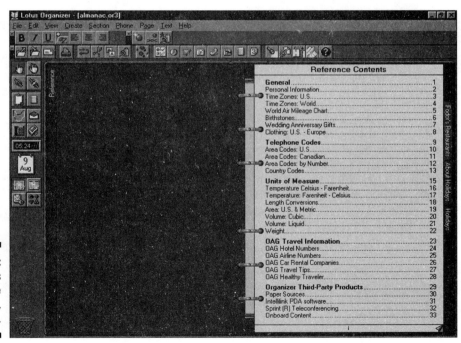

Figure 24-6:
Almanac's
Reference
Contents,
page 1 of 2.

Suppose that you want to copy a holiday from the Almanac to the Anniversaries section of your notebook. You copy the holiday to the Anniversaries section by performing the following steps:

1. **Open the file (probably ALMANAC.OR3) in Organizer.**

2. **In the Holidays tab of the Almanac, click the black down arrow in the month of May (located in the lower-right corner) to scroll to the holiday you want.**

3. **Click to highlight the holiday and then click the Copy SmartIcon.**

   Organizer copies the anniversary item to the Windows Clipboard.

   You can select several holidays to copy at once by holding the Ctrl key as you click each holiday entry in turn.

4. **Open your Organizer file by choosing File⇨Open, selecting your file, and clicking Open; then click the Anniversaries section tab in your Organizer file.**

   If, for example, you have selected Memorial Day, you do not need to turn to the Memorial Day page; Organizer performs this action for you.

5. **Click the Paste SmartIcon and watch Organizer work!**

   Organizer adds the entries you copied from the Holidays section of Almanac to the Anniversary section in your own Organizer file.

The technique above works for copying holidays, but doesn't work as well for copying some other entries from one Organizer file to another. For instance, suppose that you want to copy the U.S. Time Zones into your Notepad because of all the long distance calls you make. The normal copy procedure copies the text (the page title) but not the map graphic. Not to worry though; Organizer's Copy Special command enables you to select and copy entries (and portions of entries) that don't copy well by other means. Just follow these steps:

1. **Open the Almanac file (choose File⇨Open), click the Reference section tab, and then locate the entry you want to copy.**

   In this case, double-click the Time Zones: U.S. page in the Reference Contents to open the page you want to copy.

2. **Select the entry you want to copy.**

   Click anywhere on the U.S. Time zones page to select the page. (You can unfold the page first if you want, but doing so isn't really necessary.)

3. Choose Edit⇨Copy Special.

This action opens the Copy Special dialog box, as shown in Figure 24-7.

The Copy Special dialog box enables you to select and copy a portion of the selected Organizer item. In this case, you have only one special section to choose from (there is only one element that doesn't copy using the normal Copy command and therefore needs special handling). If, however, you were copying an Address entry, for example, the Copy Special dialog box may enable you to select just the address or the phone number to copy instead of copying the entire entry.

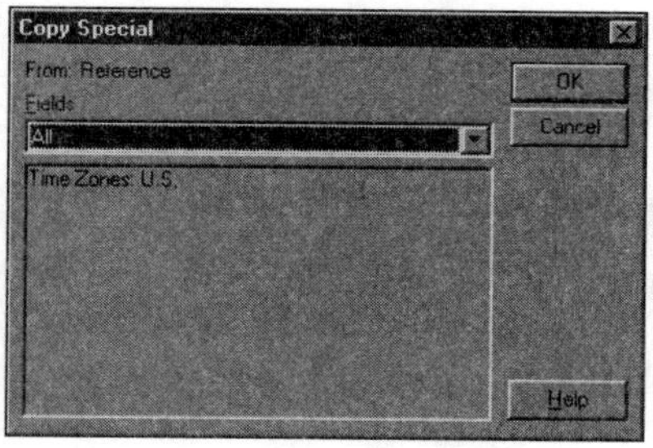

Figure 24-7:
The Copy
Special
dialog box.

4. Select All in the Fields drop-down list box and click OK.

After you select All, the name of the map appears in the box below the Fields drop-down list so that you know whether you've got the right thing selected to copy. After you click OK, Organizer copies the selected information to the Clipboard.

5. Open your Organizer file (choose File⇨Open) and click the Notepad section tab.

You don't need to use the Create Page dialog box for this action.

6. Click the Paste SmartIcon or choose Edit⇨Paste from the menu bar.

The Time Zones: U.S. page appears in your Notepad, complete with its picture (see Figure 24-8).

By using the same procedures, you can copy anything from the Almanac (or another Organizer file) to Notepad.

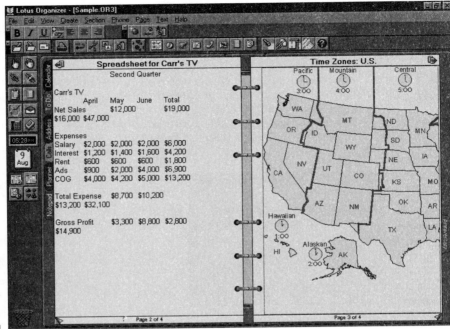

Figure 24-8:
The Time
Zones map
from the
Almanac
pasted into
the Notepad
section of
another
Organizer
file.

Tying Up the Loose Ends

This section describes some specialized topics that can make life with Organizer run more smoothly.

Filtering out the noise

A *filter* enables you to choose only particular data matching criteria you specify. For example, you can use a filter to view all the entries in Calendar pertaining to a particular project — and only those entries. You can also filter information throughout several Notebook sections at the same time. If you need to locate all items pertaining to your client, Johnathon Hall, for example, you can create a filter to locate these items for you. Then you can view only those entries in Organizer, without all the distractions and clutter of other entries.

Using a filter is a two-step process. First, you must create a filter by defining what information you want to search for and what Organizer sections you want to search in. Then you apply the filter to view only the items that match the criteria you set up in the filter. After you define a filter, you can reuse that filter as many times as you like. The next time you want to use the same filter, all you need to do is apply the filter; you don't have to redefine the filter each time.

To create a filter, follow these steps:

1. Choose _Create⇨_Filters from the menu bar.

The Filters dialog box appears, as shown in Figure 24-9. After you create any filters, those filters appear here in the _F_ilters list for you to use again.

Figure 24-9:
The Filters
dialog box.

2. Click the New button.

The New Filter dialog box appears.

3. Type a name for your filter in the Name text box.

4. Click the empty box in the first row under the Section column; then click the drop-down arrow in the Section box and choose an Organizer section in which to search (Calendar, Notepad, Address, and so on).

5. Click the Field drop-down arrow and select a field in which to search.

For example, you may choose to search the Category field. (See, we told you those categories would be useful.)

6. Click the Test drop-down arrow and select the word(s) that best suit your search criteria (such as Begins With or Contains).

Note: The selections available in the Test box vary depending on the kind of field you selected in the Field box. For example, the tests associated with a date field let you search for dates on, before, or after a given date, while the texts for a text field — such as a name — test for items that begin with a certain letter or contain a string of characters.

7. In the Value box, type the word or numbers you want to search for.

You can also create a filter that displays a dialog box and asks you to fill in the value every time you apply the filter. To do so, enter a question mark and then a value in the Value box. Suppose, for example, that you want a filter that enables you to search for a different last name in the Address section every time you apply the filter. You'd type **? Last name** in the Value box.

8. Click the And/Or field and select And or Or if you want to add additional fields or sections.

Use the *And* selection if you want more than one field or Section included in the application of the filter. For example, if you want a filter based on both the Start date and Category in the To Do section, choose *And* and define the second criteria on the next line. The filter selects only those items that meet both criteria. Click the *Or* selection if you want the filter to select items that meet either the criteria on the current line or the criteria on the following line. You'll use this option to select items from more than one Section, such as a filter based on a Start date in the To Do and Calendar sections. If you make an And/Or selection, you must fill in the next row in the dialog box to define a criteria for the And/Or choice to refer to.

9. **(Optional) Repeat Steps 4 through 8 to add other filter criteria as needed.**

   If, for example, you want to filter items in another Organizer section, you define additional criteria for each section. Each set of filter criteria takes up a separate row.

10. **Select the Show in View – Apply Filter Menu check box if you want your new filter displayed in the View⇨Apply Filter menu.**

    This step is optional. It places your newly defined filter on the flyout menu that appears when you choose View⇨Apply Filter. Then, to use the filter in the future, all you need to do is choose it from the menu. However, if you don't plan to reuse the filter (or don't expect to se it often), you can leave the check box empty to keep the filter from appearing on the menu.

11. **Click OK after you finish defining the filter.**

    Organizer returns to the Filters dialog box.

12. **Select your new filter from the list and click Apply to apply it.**

    Organizer displays only those items matching the filter criteria in the sections to which the filter applies. All the other entries disappear.

After you define a filter, you can apply the filter by choosing Create⇨Filters to open the Filters dialog box, selecting the filter from the Filters list, and clicking Apply; you can also apply the filter by choosing View⇨Apply Filter⇨*Filter Name* (provided you elected to include the filter in the Apply Filter menu, as described in Step 10 of the preceding steps).

To remove the filter and return your display to normal, choose View⇨Clear Filter. Organizer again displays all the entries instead of only those matching your filter.

Just a link in the chain

Cross-referencing entries in Organizer is called *linking*. Creating a link between data is very handy for quick retrieval of needed information. You may, for example, link an appointment in the Calendar section to the address card of the person or company in the Address section. Then, by clicking the Link icon in the Calendar entry, you can easily access information in this person's address card without having to turn to the Address section. You may also link an appointment for a meeting in Calendar to the Notepad page containing the agenda for the meeting. The Notepad page may have a link to the Freelance presentation file you're working on for that meeting. The possibilities are nearly endless.

To create a link, follow these steps:

1. **Open the Calendar section (or another section) and choose an appointment that you want to link.**

2. **Click the Link icon in the Toolbox and then click the appointment you want to link.**

   Suppose that you want to link Jonathon Hall's address card to the appointment with Hall listed in your Calendar. Start by clicking the Link icon, and then click the appointment with Jonathon Hall. Notice that the Pointing Hand cursor now holds a chain (see Figure 24-10).

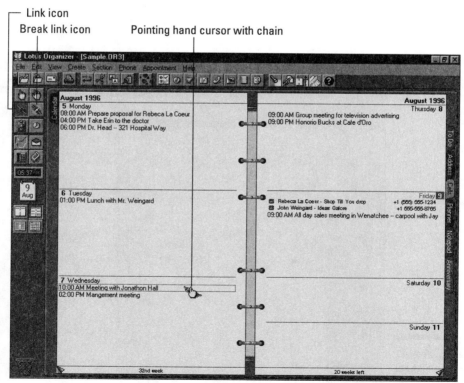

Figure 24-10: Creating a link from Calendar to address card.

3. Click the section tab and item you want to link to.

To continue our example, turn to the Address section by clicking the Address tab. Then click the H index tab and access the page containing Jonathon Hall's information. Click Hall's name on the page, and a link appears on the right-hand side of the card, as shown in Figure 24-11.

That's all you do! You've created a link between the appointment with Jonathon Hall and his address card. Now, to use the link, follow these steps:

1. Click the Calendar tab and click the appointment you linked.

2. Click the Link icon next to the appointment.

A Link box appears with Mr. Hall's name and company displayed on a clickable button, as shown in Figure 24-12. If you had created more links from this appointment, there would be a separate button for each link.

3. Click the button for the desired link in the Link box.

Organizer takes you to the linked information — in this case, Jonathon Hall's address card.

You can create a link from any section of Organizer to any other section.

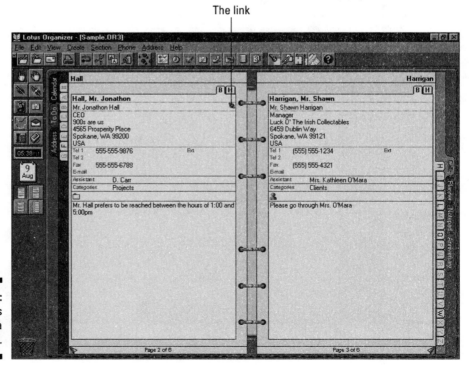

The link

Figure 24-11:
An address
card with a
link.

Link box

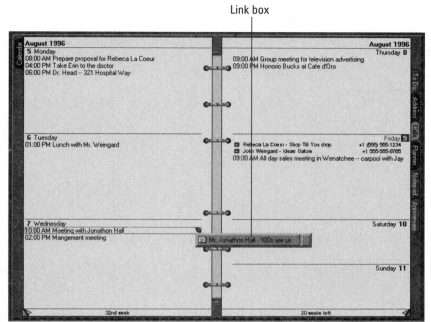

5 Monday
08:00 AM Prepare proposal for Rebeca La Coeur
04:00 PM Take Erin to the doctor
06:00 PM Dr. Head -- 321 Hospital Way

August 1996
Thursday 8
09:00 AM Group meeting for television advertising
09:00 PM Honorio Bucks at Cafe d'Oro

6 Tuesday
01:00 PM Lunch with Mr. Weingard

Friday 9
Rebeca La Coeur - Shop Till You drop   +1 (555) 555-1234
John Weingard - Ideas Galore   +1 555-555-8765
09:00 AM All day sales meeting in Wenatchee -- carpool with Jay

7 Wednesday
10:00 AM Meeting with Jonathon Hall
02:00 PM Mangement meeting

Saturday 10

Mr. Jonathon Hall - 900s are us

Sunday 11

Figure 24-12:
A Link box.

32nd week   20 weeks left

To disconnect a link, click the Break Link icon in the Toolbox, click the Link icon beside the linked appointment, and then click the link after the Link box appears. That's all you need to do!

Although the topic is beyond the scope of this book, we still think it is worth mentioning that Organizer is fully compatible with modems and Local Area Networks (LAN). With a LAN, as well as a modem, you can send and receive messages and mail through your computer by using Lotus Notes or cc:Mail. Organizer can coordinate with other Organizer users on the network to share appointment books and schedule meetings at mutually convenient times. Check with your network administrator for details on how to use these features.

Part VII
The Part of Tens

In this part . . .

This part covers several tips and tricks to help you get your work done more efficiently. You find shortcuts for all the SmartSuite 97 programs, as well as some that apply everywhere, no matter which program you're using. This part is a veritable treasure trove of neat stuff.

Chapter 25

Ten Best Tips and Shortcuts (That Work Anywhere)

* *

In This Chapter

▶ Create your own user dictionary

▶ Use the SuiteStart icons to switch among applications

▶ Open files in a flash

▶ Make a bold (or italic or underlined) statement

▶ Help is just a bubble away

▶ A file saved is a file you don't need to do over

▶ Check your status

▶ Use the status bar

▶ Use the Shift+Click trick

▶ Cut and Paste without clicking

* *

*L*est you forget that all the SmartSuite 97 applications have a lot in common, here are ten tips and shortcuts that you can use to save time and sanity almost anywhere in the SmartSuite 97 universe.

Create Your Own User Dictionary

You probably use a lot of words that don't exist in any dictionary: people's names, esoteric terms that no one outside your field has heard of — stuff such as that. For the spell-checker to have to stop every time it sees the name *Mordensky,* for example, is a waste of time, especially if that's part of your company name and you use it repeatedly in just about every document.

After the spell-checker stops on a word that's not in the SmartSuite 97 dictionary, but is a word that you use all the time, just click the Add to User Dictionary button. From then on, whenever you run a spell-check, SmartSuite 97 recognizes the word and doesn't bug you about it. (Hallelujah!)

The only application in which this doesn't work is Organizer, because that program doesn't have a spell checker. As a side note to this tip, if you're putting a bunch of text into an Organizer file (probably a Notepad page), you may just want to create the document in Word Pro first so that you can spell check the text and then retrieve the Word Pro document into your Organizer file.

Use the SuiteStart Icons to Switch Applications

Take advantage of the integration features of SmartSuite 97 by keeping the SuiteStart icons in the system tray of the Windows 95 taskbar. Then, whenever you want to switch to a different SmartSuite 97 application, all you need to do is click a SuiteStart icon.

If you don't have those little SuiteStart icons in your system tray (next to the clock display), here's how you can make them appear:

1. **Click the Start button in the taskbar to open the Windows 95 Start menu.**

   You can also press Ctrl+Esc or the Windows key (between Ctrl and Alt on some newer keyboards) to open the Start menu.

2. **Point to Programs, point to Lotus SmartSuite, and then point to Lotus Accessories to open the series of cascading menus.**

3. **Choose SuiteStart 97 from the menu.**

   Note: Your Lotus SmartSuite 97 program menu may be called something else. If it's not called Lotus SmartSuite and you don't know what else it may be, check with whoever set up your system.

Open Files in a Flash

All the SmartSuite 97 programs keep track of the files you've worked on most recently. (The actual number of files depends on the program.) What this means is that you can often avoid the hassle of going through the Open dialog box, changing drives and directories, and scrolling around to find the file you want. Just open the File menu and take a look at the very bottom of the menu. The last few files you used are listed right there with numbers next to them. To open one of the files, just click its filename in the menu or use your keyboard to press the number listed on the menu for that file.

Windows 95 also keeps track of the last few files you've worked on and enables you to choose them from the Start menu. Just click the Start button, point to Documents on the Start menu, and choose the file you want to work on from that menu.

Make a Bold (Or Italic or Underlined) Statement

Word Pro, Approach, Freelance, and 1-2-3 all use the same keystroke shortcuts for text attributes, as shown in the following list:

- Ctrl+B for boldface
- Ctrl+U for underlining
- Ctrl+I for italics

Use these keys to apply attributes quickly throughout SmartSuite 97.

Help Is Just a Bubble Away

Don't forget the Bubble Help feature of SmartSuite 97. If you're not sure what a particular SmartIcon does, put your mouse pointer on the icon and wait a second. A short description of the icon's function appears in a little bubble.

A File Saved Is a File You Don't Need to Do Over

Save, save, and save again! Save after you do a spell-check, save before you use a feature you haven't worked with before; save before you make complex changes that may not turn out the way you expect; save when the skies are cloudy. . . .

But seriously, folks, saving frequently is one of the best ways to set your mind at ease so that you can confidently play with new features and expand your SmartSuite 97 repertoire. If you save whatever you're working on before you try something you're not sure of, you don't need to worry about messing up your document. If everything turns to Silly Putty on you, just close the document without saving it. Then reopen the document and — hey, it's just like it was before it fell apart.

Check Your Status

The status bar (at the bottom of the screen) is a very cool place to hang out — those in the know know that the status bar is the place to be if you want to know what's happening (y' know?). In most of the SmartSuite 97 applications, the status bar tells you what page you're on, what the current font and point size is, and the current date and time. The status bar is often used to display error messages or messages that describe the current action, too.

Use the Status Bar

Not only is the status bar a cool place to hang out, but you can also find a lot of action going on there. In Word Pro, for example, if you click the status bar button that displays the current style name, you get a list of all the styles in the document. You can change the style just by clicking a different style name in this list. This process is much easier than going through a bunch of menus and dialog boxes for the same results.

As you work with the different SmartSuite 97 applications, check out the different status bar buttons and see what they do. They're not just pretty faces.

Use the Shift+Click Trick

SmartSuite 97 offers all sorts of different ways to select text, but the Shift+Click trick is one of the handiest and most precise. Just put your insertion point at the beginning of the text you want to select, move the mouse pointer to the end of the selection, and press and hold the Shift key as you click the left mouse button.

The only caveat here is that you need to be careful not to move the insertion point from the starting point until you're ready to Shift+Click. Use the mouse or the scroll bars to move the mouse pointer — using the arrow keys on the keyboard moves the insertion point, which you don't want for this trick.

Cut and Paste without Clicking

The Cut, Copy, and Paste commands on the Edit menu aren't hard to use, but using keyboard shortcuts for those commands is usually much faster. The shortcuts in the following list work in all the SmartSuite 97 programs (and nearly all other Windows programs as well):

- Ctrl+C for Copy
- Ctrl+X for Cut
- Ctrl+V for Paste

C for Copy is easy to remember and *X* for Cut makes some sense, even if it isn't an obvious mnemonic. The *V* for Paste must come from some strange foreign language or twisted logic, but you soon get so used to using this key that its weirdness doesn't make any difference. All three keyboard shortcuts become second nature.

Chapter 26

Ten Best Tips and Shortcuts for the SmartSuite 97 Programs

*O*kay, Chapter 25 gives you the ten best tips and shortcuts that you can use anywhere in SmartSuite 97. This Part of Tens chapter gives you the ten best tips and shortcuts — two to a program — for the individual SmartSuite 97 applications: Word Pro, 1-2-3, Approach, Freelance Graphics, and Organizer (in that order). So we guess this chapter is really a Part of Twos chapter. But they're *good* twos! Try 'em and see if you don't agree.

Get out of Word Pro Jams by Using Reset to Style

Word Pro has this really cool feature called Reset to Style, which enables you to make a total mess out of things with wild formatting changes and then say, "Yuck! I don't like any of that. Put the document back the way it was." You don't even need to stamp your feet and pout. If you make formatting changes and then decide you don't like them, just select the text and choose Text⇨ Named Styles⇨Reset to Style from the menu bar (or just click the Reset to Style SmartIcon). Your text reverts to the formatting defined in the named style applied to that paragraph. If you just want to remove the last formatting change but want to keep previous changes, use the Undo command instead of Reset to Style.

Click to Select in Word Pro

Dragging can be a real drag. Here's a Word Pro tip that can cut down on your dragging: With your insertion point anywhere in a sentence, press and hold the Ctrl key while you click the left mouse button to select the entire sentence. If you want to select a whole word, don't waste time dragging the mouse pointer through the word. Just put your insertion point anywhere in the word and double-click. Voilà!

Have 1-2-3 Adjust Your Column Widths for You

Don't waste time trying to figure out how wide to make a 1-2-3 column. Just move the mouse pointer over the border on the right side of the column letter so that it (the pointer, not the border) turns into a two-headed arrow. Then double-click. The column instantly adjusts to accommodate the longest entry currently occupying any cell in the column.

Get There Fast in 1-2-3 by Using F5

If you can see the 1-2-3 cell you want to move to on-screen, the fastest way to get there in 1-2-3 is just to click that cell. If, however, you need to make a larger leap, press F5 — the Go To key — to display the Go To dialog box. Then just type the address of the cell (or chart or drawn object) in the dialog box that you want to get to or click the range name in the list of names; then click the OK button. Hey! You're there already. (Boy, are *you* a fast learner!)

Modify an Approach Database Template

Approach provides more than 50 different SmartMaster applications and templates — predesigned databases in which to store information ranging from mailing lists and employees to art collections and musical groups. Using an existing database template and deleting the fields you don't need is almost always easier than creating a database from scratch. Each time you load Approach, a Welcome to Approach dialog box appears, asking if you want to open an existing database or create a new one. If you choose to create a new database, Approach displays the available SmartMasters in a list box. Just choose one and alter away.

Automate and Verify Approach Data Entry

To help eliminate errors and reduce work (which is why we all spend thousands of dollars on computers — and then spend an equal amount trying to figure out how they work), Approach can automate data entry into certain fields, such as dates, times, or calculations based on other fields. Just as easily as Approach can automate data entry, the program can also check for valid entries if someone types data into your database. By verifying your data as it's entered, you needn't wonder whether stored data is really correct. (For more information about verifying and automating data entry, see Chapter 18.)

Move Freelance Graphics Objects as a Group

To maintain the relationship in Freelance Graphics between several drawn graphic objects on a page so that you can manipulate them as one object, group them. To create a group, select the objects you want to group and then choose Drawing⇨Group. If you later need to manipulate the objects separately, select the group and choose Group⇨Ungroup. You can select all the objects on a page by pressing F4. This action doesn't officially group the objects but does enable you to work with the objects as a group on a temporary basis (until you deselect them).

Shuffle the Freelance Graphics Deck

The order of your pages in a Freelance Graphics presentation can make all the difference. The easiest way to get your pages in the order you want them is to switch to Page Sorter view by clicking the Page Sorter view tab and then dragging the pages to the desired positions.

Don't Type Repeating Organizer Address Fields — Duplicate!

Rest those tired fingers. Why retype duplicate entries if Organizer can do it for you? If you have several contacts from the same company, have Organizer do the dirty work. First, open the Create Address dialog box by clicking the Address tab and then clicking the Entry icon. Type the person's name, job title, and company in the Create Address dialog box. After you press the Tab key to go to the address field, the Similar Address Found dialog box appears. Select the company from the drop-down list box, and Organizer fills in the duplicate information. If you need more info on this feature, see Chapter 23.

Make a Long Leap with the Click of a Mouse

If you have sections such as Notepad set up with an Organizer index page, you can flip to any page in that section quickly. Double-click the page number in the index, and Organizer opens the Notepad to that page. Flip back to the index page by clicking the Backtrack SmartIcon (the one that appears to have footprints on it).

Appendix
Doing the Install Thing

● ●

*W*e told you in the Introduction that we assumed you already have SmartSuite 97 installed. Well, you know what happens when you assume, don't you? Suppose you don't have SmartSuite 97 installed and you can't rope someone into installing the programs for you. Don't panic! That's what this appendix is for. The steps herein give you a guided tour of the SmartSuite 97 installation process, complete with all the sights you encounter along the way. Just follow along and you can have SmartSuite 97 installed in no time.

Note: Far more installation options are available than we can possibly cover here. This appendix just describes the steps to follow for a simple, standard, stand-alone (non-network) installation. We do assume that you have enough hard-disk space and memory to accommodate a standard installation. (You need at least 8MB RAM (16MB is better) and about 126MB free hard-disk space. You can run some portions of SmartSuite 97 with 8MB RAM and as little as 89MB free hard-disk space, but that's really pushing your luck — and isn't enough horse-power for the installation we describe here.) If you're trying to do anything fancier than standard installation, you need to turn to the documentation that comes with SmartSuite 97 (ugh!) or find a nearby PC guru to give you a hand.

First, to get started, you need to find the CD-ROM disk or the huge stack of floppy disks that came with your SmartSuite 97 program. This baby is one big program! Actually, it's a bunch of big programs.

After you find the disks, follow these steps for a nice, uneventful standard installation:

1. **Start Windows 95, if it isn't already running, and close any programs that may be running.**

   The SmartSuite 97 installation is going to copy files and update your Start menu, after which you need to reboot your computer. So you don't want to have any other programs running while all this copying and updating is going on. You especially must disable any virus protection programs. Such programs can interfere with the installation.

2. **Insert the CD-ROM or the floppy disk labeled Disk 1 (Install) into the appropriate disk drive.**

If you're installing SmartSuite 97 from the CD, the splashy introductory screen shown in Figure AP-1 appears automatically after a short delay. After the screen appears, you can perform one of the following actions:

• **Click the One Button Install icon.**

This option proceeds automatically with a standard installation on your C: drive. You don't need to make any choices. Just let the installation program do its thing and then skip ahead to Step 14.

• **Click the Install Icon.**

This option starts the standard installation process, which gives you a bit more control over the process. For example, you can tell the installation program to install SmartSuite 97 on a different drive. After a moment, the Welcome to the Lotus SmartSuite Install Program dialog box appears (which is shown in Figure AP-2). Skip ahead to Step 6 in the instructions.

If you're installing SmartSuite 97 from the floppy disks, proceed to Step 3.

Figure AP-1:
The CD-ROM -based installation welcomes you with this screen.

3. **Click the Start button on the taskbar and choose Run to open the Run dialog box.**

4. **Type** a:install **in the Run dialog box's Open text box.**

   Note: If you put the installation disk in drive B, type **b:install** in the Open text box. If you don't know what this A and B drive stuff is all about, and you don't know which one you're using, find a friend who knows about computers to help you or read *PCs For Dummies*, 4th Edition, or *Windows 95 For Dummies* (both from IDG Books Worldwide, Inc.) right away.

5. **Click the OK button to start the installation process.**

   After a short time (anywhere from seconds to minutes, depending on the speed of your computer), the Welcome to the Lotus SmartSuite Install Program dialog box appears, as shown in Figure AP-2.

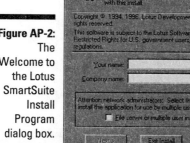

Figure AP-2:
The
Welcome to
the Lotus
SmartSuite
Install
Program
dialog box.

6. **Enter Your name and Company name in the appropriate text boxes and then click the Next button to open the Confirm Names dialog box.**

   You must enter a company name even if you aren't part of a company. You can make something up, but you can't leave the Company name text box blank. Don't ask us why.

7. **Click the Yes button if the names are correct; if the names aren't correct, click No and repeat Step 6.**

   The Specify Lotus SmartSuite Directory dialog box appears. This dialog box shows you how much space is available on your computer's hard drive and into which directory SmartSuite 97 is to be installed. If you have more than one drive available, you can select the one you want SmartSuite 97 installed on by choosing that drive from the Drive drop-down list.

8. Click the Next button.

If one or more of the SmartSuite 97 programs are already installed on your computer, the Multiple Copies of SmartSuite Products dialog box appears. (This box appears even if the entire suite is not installed.) If this dialog box appears, click the Next button to continue the installation. If no other SmartSuite 97 programs are found, the Select Lotus SmartSuite Applications dialog box appears, as shown in Figure AP-3.

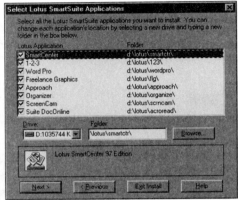

Figure AP-3:
The Select Lotus SmartSuite Applications dialog box.

9. Click the Next button to accept the standard defaults for installation.

The Install Options dialog box appears.

10. Make sure that the Default Features - Automatic Install option button is selected and then click the Next button to open the Select Program Group dialog box.

If some of the SmartSuite 97 programs are installed on your computer, you may see a different dialog box that asks if you want to overwrite existing paths or if you want to back up SmartMaster sets. Unless you know what you're doing, your best course is not to overwrite anything and always to back up everything if asked. If you choose to overwrite an existing program you wanted to keep, you're out of luck. It's gone.

11. Click the Next button to accept the default Lotus SmartSuite folder.

(This folder determines where all the SmartSuite 97 program icons appear on your Start menu. You can always move them later.) The Begin Copying Files dialog box appears.

12. Click the Yes button to begin installing SmartSuite 97.

The Lotus Install - Transferring Files dialog box appears to show you that the files are being installed on your hard drive. Be patient — this process may take a while. If you're installing from floppy disks instead of the CD-ROM, the installation periodically displays another Lotus Install dialog box to request the next disk.

13. **After you're prompted to do so, remove the floppy disk that's in the drive, insert the disk that Lotus is requesting, and then click the OK button; continue removing and inserting disks until the installation is complete.**

After the installation program copies all the files and completes any reconfiguration, the Install Complete dialog box appears.

14. **Click Done to finish the installation process.**

Next, a dialog box appears offering to register your software online by using your modem or Internet connection. To register online, select your location from the drop-down list and click Next. This opens the Lotus SmartSuite Registration dialog box (as shown in Figure AP-4) and you can continue on to Step 15. If you don't have a modem or just don't want to go through the automated registration, click Exit. (You can, of course, always register your software the old-fashioned way — by mail or phone.)

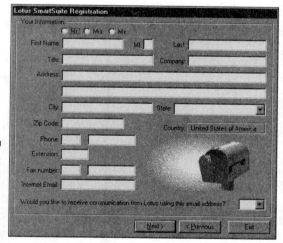

Figure AP-4:
The Lotus
SmartSuite
Registration
dialog box.

15. **To register online, fill in the requested information in the appropriate boxes and then click <u>N</u>ext to go to the next page of the Lotus SmartSuite Registration dialog box.**

16. **Answer the marketing questions on the next two pages by making selections from drop-down lists or typing information into text boxes.**

Note: You must answer the first question — the one about where you purchased your copy of SmartSuite 97 — but you can leave the rest of this stuff blank if you want.

17. **Click Next to start the online registration.**

    The SmartSuite 97 installation program finds and configures your modem, calls a toll-free phone number, and transfers the registration information to Lotus. This process happens automatically. If the installation program can't find a modem, SmartSuite asks if you want to use your Internet connection to register the software. Click Yes submit the online registration over your existing Internet connection. If you click No (or an Internet connection is unavailable) the installation program offers to print your registration information, which you can then fax or mail to Lotus.

18. **When the installation is complete, you must restart Windows 95 before you can begin using SmartSuite 97.**

    Click the Start button on the taskbar and choose Shut Down to open the Shut Down Windows dialog box. Select the Restart the computer option and then click Yes to have the computer shut down and then restart automatically.

Congratulations! SmartSuite 97 is installed on your computer and ready to run. Now you have no excuse not to learn how to use this puppy. Time to turn back to Chapter 1 to start the adventure.

Need an Internet connection?

SmartSuite 97 includes many features designed to take advantage of a connection to the Internet. Of course, you don't have to be connected to the Internet to use SmartSuite 97, but without Internet access, you'll miss out on some of the neat new features, such as the ability to share files across the Net and having easy access to news, weather, and stock quotes from SmartCenter.

You don't have to get a separate Internet connection just for SmartSuite 97 — the program can work with your existing Internet connection, whether it's a direct connection to the Internet from your local area network or a dial-up connection via modem. However, if you don't already have an Internet connection and don't know where to turn to get one, you're not left out. Lotus was thoughtful enough to provide everything you need (well, almost everything you need; you must provide your own modem and phone line) to get started with an Internet access account with the IBM Global Network, right on the CD with the SmartSuite program.

The software is in the \extra\internet\ign folder on the CD. The readme.txt file contains instructions for installing the software and establishing your Internet access account. The process is simple. You just run the Setup program and follow the instructions that appear onscreen.

Index